THE
Miserables

THE
Miserables

Damien Wilkins

HARCOURT BRACE & COMPANY

NEW YORK   SAN DIEGO   LONDON

For Marie, Patricia, Anne, and Pauline

Library of Congress Cataloging-in-Publication Data
Wilkins, Damien, 1963–
The miserables/Damien Wilkins.
p.   cm.
ISBN 0-15-160523-8
I. Title.
PR9639.3.W49M57   1993
823—dc20   93-14100

Printed in the United States of America

First edition

A B C D E

THE

Miserables

1

The
Aunts'
Tale

"STRANGE THINGS AT SUCH TIMES, BRETT." ONE OF THE
aunts had taken Healey by the elbow at the funeral reception
and pressed her head to his. He was sitting and she was bent
down to him. She was excited, her eyes wide and dry from
not blinking. The lines of her neck, usually concealed in col-
lars, or loud hand-knitted scarves, now appeared so close that
Healey thought of the flutes of a fan, or a contour map in its
crinkly, plumbable shading, or the folds in a curtain as it is
being raised.

This was the aunt about whom it was said she had a touch
of the theater, by which it was understood she had a talent

for stealing everyone else's best stories and improving on them. If Healey thought of her as his favorite actor, this did not mean he saw his aunt as affected in any way; it did not seem to be an effort at all for her to "perform"; rather, she knew her own nature and the range of her skills, had found early on their point of coincidence, and now went about things with according and quite expected excess. She had, she said, something to tell him.

Yet the drama was not the aunt's alone. After the graveside, he thought, a change had been registered. Something altered in the tenor of everyone's grief. Healey felt it too; the aunt clasped him ferociously, steering him toward a free corner of the room, not waiting for a passage to be cleared, but pushing ahead, bumping elbows without apology, stopping only to tickle an elderly man who had sat behind the organ and blown his nose through the eulogy. "A darling, absolutely, and at such short notice," she was saying as they struggled past. "Oh, Daddy did love his Bach, his fugues, so there, who's to complain? Not me. Not I." Where caution had ruled there was now looseness, extravagance—this theatrical aunt seemed even a little upstaged or was at least working hard to stay central, the leading of her nephew around giving the note of improvised action—though both periods, the stiff before, the slackened after, seemed to Healey forced somehow, as willed as the organist's squeak of delight when the aunt poked him sharply in the ribs.

Before the graveside, everyone had been on best behavior, watching what the others were doing with the tentativeness of the grand occasion. Watching not only to ensure that they themselves wouldn't commit some ghastly error—funerals, as he heard one family friend say, but only after the worst had passed, could be as bad as weddings, *etiquettewise*—and listening so that they might stop themselves before the wrong word escaped. Emotions were tender things, another observed with more glee than gravity, as helpless really as wind chimes in Wellington. There was also the hope that one's outfit had judged correctly the tone of the event—dark certainly was safe, but what sort of dark and how to pull it off *lightly?* One girl, about fourteen, had turned up at the church in fishnets and a black miniskirt. Noiselessly and without fuss she had been hustled into the ladies'. This had been the only decisive action of the afternoon, the reply to a clear transgression; otherwise caution and a crippling hesitancy had hovered over the day.

More than mere taste, however, the new watchfulness had struck because, Healey believed and was surprised that he was about to include himself here, we are interested in seeing, after all these years, how we've all done.

He had first thought that without the presence of his older brother and sister, neither of whom had been able to make it back from overseas, he would feel a certain freedom. A license to distance himself. Detachment, after all, was his natural posture. He would carry the banner, as it were, for those absent, but he would do it coolly and without fuss. None of these others gathered around the graveside had much of a hold on him. It was the usual gaggle of family, the doling out of a limited resource—a certain chin, a thickness of the female calf, a foreshortening of the male neck—amounting to an endlessness of variation but no new thing. Yet he suddenly felt himself caught up in this watching mania just like everyone else. And perhaps he was even further gone, though not as quick, of course, as those who had dealt with the fishnets, the nimble chaperones of hem. For what he first shrugged off as mild curiosity, or as the groundwork of gossip, which was always being laid whenever the relatives were brought together and which he immediately assigned to the others, he now recognized within himself as an overwhelming need to be brought up to date on these strangers.

At a certain moment during the interment the group vigilance had been relaxed. On the sloping cemetery lawns under a gray sky, one of the great-grandsons, a boy of perhaps five or six whose neck had already disappeared, whose chin had already doubled—a small emblem of them all in fact—had grown impatient with the murmuring and the slow-motion rituals. He swung a bored foot and kicked soil onto the backs of his mother's legs as she was approaching the grave with the trowel. She turned quickly on the boy, raising her hand, and for an unbearable series of seconds the funeral party seemed frozen by the audacity of both the act and the response it was threatening to call up. The trowel hung above the whole group. The boy didn't know what to do but finally ran and hid behind his father's legs. Then one of the aunts came forward and placed her arm around the mother, her daughter. "With the black, dear," she said, motioning in a pacifying gesture toward the soiled stockings and turning for support to the whole group, "it won't show." Next the aunt was bending down and had started to brush the stockings with a handkerchief, and someone else had quickly joined her, working on the second leg; then another relative was patting at the material of Healey's cousin's skirt while others approached to give advice until she was completely surrounded and had to shoo them off her so the service could go on.

In this volley something broke, so that traveling back from the cemetery toward his parents' house for the reception, after the sobriety and excessive solemnity of everything before the graveside, there was, Healey thought, a kind of thirst. Now no one could say anything to anybody without fun in their voice, a slightly hysterical edge.

"Daddy's *lighter* down here," said his aunt when she had him to herself.

Healey didn't understand what she meant, except for the new spirit of relief and modest exaggeration. Louise had been right—morbidity wasn't an issue. The living room in his parents' house was suddenly filled with the noises of intense greetings, somehow amplified, as along the corridor of an airport concourse. It was as if none of those present throughout the day had really been introduced to one another earlier, nor had even properly noticed each other during the funeral. The surreptitious scrutinizing of faces, of clothes, of gesture had been for nothing. The intensity of those studies had been blinding. Now people seemed surprised at who was here, and not, Healey believed, because they had thought that person would never come to the funeral. It was rather from that sense of awe in the face of a coincidence that is not really one at all. It was the buoyancy of delayed recognition. They themselves were there at the precise moment the others had turned up. "You!" they seemed to cry, astonished with this piece of matchless timing. On this second meeting, everyone could truly hug and make the noises so keenly controlled before the moment at the graveside when the great-grandson had kicked the soil and the granddaughter had been enveloped in women's hands.

A little later, when the drinks had gone around, a handbag opened and the sulking fourteen year old was slipped her fishnets. Now the outlandish had a place. Daddy, after all, as the girl's mother said, coming to her defense for the first time, was never maudlin around a good pair of legs.

"Won't see much up there," the steward told him on the ferry's narrow stairs.

Healey, attempting to move around the steward, felt brushed by a look of inspection that he knew had instantly taken in the paleness of his face, the panicky glaze of the eyes. He was being assessed. Of course, his type had been seen countless times before and his humiliation was simply part of the on-board drill. The steward held his ground, forcing Healey in close. Perhaps this was also training, to catch the fainters.

"But if you have to, sir, you know," the steward said to Healey, "my advice is to keep yourself upwind. I've seen some terrible accidents. Here." Almost with an air of conspiracy, the steward then pressed the white bundle into Healey's hand.

He stood on the poop deck, gripping the emergency napkins. The steward had, of course, been right. Beyond the wooden railing that fastened him to the ship it was difficult to tell much about his position; the South Island was somewhere ahead in the gray clouds; behind him, Wellington and the whole of the North Island slid from view. Healey was no sailor and had no head for heights. Yet he had chosen what they called the aftermost deck, climbed toward the very tip of his queasiness to begin collecting himself. One of the paper napkins was torn from Healey's fingers; it flew sickeningly above his head, hanging there for a time before being sucked downward.

He held tight with both hands and let the wind buffet him full on, its force inflating the arms of his jacket. Seasickness. Vertigo. Where had these come from? Sometimes Healey believed he had developed as an adult several afflictions that he might properly have grown out of had he suffered from them when a child. Growing into them as a man of thirty, he found their effects more difficult to shake off, as if, finally stricken by these infant diseases, he was suddenly prone to the delayed virulence of all those years of incubation.

Beneath his hands, the wood of the railing was as smooth and solid as a bared knee. He was thinking of the phrase "ship's timbers" and then "shiver me timbers," and for one moment he almost believed it really was something as easy as his stomach that was the trouble, the bracing air his elected remedy. Looking out across the sea, he imagined sea gulls diving for the kitchen slops in the wake. Wouldn't that be a sign? He closed his eyes on the image of the places he thought these gulls had come from: the firmness of land one hour ahead. A stream of the steward's white paper napkins continued to rise behind him, as in some mad release of hand-kerchiefs.

Healey had come up here because on the outward jour-ney from the South Island three days before—when the boat was leaving the land, moving between hills that rose steeply on either side and were so close birds could be seen in the bush—he had stood on the same spot and felt that a passage was clearing in his life, the sensation of a fresh beginning as if he had just sneezed or finally lost something to which he had attached too much significance. As a child he once left his favorite coat on the seat of a train—a cream-colored win-ter coat with fur on its collar, without which, he believed, people would be unable to recognize him. He begged his mother to be allowed to follow the train up the island. "An-other boy might get hold of it!" he pleaded, feeling the same sense of invasion as when he came across someone who had "his" first name. Yet in that moment, through his tears, Healey had suddenly said "Now!" The child had lost everything; here was the thrill of a completed disaster, the same feeling with which even now he would finish reading a book he valued— dread and relief in alternating waves.

When the boat reached the midpoint of this outward voy-age, however, and there was no sight of land, Healey felt as desperate as when they had gone the following week to the Lost Property Office of the Wellington Railway Station and his mother herself had failed to see that among the rack of children's coats, clearly his was not to be found. She could not understand that it was over. And her persistence with the clothes of *other children* in the small room that had about it the faint aroma of the men's toilets to which it was adjoined disturbed Healey. Here she was, measuring him for coats without fur on their collars and in quite the wrong color. When he protested, she turned him aside. The acne-faced young attendant, who had begun to survey the fitting with an increasing interest, leaned closer to the pair. His mother pulled him farther away and whispered fiercely, "Try it on, won't you. I can take up the sleeves." Healey saw now that, typically, the child had believed a deep injustice was being done to him when, in fact, his mother was simply exercising a kind of thrift.

On this outward voyage, he retreated below decks and did everything he could to avoid noticing the ways in which the midpoint, no matter how smooth the sailing, seemed to have affected everyone on board. That old woman, he thought, only wants to ask about the salad and no one pays her any attention. A girl can't do up her laces while her mother is watching. The purser walking around, his head in the air, a button missing. No toilet paper! The inventory signaled a kind of hysteria familiar to him from other voyages, though here it was given an added charge. This extra pressure was, he guessed, the result of the circumstances behind the trip.

Nor in the midpoint was Healey able to read any of the books he had brought with him, despite the fact that he had often heard it said of such times and had said himself that it was a good opportunity to catch up on some reading. He was, after all, the literary editor of a newspaper and, as such, had more books than he could ever hope to read, with more coming across his desk each day. "More books than underwear,"

Louise had told him, inspecting his travel bag. Yet it was something like the *transparency* of the act of reading a book in the midpoint of the voyage that made it impossible for him to do more than occasionally reach down into his bag and touch their spines, and this was an objection similar to the one that often arose in him on takeoff when his fellow air travelers began to turn the pages of magazines. Nor could Healey bring himself to go up on deck in this midpoint, since he imagined not being able to see anything but the ship itself, the very idea of which caused his queasiness to increase.

He was now returning on the Picton ferry from his grandfather's funeral in Wellington. Three days before, his mother had phoned him and Healey tried but couldn't get a flight that day—it was the August school holidays—so he had driven from Christchurch to Picton, leaving the car there because of the expense of taking it across and catching the early morning ferry. He might have waited for the next available flight and still been in time for the funeral, but even as these calculations were being made for him by his wife, Louise, he had felt he needed to be on the move that instant. More than this, the moment his mother had begun to speak, Healey had experienced a kind of giddiness, as though he was already in transit, imagining the leaving, the midpoint, and the arrival of the journey. "I suppose it's the call we've been expecting for years," his mother's voice said.

Immediately, Healey had thought of the grandfather not as dead but, somehow, sculptured, in tweed and tartan, not lying down, which seemed obscene, but standing or sitting, and of himself going to Wellington to be received by this raised figure. The materials of his grandfather appeared to his mind— damp woolens drying on the firescreen—leaving that thick taste in the mouth that he remembered receiving on running into the living room in Miramar on Sundays. And a hugeness, which was even about the pores in the skin on his face, causing the child to wonder aloud about the "holes" in the nose and cheeks. There had always been something monumental for Healey in the image, although this was not the common largeness of the adult in the child's view. A certain loftiness of spirit, rather, had always been heard in the word *grandfather*. He thought of the period in which he had longed, with an intensity he now found difficult to credit, to get up on that knee from which he hoped to gain a lookout on those, like his brother and sister, who only aspired to be patted on the head.

Yet it was an area never conquered—those few inches of cloth—except as a resting place for the grandfather's hand. For it often seemed that Healey's desire to touch the grandfather, indeed to climb all over him and thereby, as he now thought, to secure the sacred bond the child felt existed between them, was only matched by a certain physical reserve that characterized the grandfather's movements and that only further excited the child's desires to force his way in. If Healey carried in his mind one image now, it was of the grandfather coming nearer, bending down, looming closer until the child is staring up into the soft holes, and then the figure above is receding, while the child continues to dream of occupying the citadel of the knee.

Approaching and receding—surely this wasn't the story
of all their relations but only of a certain period when Healey
must have been very young. Nor was the grandfather a cold
man likely to repulse the advances of small children. "Phys-
ical reserve" was wrong. It was stateliness, it was bearing, it
was posture—that was true. Yet in all these qualities of ele-
vation there was also softness; the grandfather appearing
kindly, generous, even flattering.

Healey's grandfather was a big man physically, and in
later years, as if to compensate for bodily diminishment, had
become increasingly "large" in the indulgences he showered
on his children's children. Often he would give them too much
money with which to buy the bottles of Coca-Cola that every
Sunday they were to have in the living room while in the
kitchen the grown-ups drank their regulation one small bottle
of beer. The harshest rebuke the grandfather might attract
from his daughters was—Healey, as a boy, hated to hear it—
"You'll spoil them." Healey knew the response to this inan-
ity, would beat his grandfather to the words: "They *need*
spoiling!" The boy thus earned for himself another reply from
the grandfather, "You're quick with that! A quick one. You
watch Brett. Quick as a fox." It became so that Healey could
have beaten his grandfather to this, too, though it was best
to slow down for just a second and hear it for himself that he
was a fox. It wasn't necessary to steal your own moment,
not if you were *Monsieur Renard*—he'd looked that up in the
vain hope of impressing on his grandfather the idea of his at-
tentiveness, which was rather, a desperate sort of acquisitive-

ness, Healey never having overcome his dullness with foreign languages.

On the phone, while he heard out details of the funeral arrangements, Healey listened to the peculiar resistance in his mother's voice, something being held back by force of will; she spoke without inflection and kept repeating how bad the line was, though it was perfectly clear at Healey's end. But she forgot to say Grandfather. She said Daddy, which was private language—his mother talking to her sisters—and Healey had the sudden feeling that he was *overhearing* something, that he had picked up the phone and a voice he didn't know was saying things of an unbearably personal nature from which he could not pull himself away, but that had nothing to do with him. "I can't hear myself think on this line," she said.

Healey stretched his arms high above his head and, feeling ill, yawned in the direction of the ship's funnel. A gray mist had lowered itself to the water. The feel of rain coming. Some children were running around the funnel, chasing each other. They wore hooded jackets and gloves and the steam of their breath was momentarily visible against the funnel's fresh white paint. Everywhere the thickness of this paint, layer upon layer hanging against the salt spray and pressing against his skin with that clamminess. The tart smell of it cutting through the cold air. In the odd place where the paint was eroded—he pushed his finger into the damaged coating on an iron post— it was more than an inch deep, and the rust that ran from the hole made him think of the constant repair work that had to be undertaken to keep the boat seaworthy. He remembered from the war films of his boyhood that in slow times the sailors had to paint and repaint their ships. Whenever he had seen these images of men leaning over the railings and hanging from ropes with their hopelessly small paintbrushes—images which, he believed, were included in the films to suggest the everydayness of life at sea, a relaxation from the rigors of combat—he shuddered slightly. Knowing that the father of the friend, the same friend who was now a lawyer and whom he'd visited in Wellington, had fallen from a simple house ladder and cracked open his skull, he believed that the extras playing the sailors doing the painting were in real danger for perhaps the first time during the entire film. That they were whistling sea songs and smiling only heightened the tension.

Then a picture appeared in his mind of the ferry in dry dock, cossetted in scaffolding. Cossetted? The word was faintly familiar, though its promise seemed distant, touched by the odor of woolen dressing gowns. So tense was his grip on the railing that when he managed to let go he felt himself lift slightly and another of the napkins flew off wildly.

Healey had already walked around the poop deck several times, as if in training, he thought, though someone else had already beaten him to that. A man in his sixties, wearing a tracksuit and running shoes, was jogging slowly around the deck in the opposite direction. A sort of relationship had already formed between the two of them, since the jogger had nodded to him when they first passed each other, then called out something about the weather when next they crossed, until on the third run past the jogger said: "The wife thinks I'm crazy, but it wasn't her finished the Tokyo Marathon in Tokyo, Japan. Wasn't her stopping the traffic that day." Then the man was jogging on the spot—which had always struck Healey as silly—and telling him the various times, personal bests, he had run in races all over the world in the veterans' division, repeating the phrase "veterans' division" until it had become VD. After the man had finally run off again, Healey turned around and began walking in the other direction so that he was now following the jogger and wouldn't have to meet his eye again.

The children were circling the funnel, then stopping suddenly to make themselves dizzy. Healey watched them as they stumbled—tottering with arms out for balance, falling sideways and laughing in the new feeling of blankness. Once, he remembered, there had been a school craze for fainting. Why were children so interested in it—was it new versions of themselves? Why was he, an adult, still so afflicted with childlike fears that whenever he thought of a voyage by boat he always imagined three separate stages that never appeared to him all at once but always as pieces—the beginning, the midpoint, the end—as if someone had to cut up his meat for him before he could eat. (His sister, he remembered, could only suffer the chard their father grew in the back garden once each leaf had been relieved of its stalk—the rejected stalks mounting on her plate and forming a barricade against the father's urgings.) Was it that only by taking things apart like this he could see the whole or *make a new whole?* But he had always found that once a thing was in its constituent parts he panicked and walked away from it, just as he had walked away when his school friend had finally succeeded in falling unconscious onto the grass after they'd been holding their breath and spinning themselves around—how he had tried not to make a sound as he moved off, stumbling stupidly over his own feet, the sky turning viciously against the ground, the pale face of his friend lost to him in the deep grass.

Healey swallowed again on the nausea and tasted the cucumber from the one bite he had been able to take of his club sandwich. He didn't even like cucumber. One kid fell abruptly on his behind and screamed.

An American, a very mild man, dressed in a suit and tie, soft-spoken, reasonable—certainly he loved *reasons,* loved placing them one after another, like feet on a plank—was waiting in the bar below for him. The man would still have half a glass of beer in front of him on the table, and, if he was as slow and deliberate an eater as he was a drinker, Healey thought he would still be picking at the club sandwich with the one bite missing.

"Please," Healey had said, pushing the plate toward the American.

"You're sure?" said the man. "You know you should try to eat something. It helps, it really does."

"I'm fine. Air is all I need."

"Air is wonderful."

"I'm going up on deck, then."

"Take some good deep breaths. That'll do it."

"Well," said Healey, getting up to leave. "I'll be thinking of your—'' The word—what was the word? Up to this point Healey had thought of himself listening to the man in the suit with an attitude of "professional control." He had been careful to express neither surprise that he of all the other passengers had been chosen, nor distaste for what the American, this complete stranger, was planning. He had only questioned in the voice of the journalist, or maybe the therapist, the mechanics of the thing. This approach seemed safest. He hoped to avoid upsetting the man who was demonstrating the sort of calm that every now and then seemed to Healey the likely symptom of a deeper disturbance. Certainly the man needed help. Healey now felt, in his hesitation over what term might adequately cover the transaction without tainting it, he was somehow giving himself away.

"Proposition," supplied the American smoothly. "You do that, Mr. Healey. And if you want I can mind your things. Just leave them. Please. Here I am, eating your food."

The man eating Healey's food, then, had a proposition. That was one word for it. He had a large sum of money for Healey and all Healey had to do was say he had seen something he hadn't seen: a man, American, soft-spoken, suited, jumping from C-Deck into the blankness. Like play.

As he was walking around the poop deck of the ferry, weighing up the American's proposition—though now that he had left the dining room the substance of these considerations was proving elusive; had the man really said all that?—Healey saw there was a couple in the distance embracing. They were leaning against the railing, pressed close together, his leg between hers. Healey was about to turn back the other way, but behind him he could hear the jogger approaching, so he was forced to speed up and attempt to pass the couple and act as if he hadn't seen them. Yet the jogger also seemed to be moving faster and overtook Healey, giving him a wave over his shoulder. Then he actually stopped and addressed the couple, who immediately sprang away from each other in surprise, so that when Healey came up to them, the jogger called to him and attempted to introduce everyone, again while jogging on the spot.

On first seeing the couple in the distance, Healey had experienced a longing for Louise, which the jogger, in breaking up the intimate scene, had quickly destroyed. For a moment, then, Healey was glad of the man's overbearing manner, the way he flapped his arms, the encouragement he seemed to take from the couple's bemused looks. The jogger clearly read their passivity as a signal to explain himself further, to recite the times, down to the last second, he had run in this or that race in this or that country around the world. In Jakarta, he assured his listeners, one of the drinks stations had been contaminated, resulting in a seventy percent no-finish.

For the two weeks leading up to the time when Healey received the phone call from his mother in which he believed he overheard important messages, Louise had been working on a story about the Armed Services. It was to be another "light piece," the paper running it as a Lifestyle serial in the Features pages. Life in the barracks, she told him. What went on in the officers' mess. The feelings of an officer on getting his wings. The way she described it made it sound frivolous, though this was the way she often talked about her work, speaking as if it hardly mattered whether this piece got written or another similarly light piece took its place. It was a mistake, however, to suppose that she was shoddy in her work, that it meant nothing to her, or that anybody else could tell her what she often told them, offhandedly, laughing, that she could scarcely believe what she was working on now. When duly challenged that she was wasting herself on this type of piece and that she should move off features on to harder stuff, as she herself was often threatening to do, Louise would suddenly become indignant. She would say that she was always coming across fascinating things in her job, that you couldn't just write it off like that, and that even with the most seemingly lightweight material, there was always the serious and worthwhile task of "knocking it into shape." Often these were ordinary people's stories, she said, which, unlike the stories of this politician saying certain things, or this businessman making a profit or a loss, had never before been heard. At this point, she would laugh, surprised at the intensity of her homily. Don't take me too seriously, she seemed to be saying, but also don't judge things so quickly. Last week a story about a female contortionist!

As Healey was leaving, Louise had almost completed the Armed Services series, though she had already missed one deadline when someone close to top brass—the nice captain in public relations couldn't give a name—pulled permission at the last minute on the lead photos. These were candid portraits, she said, Joe and Jane Crewcut at war work—interesting shots, but hardly a security risk. It seemed like harassment, but for what reason? She said she was fed up and would prefer to drop the whole thing and come with Healey to Wellington for the funeral. She had met the old guy once, and he had complimented her on the pattern on her sweater and, she remembered, Healey on his choice in wives.

It soon became clear, however, that Louise would have to work through the next few days. "The thing I've learned about the army," she said, having put down the phone after speaking to the editor, "is that it really is the army. But with a severe image problem. Because although *we* don't think they mean it—all this soldier stuff—*they* think they do, and, in fact, they also know we don't think they mean it, which makes it even worse because now they don't just think they mean it, they've persuaded themselves out of sheer pigheadedness that they really do mean it and have to prove they do to us! You see the atmosphere here, don't you? For dumb violence. For war!"

Healey remembered feeling, as he listened to Louise speak, a sense of exhilaration that was out of proportion to what was being said, though he believed it had its roots in his own mounting impatience with working at the paper. Here was utterance, he felt, not already measured to a certain vocabulary, a certain grammar, and a certain column width. This was the same feeling he had several days later as he listened to the American on the return trip using the words *the authorities, a black briefcase, affidavit.*

"Funerals are okay," Louise had told him on the night he was leaving, leaning her head right inside the car window. "They kill morbidity at least. The world's lost a true gentleman. I'm the one who'll linger with it here." She pushed her nose into his cheek and laughed. "Think of me."

Healey had been thinking of her, as he looked not into the eyes of the American but at a point on the bridge of his nose, remembering the trick Louise had used many years before against the fathers of her school friends, whose lingering stares she had defeated by this "objective" studying.

Then, as he was listening with the couple on the poop deck to the best time the jogger had yet recorded in the veteran's section of some marathon, he began to think not of Louise nor of the American but again of his grandfather. Even as an adult, he thought, when he had seen his grandfather he had always adopted the posture of a child looking up, just as now, listening to the man jogging on the spot, he had adopted the posture of someone looking down. Even in the last years, on the few occasions he'd visited the old man, who had dwindled alarmingly, Healey had felt himself hunch over and his knees bend slightly, so that things between them might carry on undisturbed. And he understood, while hearing the jogger's "three-hour barrier," that whereas in working at the newspaper Louise had always looked *at* or *into* no matter how "lightweight" the material, he'd always looked up or down or sideways or even away, even though he was, supposedly, working on things that mattered to him, and for which Louise often envied him. "You have your books."

Healey now saw that the reason he had felt himself to be already in transit when his mother called him, the reason he had begun to imagine the three stages of the journey ahead of him as well as the sculpture of the grandfather, was connected to his having heard someone at the paper saying that he couldn't stand it any longer and one of these days he'd be "packing his bags." Since then, Healey himself had had the sensation that he, too, was preparing to leave. For several months now he had gone to work thinking that it would take only one word or a certain phrase for him to clear out his desk and leave "once and for all" as he often said to Louise. It was not that he disliked his job—his feelings toward it could never be such as to suggest the evenhandedness of mere preference—and while he periodically loathed *being at work,* he had found in himself a deep attachment to the idea of *going to work.* And although the open-plan newspaper office had a low ceiling lined with fluorescent lights so that he actually felt each time he entered the building as if he were lowering his head, it was, he believed, the only job he could stomach or to which he could apply himself with any measure of skill.

He now understood, while the couple on the poop deck was looking at him as the jogger went on talking about *ligaments,* hoping, perhaps, for Healey to finally say something and release them all from the jogger's career, that while first picturing the "monumental grandfather," he had been thinking only of the days he might be able to get off work to visit, as it were, one of the great sites before it was lost—a building set for demolition, a sinking foreign capital—and that he had failed to believe it already lost but rather had built in his own mind an image with which he could go to the editor, who had already cut the Books Page by twenty-five percent, and confidently request bereavement leave, and this came to him just as the jogger was suggesting to the couple some point about the cardiovascular system, which Healey instantly translated as CV.

The atmosphere at the reception had suddenly become festive. Healey, who had always fought the temptation to recoil slightly when touched by a relative, found himself initiating long, close embraces with cousins he barely remembered. As they touched and he was called upon to say a few words, more often than not the guesses he made were good ones. This was Keith, who had once worked on oil rigs and had a Filipino wife. Beth the equestrian. Peter, who was slowly ruining his father's joinery firm. Healey, too, to his surprise, was known, or guessed at in this way. Several people had him as a reporter; one or two asked him to recommend a book.

Then at a certain point, when looking about the room, he recognized, standing a little way away from the hugging, a cousin not from his mother's side of the family but from his father's side, a figure whose presence instantly rearranged the room for Healey. He did not have time to consider this odd alteration, however, since his aunt had taken hold of his elbow and was telling him about his grandfather's lightness.

"How's that?" Healey asked her.

"The coffin," she said. "Did I say coffin? Oh, dear. It's the *casket*, of course. The undertaker's is the funeral *parlor* and the coffin is the casket. Anyway, the oddest thing. The casket is definitely lighter here than it was in Auckland." She laughed.

Was it a joke? He didn't think it was. Laughter didn't mean quite the same thing anymore. Nothing did. Coffin was casket.

"Really?" he said.

"Oh, quite," she said. "By some margin."

"Lighter," he said.

"Yes. Now how would that work, Brett, dear? You're a journalist. Every day you must get information to sort. Unbelievable facts. What would be the thinking behind such a thing?"

"I can't—"

"*Heavier*. Now heavier one could understand. The packing or something. For the traveling. Poor darling Daddy would need some packing in there, I suppose. He'd break otherwise. But lighter? Lighter, Brett. That way madness lies!" His aunt laughed again, this time coming into the last of the peculiar gaiety affecting the room—the laugh without resonance.

Daddy—Healey's grandfather had become Daddy to everyone now—had died in Auckland, where he'd been living in a rest home since moving from Wellington after the death of his wife some eight years before. Nana was buried in Wellington and there was no question but that her husband should rest finally by her side. There was a place on the headstone for his details. He should come home.

There had been a memorial service in Auckland at which the weight of Daddy had been tested by Healey's aunt in her capacity as pallbearer. Healey had also learned of some Auckland disagreement over the propriety of female pallbearers, some deep pettiness, and he had recognized in the machinations of opposing camps the curious permutations of goodwill. It was so, it was just as his aunt had said: Death— she'd told him—always has about it the grimness of comedy. Apparently, some question of insurance had arisen should the casket, in the hands of four daughters and two granddaughters, somehow escape, fall to the ground. Everyone was joking about it now, though a wounded uncle had found an excuse not to make the journey down for the funeral. I've paid my respects to the old fella once, he was being quoted, life goes on. "Poor Uncle Philip," everyone was saying, the success of the female crew had almost killed him, and he was still smarting. Phone calls had been made from his house—long-distance reports on Daddy as he grew worse—and someone would have to pay for them. Philip was said to be tallying the bill even as they spoke.

"Daddy weighed seventy-eight pounds when he passed away," Healey's aunt said. "Six foot one at full extension and seventy-eight pounds." More laughter, her hand pinched to his elbow. "You don't become lighter after two days, do you, Brett?"

"Well—"

"Strange business. Maybe we don't inquire. Perhaps that's best, eh?"

"Yes, I think so too," said Healey.

It was unexpectedly peaceful, this not having to talk when in conversation with his aunts. The briefest noise of response was enough to pull them through to the next thought, although that was already likely to have been overtaken by its running mate; it was, Healey imagined, like touching matches to an intermittently damp fuse. Although an explanation had occurred to him—that perhaps it was because his aunt was stronger now, that she no longer knew her own strength, the coffin only *seeming* lighter (this happened in times of extreme stress—didn't it?—feats of unusual vigor: a man lifting the car off his friend when the jack has collapsed)—he did not offer it. Anyway, his aunt looked older than Healey remembered, diminutive in black. Despite the force of her grip, worn out. Everyone did. Joyful in the exhausted touching they were doing. None of the Auckland contingent had slept for almost seventy-two hours.

What presided was the exalted state of trance. Some mystery adhered, he thought, both to his aunt's tale and to what he had witnessed during the day. A persistent tingling of the senses or buzzing in the joints, which he had sometimes felt after working late at the paper and not without pleasure. Both triumph and depletion in the muscles, as if there had been a tapping of reserves, reserves which everyone hoped they had but no one knew for certain whether they did or not until this moment, until the reserves were called upon. A test. Yet even now, who could be sure they hadn't come through on nothing but bluff, he thought, that really there were no reserves, and that somehow, collectively, they had all cheated with this mourning. And that this, after all, was the point of funerals, or of any ritual—you got by on form alone.

It was only later, on the return voyage when he was standing on the poop deck in the rainy mist of Cook Strait, clutching the emergency napkins, and he had met the eyes of the woman who was half of the couple who had sprung away from each other because of the veteran jogger, and had seen there a look, an irritated glance that said to Healey, "You get us out of this, take your friend away from here," that he understood how easily such phrases as "You got by on form alone" had come to him in moments of unusual pressure and how such phrases had only obscured his true feelings at those times, just as when he was being embraced by his cousins he had convinced himself that he was considering only what he would say about the embrace after it had happened and how the embrace should be reported to Louise. Standing there, listening to yet another story about heat exhaustion, Healey had resolved to lead the jogger away by the arm. He would say that he was very stiff and would appreciate some company on a few laps around the deck, although of course he had no desire at that stage to run anywhere and certainly not with the veteran jogger on a circuit that would take them past the fainting children around the funnel. He imagined, however, once he had made this saving gesture, receiving from the woman a brief look of intense gratitude as they jogged off. Just as Healey was about to act, however, the man who had been embracing the woman suddenly said, "Goodness, we must go!" as if they needed to be somewhere by a certain time, even though there was still an hour before the boat docked in Picton, and he took the woman by the arm and walked off, leaving Healey alone with the jogger who was then announcing the word *gout*.

The night of the funeral, when everyone else had gone to bed, Healey stayed up listening to the aunts, the daughters, talking about Daddy.

Daddy's four girls sat in a row on the deep sofa in the living room, sinking farther into the sofa's high, soft back so that they appeared to be getting smaller, their feet lifted from the floor, except Margaret's, gangly Margy as she was known amongst the sisters, with her "pipe-cleaner legs," whose talent for volleyball was such that only now, in her early sixties, after three decades of dominance, was she starting to talk of retiring from competitive play.

The room had been cleaned and vacuumed but still had about it the smell of a recent party; beneath the air freshener lingered the odor of a crowd of people eating and drinking in a space a little too small for them, though everyone agreed that the venue, the spread, everything, had been a tremendous success. He sat in an armchair facing his aunts, looking down at the carpet where spots of white powder marked the stains being worked on. Someone had said sprinkling salt was good for red wine, so salt had been sprinkled, and Healey had the impression that when someone walked across it the carpet now smelled a little like the sea and even gave a faint crackle underfoot as if what was being crossed was a beach of tightly packed sand.

At the far end, Lillian, still the baby at fifty. It was Lillian who had told Healey about the weight problem. Next to her, Margaret, who was married to the absent Uncle Philip; Philip was something pitiable, a little laughable, among these daughters, as if he were their silly uncle, too—not a contemporary but someone infinitely, prematurely old. Margaret, insisting that the full extent of his foolishness be broadcast, spoke of her husband as she would of a naughty child, the same note of tenderness stretched to snapping. Hated him in flashes. In fact, none of the husbands escaped this humor, which may have been one reason, Healey thought, that his uncles had already sought refuge in their makeshift beds—mattresses set up on the floor of the spare room. If it were true the men didn't like each other much, it appeared they liked less the prospect of a collective assault, and this had probably urged the quick bedfellowship, which itself had become the object of the aunts' amusement. Even his own father had given up his side of the bed and joined the men, so that one or perhaps two of his sisters-in-law might continue their late-night conference while lying beside his wife.

Then there was May. No one saw much of May. Quiet, serious, a recluse, she lived out in the country with her husband, a jocular man, who had been silenced two years before by a stroke. It was an oddly fitting occurrence, since now they both went about things with a mute industriousness. May could only be coaxed from her "hidey hole," as Lillian called it, by the awful tragedies in whose path the aging sisters now walked. May had established a very profitable sideline in pottery, selling her work from a little shed on the roadside at the top of her half a mile of driveway. Occasionally, she sent pots to her sisters, though with only the briefest messages written on the backs of her business cards dropped inside them. She spoke in slow, deliberate sentences that unnerved Healey, who was used to the headlong rush of the other aunts.

Yet he came to see how even this studied speech of hers had its own place in the aunts' talk. In fact, it seemed only in the company of her sisters that May's heaviness, set against their flights, assumed a kind of momentum, so that what was slightly ponderous now had a weight, a force. Angela was the eldest daughter, and she sat on the end of the sofa nearest to Healey, her son.

Daddy had outlived the only boy in the family, Thomas, by almost twenty years, and it was this pair—their father and their big brother—about whom Healey's aunts now started to talk. "Recent ghosts," Lillian said.

Healey, a little unsure of his rights, had opened a book in his lap so as to appear to be only half listening. In this posture of half attentiveness, he felt the aunts might open up more, believing themselves to be talking in private, while at the same time grateful for at least the appearance of an audience, since he had observed that it was only when an "outsider" was present that the full drama of the family took shape and rose above the usual coded silences and shorthand communications of a life lived so long in intimacy that one sister's cough was another's rebuke, one's finger raised another's salute.

He also believed that it was only in this posture of half attentiveness that he himself could truly make something of what was being told to him. At the newspaper he often needed to be scanning some document, or finishing a letter, or keeping his head down to be able to listen calmly to what someone was telling him. It was a bad habit and one which had caused some awkwardness. This studied removal was often mistaken for indifference or rudeness and was part of what Louise sometimes called his "lack of social skills" and at other times his "petty bureaucrat act"—this *not looking up from the desk*. He might attempt to justify himself by an appeal to time—that his schedule demanded he always work on at least two things at once—but this was not it at all. Something like temperament was behind it. Certainly he feared failure, but this did not result in an unwillingness to commit to just one thing; he had rather sometimes recognized within himself a desire to entertain a range of disappointments so that no single disaster would crush him.

If at the paper he should decide one week to create a Books Page with "something for everyone," but also one that people might comment on and even be stirred by, working singly toward this aim, he believed that he would as likely discover late on Friday night just before it went to press that the page was made up of reviews of a wide range of obscure works in fields in which he had no expertise and which would appeal to only a tiny, if disparate, minority of the readership. He would again be forced to explain to people who searched for something of interest that the week was a clearing out of the backlog of reviews that had been clogging up his desk and that it had been a slow time, no decent stuff coming out, etc. He therefore proceeded as he had always done, putting together a various and inoffensive page of middlebrow reviews that drew few comments, except from friends, who were likely to note the amusing juxtapositions created by the advertising:

a notice for a speed-reading course, or women's underwear, or chicken pieces.

As the aunts began speaking, Healey looked at the page of the book in his lap and believed he was hearing the old family legends, the times-when, but recast, granted a clarity and poignancy now that both the principals—Daddy and Tom—were no longer there to speak for themselves or to add one more particularizing detail and lend that note of authenticity to the fables of their own pasts. At this moment it was not loss he felt in the room but rather a swelling of narrative powers. The stories seemed to take on a kind of incantatory drive that might only have been diluted had there been more certain recourse to the facts. If there were facts, they belonged to the uncles, and the uncles were asleep.

The aunts were telling each other things they already knew. And the familiarity—here Healey paused, in the intricate roots of that word—was a force in itself, yet added to it was now this integer of circumstance, this twist of plot (a plot was what you booked at a cemetery, a coffin was a casket) that deepened and renewed the connections between themselves and what they were saying, connections that, otherwise, lay obscured in simple repetition. With the result that the figure of the grandfather was so magnified in its own absence that Healey, looking at the four women sitting opposite him on the sofa, thought they were, indeed, Daddy's "girls" and that big brother, Tom, who had suffered mysterious blackouts from which he had never fully recovered after returning home from the War, might bound into the room at any moment, quickly followed by Daddy himself, dressed not in the layered woolens of old age but in flannels and cottons, in ordinary men's working clothes, got up as a regional inspector of bridges circa 1947.

"So Daddy must have been holding the ladder while Tom climbed up to the bathroom window with the hose," Lillian was saying.

"The bathroom was on the second floor. This was our house in Miramar, remember," said Margaret.

"In Carlysle Street," said May.

"Number forty-six," said Angela.

"Forty-six Carlysle Street, Miramar, Wellington," said Lillian. "May I continue?"

"Go on," said Angela. "Tom's got the hose. With the sprinkler thing on the end."

"With the sprinkler thing," said Lillian. "Okay. We're all getting ready for the party. It's too exciting to wonder about what might be going on in the garden with the men."

"I knew they were up to something," said Margaret.

"But your hem had come down. You were screaming about your hem," said Angela.

"That's right! How can you remember that? But, yes, Mummy had to pin it. So I forgot about Tom."

"Which was a dangerous thing to do with Tom," said Angela.

"Thank you," said Lillian. "Well now. The party is under way. It's girls only. Margaret, your dress is beautiful."

"I know, but I'm worried about the pins."

"No one can see the pins. It's perfect. We're perfect.

Aren't we? Oh, make your leap of faith with us, May! This is a very special party. A kind of warm-up to coming out. Or the Wellington equivalent of coming out. Such days!"

"Lillian," said May, "I was eighteen years old and Angela must have been almost twenty—we were quite *out* by then, I'm sure. In fact, I have vivid recollections of the disappointment even now."

"Yes, May's right," said Angela. "There wasn't much *out there* in the end to come into, I'm afraid."

"It was a nice party anyway, that night," said Lillian. "Except for Daddy and Tom and, well, visits to the ladies' room."

"I can't believe Daddy helped him," said Margaret.

"I can," said Angela.

"You see they had a system," said Lillian. "Both of them lurking outside in the garden like Peeping Toms—well, one of them was called Tom, wasn't he—so that whenever the light came on in the bathroom, Daddy must have been signaling to Tom, who was waiting round the side of the house by the tap. When they heard the flush, Tom would give a quick turn to the tap and send a short burst of water up the hose and into the bathroom. The sprinkler nozzle was—where? It was hidden in a potted plant hanging over the cistern, I think. I can't remember. Anyway, the result: you got rather mysteriously and rather embarrassingly wet every time you went to the bathroom."

"I got hit in the eye," said Margaret.

"They got May on the behind, didn't they, May?" said Lillian.

"Oh," said May. "Yes."

"I thought it was the stupid toilet," said Angela. "Remember that stupid upstairs toilet? The strength of the flush was a little . . . unpredictable."

"And no one said a word," said Margaret.

"How could we?" said Lillian. "We were girls, in our best party frocks. We were—"

"Humiliated," said May.

"Well, I'm not sure, May, that it was quite as bad—," said Angela.

"Mortified," said May.

"Bathrooms in those days had a certain . . . strictness about them, didn't they. A code," said Margaret. "We were all little Queen Victorias when we visited the smallest room."

"Taboo, my dear," said Lillian. "They were quite taboo! What awful secrets went on behind that door! What *operations,* eh. Remember Great-uncle Eddie? Ten o'clock Eddie we used to call him."

"Was that Eddie?" said Margaret "I thought it was Uncle Frank."

"Oh, it was Eddie," said Lillian. "Eddie and his great suspenders. Do remember and spare a thought for Eddie. That hat of his which someone said doubled as a spittoon. Oh, yes."

"I do believe you're confused now, Lillian," said Angela. "Eddie never wore hats. But go on. The plumbing—"

"The plumbing!" said Lillian. "Exactly. That was the secret power of their plan. *I* didn't know where the water was coming from. The spray hit you so fast. And in that kind of

situation, well, your mind starts to . . . boggle. I dried my-
self as best I could, then I went down to the party again.''

"Everyone was spending ages in there!'' said Margaret.
"What on earth were we thinking!''

"I was flapping my dress, trying to get the wet patch out,
standing at the window,'' said Lillian. "I couldn't believe it.
Not tonight, I was saying, not tonight, God, please. . . . Oh,
how simply, how quickly and completely can the wonderful
heart of youth be punctured, its dreams so silly and precious
and quite, quite without defense.''

"Yes, yes. Until Mummy went to the toilet,'' said May.

"And she knew immediately,'' said Angela.

"She came down those stairs—,'' said Lillian.

"And got that hose, and Tom told us later she put it right
down his trousers, full on!'' said Margaret.

"Which I think Tom rather enjoyed,'' said Angela.

"And Daddy?'' said Healey. "I mean—'' The moment
he spoke the aunts all turned to look at him, as if they had
just discovered an intruder in their midst. But this was not
quite it, he thought, since there was no hostility but only a
brief surprise, the hitch of a minor interruption as if a child
had put his head around the door and quickly retreated. Then
they were off again.

"Oh, Daddy must have seen trouble coming,'' Lillian was
saying, "Mummy glaring out the bathroom window. Any-
way, he reckoned he had nothing to do with Tom's foolish
prank. He was checking the roses or something.''

"He said he was worried about an unseasonable frost,''

said May. "Those were his exact words. I can hear them now—how strange."

"A frost!" said Margaret. "The night was positively balmy! Oh that was Daddy."

"We were all inside with our summer sleevelesses on," said Lillian.

"Drying," said Margaret.

"And trying not to show!" said Lillian.

Then, as Healey was considering walking across the carpet and was listening for a gap in which it might be appropriate to say his good-nights—not because he wanted to leave, but because the richness of the day's food, the heedless mixing of the drinks, were making him feel a pressing need for fresh air—it struck him that he was waiting as if for the interval in a play. Each aunt had her lines, which she spoke with a sense of timing made impeccable, he guessed, by time itself, cued in by the habitual rhythms of sisterliness. For this moment, sitting close together on the sofa, their husbands were superfluous—odd, amusing things off to the side, but hardly to be taken seriously—which caused Healey to experience a small, disturbing thrill, as if he might be reporting back to the husbands, the excluded men, the only male in an all-womens' club! It was as if he was listening in. But, of course, he was in a different category from his uncles. He was Angela's son and therefore belonged to the set apart, sometimes indulged community of nephews. He did have rights, access, and—feeling it most strongly now, though it had been with him his whole life—a certain sympathy with what his uncles called his aunts' "nonsense" from which he had always gained an odd calm, as if he were being cossetted.

"Of course, Daddy was always in the garden, *checking on the roses* or something," said Angela. "Figuratively speaking, that is. He didn't know a thing about actual roses. *Radishes.* He was an expert at radishes. Put them in the ground, come back later, and there you have your radishes. Food on the table. He was pretty proud of that! When he was home, that is."

"What do you mean, Angela?" said Lillian. "*When he was home.* How melodramatic all of a sudden."

"Maybe you were too young, Lillian. But Daddy . . . he was away a lot when we were little, when Mummy had the five of us on her hands, by herself really."

"He was away on business, Angela. It was his job," said Margaret.

"Some of it was that," said Angela. "But a lot of it . . . Well, he just loved to be away. He just wasn't there a lot of the time."

"Yes, Daddy loved those trips," said May.

"You two!" said Lillian. "Painting him out to be some sort of absent father! Really, in front of Brett here."

"Absence is a good word," said May.

"Oh, I think neglect is better," said Angela. "Maybe a touch strong but—"

"Really!" said Lillian.

"I think that, periodically, at least, Daddy neglected some of his . . . responsibilities," said May.

"Don't we all!" said Margaret. "Don't we all periodically, well, cheat a little on our families."

"Margaret!" said Lillian. "You've been watching too much television."

"No, it's true. It's a sort of . . . well, this is too much, but it's like an adultery we commit with ourselves," said Margaret.

"Margaret!" said Lillian. "Are you suggesting that Daddy—and Daddy, bless him, must forgive me and all of us for these thoughts; it's the alcohol, it's the stress of this whole business—*had something on the side?*"

"Only himself," said Angela. "I think Margaret is saying Daddy had himself on the side."

"Am I? I think so, yes," said Margaret.

"Okay, you're talking about a private life," said Lillian. "We all have those. It's the one thing God gave us all—a private life. And then, to escape from ours into other people's, we had to invent gossip, which is wonderful in itself, of course, but—"

"Sometimes I wonder, you know," said Margaret. "If Philip has a private life."

"Oh, Margy!"

"What I believe about Daddy," said May with a sudden firmness, "and this is not the Daddy you others looked after these past years, which has always made me feel selfish, which I am, and mean, which I know I can be, the way I never did my bit—no don't stop me now little Lillian—"

"Oh, well don't call me that, May, and you're not selfish and—"

"But see how mean I can be, still calling you that. What was I thinking of, still talking down to you as if we were children?"

"Go on, May," said Angela.

"Very well. What I feel about the Daddy, who was our young, then middle-aged father, is that he was prone to a kind of . . . amnesia. It was as if he sometimes forgot he had a family. Angela's right. It was neglect. But neglect of a certain quality, almost impossible to chastise, or even identify as a failing on his part. I don't know what I'm saying, really. Is this making sense? Poor Brett is sitting there trying to read his book and having to hear all this."

Everyone was now looking at May. They had not heard her speak like this in years—perhaps she had never before spoken in such a way—and as her words came out, Healey imagined them arriving as if from the long, winding distance of the driveway that he had always thought of as the arm's length at which May kept the world, but which he now saw as a kind of telescope bringing the far things almost painfully close so that he had the impression his other aunts were all now moving back slightly in their places, as if correcting their own longsightedness.

"Oh, I talk to myself a lot these days," said May. "And, no, I don't deserve your pity for that circumstance; it's just that I've developed the habit of *speechifying,* I suppose— which I always resented in Daddy. You know, you're sitting looking at this pot spinning around all day and things come out, things you never knew were even there. But, anyway, I think we loved Daddy strongly *because* he came back. And that's why it's so hard to get it clear in our minds—he forgot, and, somehow, it made us forget."

"He was infectious," said Margaret.

"We forgot we were forgotten," said May, "since his return remembered us. Goodness, this is getting—"

"May, I'm going to cry," said Lillian. "And don't you try to stop me."

"You know, I remember loving Nana—Mummy—perhaps, a little less," said Angela.

"Angela!" said Lillian.

"Of course, of course," said Angela. "Is this something to bring up now?"

"Oh, I don't know," said May. "If it's what happened, it's what happened."

"It happened, and I never really knew why," said Angela. "I was ashamed I felt this way. But maybe it's as you said, May—I think it is. Mummy was always there, wasn't she. Always. And how could such a constancy compete with the excitement, the intoxicating fickleness of Daddy's comings and goings. It's terrible to admit this, and of course I do not believe in what I am going to say—I never have—but her love seemed positively *dull* in comparison. There, I've said it."

"Oh, Angela, now I really am going to cry," said Lillian. "Though I've nothing left. I'm utterly dehydrated and all I want to do is this—start up the waterworks! It's the alcohol and the traveling which has made us all lose our heads. But that isn't stopping me. Just watch. I'm silly, Brett, dear. I'm—what did Mummy used to say—I'm overtired and need a nice lie down. That's it.''

"Now one thing this is not, Mr. Healey; this is not someone hurting someone else. I want to be clear about that much." The American was speaking to him in the bar of the ferry. "The hurt? That's all done and gone. There, that's in the past. So long. Leaving what? Leaving this business. Because that's one way of looking at it, Mr. Healey, as a business venture. Fine. Here's another: as what follows on from a marriage that should never have happened. That's another way. You can always give something a spin, the spin you want, Mr. Healey—I have no problems with people doing that. See, what we have here is unfortunate, but also, in its own way, kind of natural. Natural for a man to follow his heart is what I mean, Mr. Healey. Which is my spin on it."

The man was in his forties, though this could only be guessed in profile. When he turned his head, the full weight of his jowls appeared, the beginnings of a roll of gray skin pressing on his shirt collar. In this pose, Healey thought of a heavy-set accountant searching for the layman's language to explain to a client a column of disagreeable figures.

Healey looked steadily at the bridge of the man's nose. "And the fraud aspect of it? This is something, you know, to consider."

"Now, Mr. Healey," the American said, moving in closer over the table, showing his palms, "of course you have something there. A certain amount of this, you're absolutely right, is going to get taken on trust. And trust is trust. Can't buy trust, because if you could it wouldn't be called that anymore. But here's what I'm saying. If all the background information came to light, I wonder if anyone could judge so quick. I wonder a lot about that. And you say—go on, Mr. Healey—you say I'm holding out on you. So I say, see, it's because I don't want to involve people more than would be advantageous to them—it's as a *protection,* Mr. Healey, that the full story has to remain here," he tapped his temple with one finger, "with me."

Face on, the man lost ten years. When he spoke, his chin had a habit of pointing at whomever he was addressing and making small upward movements in emphasizing certain words. Now the skin was stretched, except for around the eyes, where the puffiness strengthened the impression of a kind of overworked, overtired youthfulness.

"Can I ask you a question?" said Healey.

"Shoot."

"Do you know what I do for a living?"

"You're a man of intelligence, Mr. Healey. You're a sensitive person. Nobody's fool. Heck, certainly not my fool—that's not the plan!"

"I work for a newspaper."

"You're a people person. I knew that."

"I'm going to suggest something. A hypothetical situation, okay?"

"Sure. A thinking man."

"Say I'm your man. No, say he's just like me—the man you want. What's to stop him taking this straight to the paper, then getting the police on to it? Or what if he refuses to go along with it and then a few weeks later he sees a notice that a certain American visitor has gone missing, presumed dead somewhere. What's to stop him telling his story of being approached by the same American visitor, who politely asked him whether he wouldn't mind saying he saw him jump. You see how this might pan out?"

"Absolutely, Mr. Healey."

"Well, I don't mean to be rude, because for all I know, for all your newspaperman knows, you have these angles, as they say, covered, but in the course of your research, you know—"

"Research?" said the American. He turned away, ran a hand through his boyishly full hair, then faced Healey once more so that in the moment of preparing to answer he seemed to have advanced in years, then shed them in equal time, a performance that held Healey and made him eager to learn the trick here.

"Please," he began with a sigh, "I'm a businessman back home, Mr. Healey; I'm no gangster, no shyster. What do I know about crime? I read it, I see it on TV—I'm like you. I'm personally shocked by it, yes. It's disgusting—what one person will do to another. Let me tell you a story. A short story. I have a sister got mugged in the park outside her apartment by some kids. She's wheeling her six-month-old baby on a beautiful sunny day. My niece. They arrest some twelve year olds. *Twelve years old,* Mr. Healey. I'm sorry to preach. But I hate it that it's my little sister and her baby. I hate it that these kids have to do this. What's got into us?

End of sermon. Another thing I hate. I hate it that we have to talk like this, about such things. This here's the first time I've even considered anything like this, so, no, I didn't research you. Maybe that was crazy. That was crazy, of course. I saw a man with a book open in front of him and I had a hunch—there's my research right there. My plan comes from . . . well, passion, I guess. There's a word. Passion. I'm not an artful man. I'm not one of those clever get-something-for-nothing guys. I feel guilty reading a paper someone's left on the train. Like I said, I have debts: I owe my ex-wife back home. There's this bunch of creditors after me, and for what? A few honest mistakes, Mr. Healey. Business is tough. It's tough. No one tells you about that toughness. And here in your beautiful country—which is no empty phrase, I can tell you, though why should I be trying to convince anyone of the obvious?—there's a woman here I love very deeply and who I'm going to lose otherwise. See, they'll deport me. And, Mr. Healey, what would you tell your paper anyway? That a crazy American—because this is crazy, right?—had tried to involve you in some insurance scheme, though you couldn't be sure of any of the details? It's the stuff of dinner party conversation, perhaps, a few close friends around on a nice evening. But a newspaperman such as yourself, well, you know your trade better than I do Mr. Healey—what am I telling you your trade for?—but is this really going to sell the evening edition? I mean no disrespect to your profession, I'm a reader, I love newspapers, but they'd want something bigger, wouldn't they, something more substantial, wouldn't you say? A random meeting in a bar on a ferry and *that's* news?"

"And if I see you've gone missing later?" said Healey.

"Mr. Healey, for obvious reasons I do not plan to approach everyone aboard this boat until I find someone who'll say they saw me take my dive. That would be some running gag, wouldn't it?"

The man was so close Healey could smell his breath. Mint. He could feel it against his cheek. The American was as near as his aunt had been when she had cornered him with her secret about Daddy's weight. He was as close as a cousin. As Keith and Beth and Peter. Healey fully expected to be taken by the arm.

"I promise you, Mr. Healey, that if you read a notice in your paper saying that I'm missing and am presumed dead, it won't be faked. I'm near the end, you see." He let his head drop. "Sheila. I mean, the woman I love. You didn't need to know her name. That was sloppy. See what an amateur you have here? You understand how it is. Desperation. Sheila— her hair is falling out. She's taken to wearing hats. But now I'm talking nonsense. Really. I apologize."

Healey waited while the American completed his characteristic looking-away movement. His suit was a little small, that collar too tight, the knot of his tie seemed so fierce as to function almost as the buckle on a belt, restraining, upholding. Looking at it, Healey felt a constriction in his own throat, which he had to swallow to overcome. So Sheila was wearing hats because of her hair. Had the detail really slipped out accidentally? Was she ill? Was this emotional blackmail? Even Sheila was a little weak, as a name. The man's own hair fell in a dark mop behind which his fingers were now working on

the skin of his forehead, smoothing it as if applying some
cream. There was, Healey thought, a curious vanity in these
gestures that did not quite qualify as self-regard but was a
sign of that confidence he had always thought of as peculiarly
American and that he had witnessed in his own time there. A
confidence that allowed the man, even out of his own con-
text—a context that perhaps might have made sense of the
suit, the tie, the hair—to nevertheless import his own sense
of occasion, to create what was missing. It was this act of
improvisation that was providing the atmosphere in which
Healey, too, found his own attitude. He couldn't be sure
whether he was being played with or not, and so he heard
himself playing along. Only now he could also feel the tight-
ness communicated by the other man's tie traveling down
through him so that he actually pulled at his own shirt, as if
to increase the circulation, while his head continued to grow
lighter.

"You'd really jump?" Healey said with difficulty.

"Some other way, I think. I'm a swimmer, Mr. Healey.
College team, four straight years. I hit the water, I'm like a
duck. I'd find it difficult just sinking, you know. It would feel,
somehow, unnatural to me. Like I was letting the school down
or something. Isn't that the craziest? These connections. I
swam the individual medley. In the relay too. A lot of pride
in those days, Mr. Healey. Very tough in the swim team we
were. Funny how that old stuff comes back to haunt you,
isn't it. Won't ever let up."

But now Healey was having trouble concentrating. He
heard himself asking the American what school he had been

to and then he wasn't sure whether he had waited for the reply. Anyway, he was already telling the man that he, too, was an alumnus of an American university. There was some general reaction of surprise, perhaps delight. Healey tried to smile. The cucumber came back. He needed to move. One of them—could it have been himself?—was saying something about Ivy League schools, tuition fees. "But, Mr. Healey," he heard the voice say, "you're not eating. I didn't mean to sit myself down here and ruin your meal. I'm sorry. You're not well, Mr. Healey?"

He felt better on the stairs, and climbing to the upper decks, he was diverted from the nausea by thoughts of those other ascents that had concerned him in his time in Wellington, chief among which had been the object he had first aspired to, the grandfather's knee, and from which, he had believed, all the others descended: the repeated climb up through the Aro Valley to the university when he was a student ten years before; the tall, cursed steps to his parents' house on the hill overlooking the harbor; the almost desperate push to the summit of Mount Edgeware as a young boy, following in the steps of his mad cousin; overtaking the tourists in the race to the summit of Mount Egmont; the rise of the Millard Stand; the incline of the cable car. It was absurd to hold to the notion that his whole life might be arranged around such a device, and yet he could scarcely disown such distortions. Indeed the solace he found in considering this "false" life of climbs now provided him with a lucidity about the present moment.

He thought clearly for the first time of what he was being

asked to do, never once believing that the Healey he saw acting out the American's directions was the same man imagining himself, the same man who could barely stomach a bite of sandwich, but who had nevertheless given the impression that he could, if it appealed to him, take part in a criminal scheme.

When the ferry berthed at Picton, the American was to purchase two one-way tickets back to Wellington; one under Healey's name and one under his own real name; he was at present traveling under a false name. He would pass over both these tickets to Healey and then disappear for good. Healey would deposit the American's ticket in a trash can on board. Then at a certain point in the voyage, when it was dark and they were toward the middle of the Strait—this was important, the American had told him, because of the currents that might easily drag a body far out to sea—Healey was to raise the alarm that he had just seen a man jump overboard.

The ferry would most likely be stopped and Healey would have to take a role in looking for the missing man. He would have to be ready to indicate how the figure fell and from where exactly, what he was wearing, what he looked like, and in none of these details should he be too precise. It was dark. No one else was on this part of the deck when it happened, and Healey himself was on an upper deck and saw it more or less out of the corner of his eye. No, the man did not shout or make any noise as he jumped.

In Wellington, he would accompany the captain of the ferry to the police, it having first been ascertained through a full passenger check the name of the missing man, whose suitcase was to be discovered the next day in a toilet in Picton. Healey would tell the police what he had told the captain as the spotlights swept over the black, churning waters, that he was certain of only one thing—a man jumping from the side of the ferry. And had he heard a splash? No, nothing over the sound of the engines. This, the American said, was important for verisimilitude.

Would they ask him about his own movements? Why he had come back to Wellington on the return sailing when he lived in Christchurch? It was unlikely they would be thinking of anything but the man overboard, but he would have an excuse ready, something about his grandfather's funeral and forgetting something in Wellington, something he needed for his work. Then, after it was in the papers that a certain American tourist was presumed drowned in Cook Strait, an advertisement would appear in Healey's own newspaper giving a box number where Healey would use the key he'd been given to open the security box in which the money was waiting.

Running it through like this, Healey now understood that, from the vantage point of the poop deck covered in darkness, to say he had seen a figure jump noiselessly from the side of the ship was the same as saying he would never be able to come down from this terrible position of false observing. He would, finally and forever, be aligned with the words of a story which was neither his nor true. And this, without even looking into the water, without even completing the thought, Healey had rejected.

———

Leaving Wellington after the funeral, Healey had stood on the upper deck at the rear of the boat as it moved away from the land. His parents, who were not present on the wharf— a large backlog of relations still needed to be cleared—had always been great farewellers, often feeling it necessary to watch guests driving away. Seeing them off at the door was, somehow, not enough—they had to actually accompany people out onto the street, following the taillights until the car disappeared; only then could they afford to think the evening satisfyingly concluded. Perhaps in this way he was also now making sure of the ferry's departure, watching while the once familiar city, lying without sound against the murky hills, the melancholy effect heightened by the lights that shone in the windows of office blocks and houses even though it was only midafternoon, slipped from sight. In some of those windows—it seemed impossible—were people he knew.

When the ship was on its own, he sat down at a table in the bar. There were a few other passengers at the surrounding tables, but the ferry was surprisingly empty for this time of year. The special holiday airfares had cut into the trade, he'd heard a steward tell another passenger, though learning this Healey felt, for some reason, not that he had *missed out on the better deal,* as someone said, but that he was part of a select on-board group, people of discernment who had chosen this means to bridge the twenty or so miles between the two islands in no less than three and a quarter hours—connoisseurs almost. With a sudden confidence, he had bought a sandwich with his beer. After several minutes, however, he hadn't started on either, and he knew that the longer they sat there untouched the more likely it was that he would soon have to get up and move to a clean table. From his satchel he took out a large scrapbook bound in thick cardboard covers that were marble-patterned and stamped on the front in black lettering with the initials J. J. B. He traced the hollows of the letters with his fingertips. Julian John Banks. Jack.

The aunts had pressed the scrapbook on him. They had brought it down from Auckland specially. They told him he was "qualified." Qualified for what, Healey wanted to know. He was a literary editor fighting a newspaper management that existed solely to initiate cuts. Daddy could have been a writer, they said. And the number of letters he wrote to the editor! Letters about drainage, about the rugby selectors, about politics and morals. Of course Healey was honored to get the chance to read it, to have it in his possession for a little while; it meant a lot, he told them truthfully. But what exactly did the aunts have in mind here? Was there a plan? They said they had no plan except that of—? Preservation, his mother said. Yes, they agreed. Well, maybe there was a story in it, Healey volunteered, not wanting to appear above the spirit of loving attention that was being invoked. Indeed, the aunts said, indeed.

Maybe he had been right after all, he thought, in the beginning of the middle stage of the journey, before the American approached him, the beer and the sandwich set casually on the table as if he might be the sort of person who could eat and drink and generally behave as if he wasn't on a boat at all but in a bar or restaurant which, as a matter of course, tipped and creaked occasionally. Perhaps there *was* something here, though remembering the evening with the aunts it was already a narrative of a different order to the one he might have previously imagined. His own mother's steady insistence about her father's qualities, even over Lillian's tears, had changed what he was about to read.

Yet hadn't he felt curiously dispassionate in learning about the grandfather's "life of neglect" from the aunts on the night of the funeral? Wasn't it that lack of surprise that had, itself, been surprising, none of the words of his aunts' tale seeming "wrong" exactly, but simply a little out of place, orphaned—if he could use that word—lacking context. Was this what he was now being asked to supply? Yet it also struck him that he had been listening to their talk as if for clues to his own life. Perhaps it wasn't his grandfather that he had come to Wellington for at all. It was for himself, just as the aunts themselves were really interested only in a story in which they figured. Was it only now that he could begin to understand that his time in Wellington had been, as they say, a kind of sifting of the evidence?

Healey looked at the album laid in front of him on the table as if he might be the sort of person who could read or study while the boat was in motion. Immediately, however, he thought it was impossible and that he should walk away from it. Why should he consent to being held hostage, as it were, by this memorabilia? Didn't every young boy fall in love with his grandfather and imagine a bond when there was none? His obsessions had been so common—hadn't they—as to frighten him into attempting to impart a kind of uniqueness to them, which he now saw as unwarranted, pathetic. He would put the album in his satchel and when he was home post it back to the aunts with a note expressing his thanks and excusing himself by way of the pressures of work, which made it impossible for him to do anything with the material at this stage.

Suddenly he thought, *I'm going the wrong way!* He got up from his seat and slid into the opposite side of the booth, so he was now facing away from the city in which he had spent most of his life and which he felt he was again leaving prematurely.

He was opening the album, and though the paper was stained and brittle to the touch and he knew it was, in a sense, archival material, he found himself handling the pages roughly, as if it were that day's edition of the *Post* he'd bought and would leave on the table after finishing. He opened to a page near the beginning of the scrapbook and, distractedly, began reading from the clipping stuck there. This, he felt, was the only approach. To come at the material unexpectedly, by chance almost.

From his previous experience as a child furtively examining the contents of the top drawer of his grandfather's highboy—an activity he had admitted to no one and which made "legal" possession of the album a faintly shaming circumstance; surely there were more worthy cousins—he was convinced that he would find here only the most obvious things and that the real story, as it were, lay in those items carelessly cast aside. Nothing that was *placed* here would be of any use. Only what appeared forgotten or had the feel of being last-minute would be of any value. Then, on the half empty ferry, thinking of the people beginning to turn the pages of magazines in the air thousands of feet above him, Healey had a sudden image of himself at sea level, connoisseur of the fugitive!

The clipping he was looking at, or rather glancing at, appeared to come from the sports section of an old newspaper—a report on the all-Universities Easter Tournament, a portion of one column ringed in faded red ink.

By a matter of mere inches J. J. Banks, Otago, won the Triple Jump Crown from S. P. Flynn, Auckland, who fouled his last attempt. It was a brave and thrilling contest conducted under weather conditions whose inclemency only serves to underline the achievement, wrote the student newspaper—20 May, 1915—Mr. Banks securing not only this year's title but also a record which we are certain will last for a very long time. Surely Mr. Banks has hopped, skipped, and jumped his way into the future. Ahoy there, Jack Banks! What news, sir, of us ahead?

2

The
Lesson of
John A. Lee

A WELLINGTONIAN IS KNOWN BY HIS WALK—A FORWARD
lean of some fifteen degrees. The figure whose formulation
this was, Healey's grandfather, himself remained upright, even
against the stiffest southerly, and would thrust his cane through
the wind as if—and this was another of his pet phrases—
cutting a cake. When the ferry came through the narrow, rocky
passages into the wide bulb of the harbor, Healey saw that
those who had joined him on deck were all bent at this char-
acteristic angle, tipping toward the city that appeared, as al-
ways, without warning—a cradle of light floating a few feet
above the winter morning cloud.

The man beside him was an architect. He said he lived in Nelson now, though he was a Wellingtonian through and through and did most of his business in the capital. Without any introductions and without even looking at Healey, the man had simply started talking. "The Nelson thing," he said, "was for the kids, you know. A healthier environment. Now they're fifteen, sixteen—girls—they hate the place. We're going to have to move back. Apparently it's *unhealthy* once they pass that age. Small towns. I'll miss this, though." He pointed at Wellington. "Coming in like this. I always bring my clients out here first. It's the only way I can explain what I'm trying to do. I don't care if you're not going to be able to see their project from the water. Look at the lines, I tell them. I'm a bully. Look at them!" Healey followed the man's arm. "What are you struck by? What is it that gets you in the eye straight off? Not just the precipitous arrangement, not just the idea the whole show's up there by some sleight of hand. It's the *orderliness,* too, isn't it? The vertical lines! That's what I show my clients."

He was right, though Healey wished the architect might leave him now. Something in the approach to Wellington required privacy, silence. Healey thought his grandfather should be the presiding spirit of the place. Yet he was seeing what the architect wanted him to see, the shapes appearing with greater clarity now that they were getting closer—the elegant veranda posts, the tall rectangular windows, the chimneys, the arrows of corrugated iron roofs, which did indeed seem to point, lines that pulled the eye constantly upward. It was exhilarating.

"This," the architect said, "is the way the houses speak for the relationship of hill to sky. How movingly the architecture articulates the effort of the land's settlement. What cheek! we want to say. Wow! And the whole lot could come down at any minute. While we're watching right now. Just slide into the harbor, like plates off a tray."

A Wellingtonian, Healey thought as he listened to the architect talking about the land on which the city had been built as nothing more than a pretext for some show of natural violence, might also be known for the modesty with which she arranges her shelves. His mother, even when traveling to other cities, would never sleep in a bed that she considered to be in the direct line of any falling objects. After one period of extended tremors, she removed the overhead-light shade for fear that it would crush her feet in the night. She also had a permanent faith in the capacity of the harbor to one day flood the downtown area and wash away most of Thorndon and Oriental Parade.

The day the *Wahine* went down, a day unfailingly recalled to his mind whenever he set foot on the ferry, the only tree in their backyard had fallen through the windows of the sun-room. Healey and his brother had gone out the morning after the storm and stood on the trunk, much as they had seen the passengers in the newspaper photos crawling onto the only side of the ferry still above water. In Eastbourne and around the bays of the harbor, for several weeks following the sinking, people had gone souvenir hunting. A boy at school had found the captain's wristwatch, stopped exactly at the time his ship had gone down. Later, this was uncovered as a fraud, though not before the watch had changed hands for a sum of money that the headmaster, in full assembly, labeled "scandalous"—especially since it turned out, though there was no allusion to this in the speech, that the sum had been extracted from a senior member of staff. The only souvenir Healey had was the sound of gunfire in his sleep on the night of the storm. This was the noise of the branches from all the trees on their street snapping.

The architect was saying how the restricted approach of the harbor always gave him the feeling that he was entering something a little private, perhaps even forbidden, but also somehow familiar, like a parents' bedroom. His commentary, though it continued to run on at salesman's pitch, was no longer such an irritation to Healey. He found himself working off the architect's phrases and recovering something of his own responses. Wasn't it true, he felt on hearing the word *bedroom,* that the first sight from the ferry, the first suck of breath—it had even winded him slightly—was a key to the city? Only now, returning for his grandfather's funeral, had he been able to identify it: Wellington was all vantage point. Places to look *out from* and *into.* The experience of coming upon something would be repeated throughout the city, as the hills rose and fell and the houses that covered them appeared to be standing on each other's shoulders, craning for the best view possible without falling off. Of course, there was a secret pride among the citizens, a feeling of worth through work, which made a virtue of such an inconvenient location. The most outlandish elevations, the most extreme colonizing, the unlikeliest sections were also, as the architect said, the most sought after.

"I want a piece of rock suspended some place you'll need a helicopter to deliver the mail," he told Healey. "That's where I'm building and to hell with the kids!"

Hadn't Healey been a little overpleased, he now thought, when he came across this sentence in the Christchurch Public Library in an old guidebook: "A gaunt, almost alpine beauty is present as the hills rise sharply from the water's edge." He had looked hard into the badly reproduced black-and-white photographs and even found himself trying to recognize faces in the street scene, which he guessed from the publication date to be around 1967. Wasn't it possible that among this group of well-clad figures, bundled up against the cold, crossing Willis Street at Stewart Dawson's corner, he might spy a certain eight-year-old boy whose obvious momentum derives from that attachment Healey glimpses and then recognizes as his mother's arm? But there was only the half-caught image of a little girl trailing behind a large coat and using as her guide through the crowd the end of an umbrella. She was holding on with both gloved hands, as a water skier follows the boat. Healey stared harder. He thought he could make out the No. 1 bus to Island Bay coming along the Quay, though finally the only things marked with any clarity in the murky shot were the neon signs for diamond rings and Omega watches shining above the heads of these familiar strangers.

None of this seeing, he thought, had been possible before he had moved with Louise to Christchurch and begun living on the directionless Canterbury Plains. There in that South

Island city, as people had told him he would, Healey got lost. You had to know the names of a great many streets, to have worked out a complete mental grid. It was like walking with a book balanced on your head. And Healey somehow never managed this, or resented the imposition. In Wellington he only had to look up.

The architect pointed to Somes Island and said that although only a few sheep and a ranger lived there, that little blob was vital to the city. The aspect of Wellington's spatial arrangement, the force bringing together the major tropes of sea and hill, which could only be understood from this position on the deck of the ferry, the architect said, was the notion of *island*. That goat station introduced in miniature the idea of the capital city as island. And this prefiguring was important. Just as the harbor, due to the curling narrowness of its entrance, appeared almost as a lake, so the city, according to the architect, appeared almost totally surrounded by water.

"The island is a place *par excellence* because it appears isolated and clearly defined; *existentially* the island brings us back to the origins; it rises out of the element from which everything was originally born." Healey had found this sentence when he had been living in a city in the American Midwest, where he was then studying the books of a writer who had grown up thousands of miles from the coast. When he showed this sentence to the writer, Healey was told that the person responsible for it had "taken in too much undigested Heidegger," a comment that was enough to make Healey vow never to deliberately seek out the sentences of Heidegger, but to smile and join in the guffaws of the writer who was now almost choking, as if he had just swallowed something that didn't agree with him. He wondered if the architect standing beside him would have similar problems, though he had already lost his chance to find out, since the commentary had reached Lambton Quay.

"The unifying street," the architect was saying. "A curve as beautiful as the instep on a girl's foot." The Quay ran the mile from the Beehive to the Bank of New Zealand and took its name and shape from the fact that at the time of settlement it marked the seashore. Following the reclamation of the harbor in the early part of the century, it found itself a distance from the water. "Kind of orphaned, isn't it?" said the architect. "But you know what? I still feel it, just an occasional sensation, if the wind is right, passing the jewelry stores, the lunch places, whatever, stepping over the brass plaques that tell you one hundred and fifty years ago this was the beachhead, I still get a whiff of it, you know, of walking a coastline. Not just the smells, either, but the *light*. Hell, everyone knows about the light—I'm not saying anything new. But I like to say it anyway. I say it over and over to myself so I don't forget it. The light is what I try to tell my clients about. The proximity of the sea and the quality of the air— that's a killer formula; it can hurt your eyes, that light."

One of his father's sisters, Healey recalled, had been forced to wear dark glasses whenever she came into town for the sales so that, prowling in the aisles of Kirkcaldies—the only place she would shop since one could no longer obtain an honest bargain anywhere else and for which she'd traveled the hundred and forty miles specially—Healey had imagined her as some kind of special agent sent down from Palmerston North, where otherwise she was occupied as the manageress of a beauty salon. The salon itself was something of a sore point between brother and sister, since the aunt evidently made enough money from her business, Healey's father said, to jolly well pay full price for any item she fancied. "She could have Kirkcaldies deliver the stuff in a taxi and still not be hurt in the pocket."

Yet even Healey's aunt, as she herself said with some impatience, could never be sure of the light here. It depended on where you were, since Wellington's hilly terrain offered a complex pattern of refuge from this harshness. The vertiginous city chopped the sky up into portions, as it were. This dissectional quality served to dramatize not only light but all aspects of the weather, channeling or obstructing wind or rain, sealing a valley, then reopening it, showing a side to the elements, then hiding it. Wellington, Healey thought, getting ahead of the architect now for the first time, riding on his language, was *tactical* space. The same storm that had run the *Wahine* on the rocks of Barrett Reef with the loss of fifty-one lives and which had caused a quick trade in souvenirs, as well as a river of branches, leaves, signposts, and trash cans to flow down their street, had yet been unable to find its way into a neighboring street on the other side of the hill where the pavements remained dry, with the result that several of these untouched residents at first believed the whole thing to be some sort of sick hoax practiced on or even by the Wellington Harbour Board.

As a manmade place, the city was also full of a kind of spatial strategy. The hillsides were a tangle not only of winding streets but also hidden paths, endless steps, concealed exits. Here, Healey thought, was the image of the bureaucracy of downtown; in the twisting, bushy passages high above the places of government "the corridors of power" were emblematized.

"Too many places to hide," he had once heard his grandfather telling his father over their Sunday beers. The latter had been a civil servant, working in the Education Department, where he found himself often at odds with what the grandfather, in sympathy with his son-in-law, called "the powers that be." "They got me, too," the grandfather was saying as Healey approached with the change from buying the Cokes. "Don't ever underestimate them. Don't ever think, these are my own people, because that'll be your first mistake." The two men turned toward Healey. "Now what's this, young Brett?"

"This is the change." Healey held his hand out, offering up the coins.

"That's not change, that's a fund, isn't it," said his grandfather. "That's what we say is in the coffers. Find somewhere safe. I'm appointing you treasurer. Keep it and next week we'll do the books. That's an investment is what that is." The grandfather turned back to Healey's father. "You've heard me before on this, David," he said, lowering his voice. He never said "David" unless it was something serious, or he was inquiring after golf scores. "But remember John A. Lee. You think he was safe with his own people?" There was, Healey now recalled, the letter he had found in his grandfather's drawer some years after he had heard that name, magically punctuated in its middle, in the kitchen at Miramar. He'd been helping his mother tidy up her father's papers prior to the move to the Auckland rest home. The letter was still in its original envelope, postmarked 4 November, 1964, with its one-penny stamp showing a twig from the karaka tree—the red and gold berries against the green leaf— and a three-penny to make up the postage, the yellow trumpets of kowhai against a blue background. The envelope was spotted and soft and whenever Healey turned it over in his hands the paper had the hairy feel of overripe fruit and left a powder on his fingers like pink chalk.

The letter inside was handwritten in blue ink on lined paper and signed John A. Lee. There was the initial again, the flourish at the peak, the stab of the full stop. Lee, a Cabinet Minister in the 1935 Labour Government, who had been controversially expelled from the party five years later following a bitter feud with Savage (Lee had written an article that was said to have indirectly attacked the Prime Minister as mentally unstable), was replying to a letter of sympathy from Healey's grandfather. The grandfather had apparently read a recent account of Lee's ousting and been sufficiently outraged by "the powers that be" to send the great man his belated condolences. There would undoubtedly have been in this communication, Healey considered, that note of satisfaction which entered the grandfather's manner whenever he came across another victim of the conspiracy; this, he always hinted, was what lay behind his own slightly premature retirement from the Department of Works and Services.

The grandfather was an admirer of Lee's fiction, to which the letter also referred. Healey recalled that *Children of the Poor,* Lee's partly autobiographical 1934 novel, a book praised by Upton Sinclair and George Bernard Shaw for its "passionate sincerity" and its "intensely alive" narrative, which revealed for the first time the "gutter" side of New Zealand life, would periodically appear on the arm of his grandfather's reading chair. This was also a book that Healey himself had finally bought from a secondhand store in America at the height of his homesickness.

He had come across the book by the sort of accident that seemed to guarantee significance. The book had been misfiled under sociology, or rather it was on top of a pile of books yet to be shelved in sociology. Healey was a frequent visitor to the store over the two years, although each time he entered the place the owner would greet him with the same statement about holding eighty thousand titles and buying in over one thousand books per week. It was as if the owner failed to recognize even the most regular customer. At first Healey thought this failure was due to the fact that the owner held these eighty thousand titles in his head, which feat left no room for anything else. However, on the occasions that Healey had asked for assistance in tracking down a certain book, the owner had simply waved his arm in the general direction of the shelves, never moving from his chair and showing no sign that he knew anything more about the titles he bought and sold than that they exceeded this large number, a number that he had to keep repeating to everyone who walked through the door so that he could convince himself, at least, of the magnitude of his mysterious holdings.

In all the hours he spent in the store, Healey had never looked closely at the sociology shelves, but on this day the title caught his eye and he recognized it as the book whose first pages his grandfather was fond of saying he knew by heart: "This is the story of how I became a thief, and in time very much of an outlaw, running and skulking from the police."

Healey read this first page while standing in the secondhand bookstore. Then he turned to the last page, which he remembered his grandfather praising as being the equal of Dickens and even of his favorite writer, Victor Hugo.

"Stop thief!"

Did that cry ever resound in your ears? Have you run with the man in blue running after you? Have you driven your scampering legs across country as though they could out-distance galloping horse and barking and yelping, if not very vicious, sheep dogs? Have you won to fancied security and suddenly found a hand at your shoulder, a voice saying "Come on?"

Tallyho!

What do you know of the chase if you have never fled with the hare? What do you know of the desperate urgency

of speed if you have not felt hot breath and cruelty gaining
on you, and walls closing around you?

"Run! Run! Run! The Police!"

Have you been driven by that fear?

I rebelled. I ran away. I was dragged back. I ran again.
Tallyho. What a hunt it was! For the law was after a boy,
and the boy was a thief!

He thought how in the whole of America there was no
one else for whom these words would carry anything but a
strict fictional weight, or perhaps a vague sociological import.
He was the only one on the continent to whom these sen-
tences really spoke. The book already belonged to him. It
had made it to the top of the pile on this day so as to escape
the oblivion of the sociology shelves. As a student in Wel-
lington he might have made the decision to steal the book,
which was already his, but now he thought it would be a mark
of respect both to Lee, who had lost an arm in the War, and
to his grandfather, to pay the four dollars.

In Lee's letter there was mention not of this book but of
his Shiner books, which the grandfather similarly rated along-
side his favorites and which he must have asked about when
offering his condolences. The Shiner, Ned Slattery, lived in
the grandfather's mind as one of the most vivid characters to
have ever walked through the pages of a novel, not least be-
cause when he was a boy, the grandfather had heard the sto-
ries about this hobo figure, part philosopher, part rascal,
traveling the countryside, getting into fixes. That he had per-
sonal knowledge of such a character only served to increase

his admiration for the writer's talents. There was even the suggestion that his own father, Healey's great-grandfather, had discovered the Shiner sleeping in his barn one morning and had shared breakfast with him.

The idea that in a novel one could meet a real character like this seemed quite thrilling to the grandfather and had obviously caused him to ask the author whether he didn't have a third volume of Shiner stories ready for the publisher.

Lee, in the letter Healey held, said that although a few anecdotes had yet to be collected, a third book was unlikely. He also wished to make it clear that the figure his kind correspondent's father had met in his barn was not to be confused with the Shiner as he appeared in the fiction. The legend, Lee wrote, is the real basis of the books. The Shiner was far more significant as a legendary figure than as an actual existence and Lee said he had used him really to fix an historical background. The background was real even if the stories were apocryphal. The *legend,* he wrote again, stressing that word, was more important than the man, and this in itself reflected the times when characters were known up and down the country in a way not possible in our crowded days.

Healey was to weigh the letter and its contents later on in the privacy of his own bedroom. For now, he had scarcely taken in the name attached to the page than he found himself pocketing it. He felt, somehow, compelled to do this and yet if questioned at the time he might have come up with no better reason than, as in the case of the boy with the captain's watch, he hoped to gain some personal advantage. Occasionally, he was also to imagine himself at some point in the future showing the letter to a person to whom it might mean something, though until that time, he would act as if the name it bore was without significance for him.

The architect was moving off now with nothing more than a wave over his shoulder as the ferry berthed, the backward thrust engines coming on and the other passengers grouping near the gangplank. Healey remained where he was, feeling an odd moment of peace in standing still in the midst of all this activity. A sentence from John A. Lee's letter, whose text he had once known by heart, came back to him: "I gave my life to a cause and was evicted by gangsters who won control of the machine." He saw again the way his grandfather leaned in toward his father, their faces now close together, as if the very weight of the name being spoken might only survive the shortest journey between them. It was a serious city he was entering, Healey thought—the seat of government. Looking back into that earlier kitchen at Miramar, he was convinced that Wellington was the only place where such gestures might even be considered. Only here could two people lean in close with some pressing matter between them. Nowhere else would that name have had the necessary resonance as it passed across the tops of two half-full bottles of beer.

It also struck him, as he searched the skyline for a certain row of windows that only a few moments before had appeared with a remarkable prominence, that the city at every turn was conspiring to disappear on itself, much as his father had disappeared to "battle the machine" each day inside the giant wooden building—"the largest structure of its kind in the Southern Hemisphere," as its incumbent would say with an odd mix of pride and self-mockery—set at the northern end of Lambton Quay. Here was housed the mysterious Department of Education. Down these broad, shiny corridors Healey had once been sent to look for the man who'd left the house as usual at around 8 A.M., with his briefcase whose chief burden remained, until around 11 A.M., the four large sandwiches packed for him by his wife. Roast beef or Wiener schnitzel or mince—meats from the night before pressed between half-inch slabs of white bread.

On this occasion Healey was to carry some message from his mother who was waiting in the car outside the building, a task that proved too much for the child whose own footsteps on the linoleum seemed to echo with terrifying resonance, as along the halls of a great school, the sure outcome of which he imagined to be some swift punishment for trespass. This was, after all, the place from which all education originated. What every teacher said in every classroom around the country had its source in these rooms. This was where the whole awful mechanism of school was housed. Where the light was reflected on the floor, great pools of glue had formed. Somewhere here they would be discussing the case of his brother. They would force Healey to give evidence against him. They would want to know about the scissors and about the conversations the brothers had when they were lying in their beds at night. His father would be no help to him. They would get Healey as they got John A. Lee, *his own people.*

Hearing those telltale footsteps, seeing in his mind this

boy peering hopelessly through the frosted glass panels of an endless succession of doors, and looking up at the populated terraces ranged above like seating, Healey suddenly thought of Wellington as formed in the image of an arena in session. As they sailed in, the city was immediately convened. The city of judgment!

A few years before the *Wahine* went down, Healey stood one morning in the middle row of school assembly, among the Standard Twos, while the headmaster was making some announcement. There was a scuffle at the back, and the Standard Threes fell into Healey's row, causing that row to tumble against those in front. "What's going on? What's going on back there," the headmaster was shouting over the confusion. A little boy in Standard One had fallen against the headmaster's leg, banging his chin on the headmaster's knee and coming to rest with his face on the headmaster's shoe. The headmaster carefully removed his leg, giving his foot a little shake. "I tell you boys," he was saying, "I'm warning you all. What is this?"

The girls, who were lined up on the other side, had retained their rows, though some were giggling. Then one of them piped up, "It's a ripple effect, sir."

Meanwhile a teacher was bringing two boys to the front, and Healey saw that one of them was his brother. The teacher was brandishing a pair of scissors, waving it above the boys' heads, and there was some confusion as to what punishment might be taken out on the offenders. The other boy was whimpering and hugging himself in an odd way. He had long hair, hair which had often been the cause of official threats. Were they to witness a public barbering? Healey's brother looked on with bemusement. It seemed like a mistake that he was there at all. He put his hands awkwardly into his pockets.

"Hands at sides! The pair of you!" said the headmaster.

The other boy didn't want to let himself go. He was trembling. The headmaster pulled at the boy's arms. "At sides, I tell you!"

When the boy's arms did come down, something remarkable happened, making this particular moment one of the most memorable in the school lives of all the children gathered for assembly. The boy's sweater began to slowly peel off him. The front was falling forward, collapsing of its own weight. It seemed to fall for a morning. The whole school watched the terrible disrobing in silence. The beautiful, thick winter sweater sagging and dropping to the ground. The boy himself helpless and still as if in the grip of some hideous transformation. It was only his sweater somehow detaching itself from his body, slinking off, and yet afterward the boy seemed different. He stood there revealed, oddly undressed, painfully changed, as a snake or a cicada.

"He cut my jersey in half," the boy cried quietly. "Healey cut it with them scissors right through at the back." It still seemed more in the way of an amazing transformation than an offense which Healey's brother had effected. The boy's wounded tone even carried a touch of admiration.

The headmaster looked from the scissors on display, back to the sweater, which now rested in a sad heap at the boy's feet. The school followed his gaze. It was an unusual act, one of strange daring, and it had caught the headmaster slightly off guard.

"He cut my bloody jersey right off, he did," said the boy, a little more defiant now, sensing his case was in the balance.

"Language!" warned the headmaster.

"That's my new jersey, that. Don't want it now, do I."

A girl giggled. Healey's brother now looked thoughtful. He seemed to be considering the likelihood that he had, indeed, taken the scissors and severed the sweater from the long-haired Standard Three boy in front of him. He was actually rubbing his chin over the evidence. Yes, there was a good chance he had done it. He was nodding his head in agreement with the general consensus, then shaking it in the negative. The results of the experiment—because it was that, a testing, perhaps, to see how the business of wool worked— seemed to puzzle him. And as he was to explain later to the headmaster and to his parents, though it gave neither party any satisfaction and only increased their concern about this "odd" boy, he really couldn't say what his original intention had been. "Guess I wanted to see something," he told them.

"It wasn't like rope, though," he told Healey when they were lying in the dark. "It wasn't like cloth or material at all. It was like cutting through cold spaghetti," he said, "or old porridge. But that's not it, either. There's nothing like it. A unique experience."

Of course there was no one to meet Healey at the terminal. He hadn't told his parents when he was arriving because he hadn't known whether he would make the early sailing. He preferred it like this, to come upon the city by a kind of stealth. Yet he was disappointed all the same. One face. He wanted just one Wellington face. Perhaps an Aro Valley face, or a Kelburn face. He felt sure he would recognize these addresses, these specific neighborhoods, in certain looks, in the habits of flesh.

He went toward a taxi. The driver, a darkly bearded man in his fifties, was drinking from a paper cup with an odd furtiveness that made Healey decide to walk past and try the taxi behind. But the first driver had his window down in an instant and caught Healey's eye. "Where to?" he said. Immediately Healey thought it was a Newtown beard, that the way he put the cup to his lips was a Newtown thing. If the driver got out of the car, he was sure to have a limp. He almost said the word *Newtown,* thinking of the hospital and the various clinics whose patients were often to be seen hobbling around the streets.

"Kelburn," Healey managed. The driver nodded his head at Healey's suitcase. The trunk popped up. "Throw it there," the driver told him between mouthfuls. "I help except then I ask you to hold my breakfast. I'm finishing in a minute. You hurry?"

"No," said Healey. "Not really."

"Good. You make my doctor happy man. He tells me it's my . . . what do you call it?—nodules. I drink it hot too fast, like this." The man brought the cup to his lips and mimed taking several quick gulps. "Says I have the pop singer's nodules. I tell him opera, you know, is the thing for me. But

no, opera, these singers is all in breathing, he tells me. Pop
singers, these peoples is all with throat. Bad. Like me. Ahh,
this doctors! Scare the hell, eh? My wife, a Kiwi yeah, her
father is seventy years of age and he is drinking all the time
like this, bang, bang, bang. If he's got a bus to catch. What's
matter with him? Nothing. Is still singing like the canary!"

Healey had got into the back of the taxi. There were white
lace doilies on the headrests and a fringe of material around
the back window.

"You know Greece? Hi! This is me." The man was put-
ting his hand over the seat and Healey was shaking it.

"Hi," Healey said. "I've come from Christchurch, but
this is me, Wellington."

"Sure!" said the driver. "I live here twenty years. But
not to worry, my friend Wellington, none of this on the meter
okay. You don't pay yet. But you help because there's no
hurry, good. Pleased to meet you." The man took another
quick drink. "They say food's better on inter-island now."

"I didn't have anything," said Healey.

"Of course! No one is telling you can eat it already, no!
But you can only look at it, yeah, without wanting to nau-
seate, so progress. Personally I am telling you that all real
food never make it far as the table. Have you seen these bel-
lies on the cooks and stewards fellahs? *Crooks* and stewards
is better. They are feeding oh so well those big bellies. Noth-
ing good left over for passenger, see."

Healey had never been in the business of taking taxis,
inheriting in some measure, despite himself, his father's atti-
tude that to pay some fellow for giving you a lift was to intro-

duce into a perfectly affable relationship the murky stuff of money. His father was always embarrassed about these exchanges; he didn't know quite how to pull it off. To take a taxi was also a sign of defeat. Wasn't there always some alternative, some combination of buses perhaps, no matter how complex, a trick of timetabling, which might do the job and for considerably less? His father was irritatingly cheap when it came to such matters of convenience and hopelessly extravagant in everything else so that by mutual consent the domestic budget was freely given over into his wife's care. Any inquiry about pocket money or loans when they were children had met with the same cheery, invulnerable response: "That's your mother's department."

Being driven through the streets of his hometown in a taxi suddenly felt unearned, frivolous, and even a little wicked. It also had the unsettling effect of making things seem less familiar than they might have had Healey been walking. What he had seen and recognized and thought from the boat while the architect had been talking, now had to be seen and thought again. It was as if the city had been caught in a succession of grainy exposures, insufficiently lighted to allow the viewer anything more than a vague sense of his own position, which nevertheless he had to constantly check against certain landmarks, as if returning to the caption beneath a poor photograph. And the landmarks themselves seemed somehow transitory, a little out of place.

He tried to ask questions about what they were passing. He wanted to know what had once stood on lots that were now vacant. Hadn't that corner been widened? Why so many one-way streets? Yet he found he could not give his full attention to the answers, which were coming anyway in an unbroken flow and were attached to some general tirade against the stock market and big business. Healey was hearing the driver's voice as from a distance. It might have been Greece out there after all.

Several years after he had cut through the boy's sweater at assembly, Healey's brother had become friends with a Russian boy called Peter. Peter said he wasn't Russian but that he had Russian parents and that was the crucial difference. He threw fits if anyone persisted in calling him Russian. He didn't know a single word of the language, he said. Ask him anything, he demanded, he didn't know. He didn't like Russian food. The music, he said, drove him nuts. It didn't make any sense, all that Russian music. One day he brought a small doll to school—a figure in a full beard, dressed in a long gown that glittered with tiny jewels. On his head the doll wore a pointy, jeweled hat. In one hand he carried a sparkling stave. His feet were clad in red-and-gold curling slippers. There were private showings of the doll at lunchtime. Peter said he hardly knew what the thing was, cradling it in his big hands, but he guessed his parents would call it an icon.

Peter had a violent temper and was not afraid of getting hurt. These were seen as peculiarly Russian traits. He was big, though also oddly soft looking, plump around the eyes, and such soft size, for some reason, incensed the others. They wanted to touch him, to push their fingers into that mass and test its consistency. Few, however, dared. Mostly they pressed against him with taunts, speaking and running. Peter, for his part, never seemed able or willing to learn how to absorb this attention. He lashed out. He confirmed exactly what his excited accusers guessed—that he was truly Russian. He revealed himself every time he raised his voice or lifted an arm in anger. When Healey learned that his brother had been around to Peter's house, he was horrified. His brother was already on the edges and this would push him irrevocably from the center of school life. Healey resolved not to tell his parents. He would wait until his brother drifted away from Peter, just as he had drifted away from any number of surprising attachments. But he was also forced to admit that this new union made a sort of sense. His brother was the only one who didn't call Peter a commie, or the Russkie freak. His brother, to Healey's knowledge, had never had to dodge the desks that Peter threw across the classroom. One boy had lost a large fistful of hair to the crazy Russkie just because he happened to be the nearest thing to Peter's heat. It wasn't going to grow back properly. Russkie had made a monk of him.

The drift was taking longer this time. It seemed the brother had found a friend. Then it came about that Russkie, Monk, and Healey's brother formed a war-gaming club. They kept this secret for a while, until Healey one day found his brother constructing a mountainous valley from papier-mâché and was told that this was a region in Italy. The brother said Healey could come along if he really wanted, since they were enlisting the occasional participation of Russkie's two brothers when they needed lesser generals, and Healey was sure to be better than them. This pair, Dimmy, the younger one, and Alex, who had left school and lived in his room, had no understanding of strategy, the brother said, and little interest in learning from past mistakes. They were suicidal in their eagerness and could be relied upon to furnish a massacre when required. Healey told him he would come along but only as a neutral observer.

Russkie's parents' living-room floor had been converted into a Napoleonic battlefield by means of a green felt cloth. There were the papier-mâché hills and rivers of blue cellophane. Beside the battlefield were books opened to reproductions of oil paintings showing the original sites of war. The living-room details had been worked out with some care. Where a painting showed a bridge knocked out by cannon fire, Russkie had pressed his square thumb delicately through the matchstick bridge, fracturing it precisely. Then a model horse had been laid on its side just as it appeared in the painting, the animal's head trailing in the river. The fortifications were positioned with painful exactness, and the movement of troops was a slow business of measuring everything to the last centimeter. The fighting was not under way for hours. Then when it did finally begin, the choice of firepower, the retreats and advances, the infliction of losses were all given over to the endless throwing of the dice and lengthy consultation in reference works. Healey was bored. The brother told him afterward that this had been a day of preparations, of mainly preamble, and that next week it would begin in earnest.

Next week it looked the same to Healey. Even the little

men, elaborately hand painted by Russkie, and, when needed, carefully removed by their creator from small wooden felt-lined boxes where they lay in individual compartments according to rank and insignia, could not hold his attention through an afternoon. Occasionally there would be an argument about some matter of the rules but it was so much math and technical language, and Russkie and Monk and his brother, lying on their stomachs, were so studious and so polite to each other, that Healey found himself wandering about the house, hoping that the shape of the little soldier he had slipped into his pocket would not show against his jeans.

In this time he would also talk to Dimmy, who had by then succumbed to some foolishness in the battle and been forced to retire with the sulks. Dimmy, as it turned out, was also in the business of stealing his brother's army piece by piece. He and Healey found they had formed a club of their own.

"I can always blame it on Alex, see," Dimmy told Healey. "Alex has a history. Me, I'm clean."

"What history?" said Healey.

"What history! My brother, in case you haven't noticed, is a bit, you know, loony," said Dimmy. "He does things."

"Like what?"

"Like our cutlery was thinning out once, right? There suddenly weren't enough of things. Mum goes into his bedroom and finds all the spoons in the wardrobe."

"Yeah? What did he want with them?"

"Who knows—he doesn't. He dresses in a suit and leaves every morning as if he's off to the office. He hasn't ever had a job. He bought a briefcase. He should be on sickness, then at least we'd be getting something for our troubles. Even Monk's kind of okay beside him.''

Monk was tall and thin and anemic. He wore glasses so thick that Russkie said he could look at women and see what they had on underneath. Most kids who wore glasses, Russkie said, looked brainy, but Monk, peering through those fishbowls, just looked stupid. Monk never laughed except when he was with Russkie and then it was a secretive sound that usually ended up strangled in Monk's handkerchief, which he would bring to his mouth as if to spit. When Russkie pulled Monk's hair out it was less an act of hostility than a sign that they belonged together.

The Saturday war games, Healey thought, were the only times Monk became more than himself or perhaps his true self. For these hours his glasses seemed the reflection of a searching intelligence, a magnification of some natural cunning. He was the intellectual general, a theorist, a plotter, tough-minded and sometimes even bold. With his sickly pallor and his quick handkerchief, it could be pretended, at least for the afternoon, that he had been up all the previous night working on regimental business. His thinness was battle fatigue, his spotty skin the result of poor rations, long campaigns. When they met on that green felt field as opposing commanders in chief, Russkie would shake Monk's hand without trying anything. How many great military figures, after all, had died of tuberculosis, coughing up their last into handkerchiefs dirtier than the one Monk carried. Healey waited in vain for hours for something to happen.

Monk's twin brothers were in Healey's class. They were smart, athletic types who captained teams. Hardly anyone knew Monk was even related to this bright pair, and certainly no contact was initiated on either side during schooltime. They might cross in the corridor without a second look.

Years later, Healey was to meet one of the twins in a crowded Wellington pub on a Friday night. They were now in their early twenties. The twin had gone into insurance. He was married. Healey could not remember the twin's name, nor did the twin ever use Healey's name. If they had passed each other in the street, Healey felt sure that neither of them would have done anything but quickly shift his gaze and walk by without a word. Yet something in the atmosphere of the pub cornered them and made them admit to a shared past. They had had nothing in common when they were twelve years old, and in the intervening years the distance between them had only grown. Healey remembered how he had hated one of the twins, though he could not recall why, nor could he be sure that this was the one, despite the fact that they were not identical twins. Still, the feeling of dislike was intensifying every moment he stood there making small talk with the twin. After a short time they were both looking into their beers, searching for a way to end the unfortunate meeting. Finally Healey asked about Monk. The twin looked up suddenly and stared at Healey, as if only now he knew who he was talking to and understood how unpleasant and senseless it was.

"Richard," the twin told Healey, who now realized he had never heard Monk's real name until this point, "is still inside." Then the twin was calling out to someone across the pub and quickly moving off through the crowd before Healey had a chance to say anything more.

Healey's mother, who kept a running tab on everyone who had ever come into contact with any member of her family, told Healey when he asked about Monk that of course he had known about poor Richard. She herself had told him. "Held up a bank with a toy pistol," she said. "You know, the drug thing. The twins are doing well, though."

Shortly after he heard about Monk, Healey was in Auckland, where the Russkies then lived, and looked them up in the phone book. He had kept in touch with Dimmy on and off after the family had moved north because of the father's lungs. Up until a year ago, when the letters stopped, all three brothers were still living at home. Alex would be over thirty by now. Russkie was working as a night watchman at a factory and, according to Dimmy, had either been "on the lookout" for flats, or talking about going overseas ever since they had arrived in Auckland. Dimmy himself said that he would move only once and that would be into his own house, bought and paid for by the money he was saving living with his folks. It was a hell he was living in, but at least his mother was too dumb to charge him anything more than a nominal rent. He was a kitchen hand in a hotel downtown.

Healey found their address and decided against calling first. He would arrive on their doorstep as a surprise. Or perhaps he would not even be able to make himself go inside. Maybe he would simply sit in his car and watch the house for a while.

Russkie was the only one home when Healey did ring the bell. He had the door on the chain and was peering through the crack. It was obvious he didn't recognize Healey. He'd been woken up. Healey was already backing away, apologizing, saying he would come around some other time when Dimmy was home. Russkie, however, suddenly had the door open and was pulling him inside. He was telling Healey that you couldn't be too careful around these neighborhoods. A lot of coons around. A lot of racial stuff. Now they were going door-to-door. They didn't wait until you were walking down the street anymore. "House calls," he said with a grin.

Russkie seemed even more threatening than before. In his bare feet, which were covered in the thick black hair that had been seen as yet further proof of his origins, he appeared wild and unkempt. He kept slapping his belly. They sat in the living room and Russkie talked at great length and with some ferocity, but without ever meeting Healey's eye, about the level of precautions necessary just to get by in the city. He said he was saving for an AK-47 and he would know how to use it, too. There had been "incidents" on buses. Peter was preparing.

Healey found that after a time he could only half listen to what was being said. He was aware of an increasing discomfort brought on by this show of paranoia, by the way Peter seemed to embrace it with such conviction, rehearse it with such extravagance and even a kind of joy. Finally, when he stopped, Healey began to search for something that might compete with Peter's urgency, or rather set his violent designs in some lighter context. The only thing he could think of, however, was the old war-gaming club, and so he began to tell Peter about Monk and his own brother. Monk with his toy pistol. His brother and his interest in native flora and fauna. He tried to make a joke of these things, to give the details the sort of tone that might lend a cozy nostalgia to the talk. Peter, however, seemed barely interested enough to follow the names attached to each story. At one point, he interrupted Healey to say that he couldn't understand why someone would use a *toy* pistol in a robbery.

All the time Healey was talking, Peter was looking for something he wanted to show him in one of the military magazines, which were scattered on the table. Then he was running through the house, shouting for Healey to go on, that he was listening. And Healey began to feel that at any moment he might look up to find Peter standing behind him with a fistful of Healey's own hair falling from his hand. Finally, Peter gave up the hunt and said that he was sure to find it later on and he'd get Dimmy to show it to Healey when Healey came back that evening for dinner. He would have to come back for dinner. Peter would tell Dimmy that Healey was coming. There was no problem about food. His mother would love to have another mouth to feed. Peter himself would, of course, be at work by then and, he added with a yawn, perhaps it was time he went back to bed. First, however, he wanted to show Healey something else.

In an alcove off the dining room were three bird cages, each containing one bird, parakeets. Peter led Healey to the biggest cage.

"This is mine," he said. "This is 'Arold. I drop the *H*. Like he's an English bird. A Cockney." Peter opened the cage door and his large fingers closed gently around the bird.

He drew out his hand and pressed the bird's breast to his cheek, rubbing it lightly across his skin. Then he put it back. They looked at 'Arold for a few moments.

"What about these?" said Healey, pointing to the other cages.

"This is Dimmy's," said Peter. "He's okay. Though I don't like the plumage. You see underneath, that's a congenital defect. But that's okay." Peter turned to walk away.

"And this one?"

"What? That? That thing? That's Alex's, not that he'd care. Bird's a fucking disgrace. A real mongrel."

"You each have one then."

"Mum bought that one for Alex so he wouldn't feel left out, but he's fucked in the head so how would he know? Still, she got the right bird for him. A loser. Look at the shit in the cage. The smell really affects 'Arold."

"Shouldn't you clean it out?"

"Someone should."

"Doesn't your mother?"

"She used to, but the bird started pecking her. No one feeds it properly. Vicious monster. Mum's scared now. Doesn't even take the cover off most days. See how he looks. I think he's blind."

"That's awful."

"It's a mongrel, all right. A cripple." Peter banged his knuckles sharply against the cage and the bird slowly cocked his head. "Monk was always crazy, you know," said Peter, looking at the bird.

"What?" said Healey.

"Just like your brother. No offense, eh. I mean look at mine. I think Mum's trying to poison this cripple with that Russian soup. It's all she feeds him. When you come for dinner, pass on the soup. Dad's already sick on it. Leaked into his lungs, I bet. She can't get me, though, me and 'Arold. We're off to London soon, you know." He slowly lifted his hand so that the bird shuffled away in anticipation. "Sees another one coming, does he?" Then he quickly brought his other hand around and smacked the side, sending the bird to the bottom of its cage. "A toy pistol!" said Peter, shaking his head. "That just wouldn't happen up here. That's a Wellington thing."

The driver was talking about the flashy stuff they'd put up before the Crash. He was saying that in those days the bigwigs had their minds on nothing but quick profit, then they were off to Sydney or London to watch the cricket in their private booths. "All the time is cricket." Then he was on to the Rural Bank Head Office in Manners Street. He said it was bloody criminal. "This building is being submitted into evidence, yeah." Everything was for image, but where was the image of the country's farmers now? He had a brother-in-law who was a farmer in Hawkes Bay for eighteen years. Now he owed a million bucks, and was working in a shearing gang for seven dollars fifty an hour. That was okay with the boys at head office, of course. The foyers, he told Healey, cost a million, no change. Italian marble. Gold on the fixtures. "Step in here it's like being in, you know, some bathrooms from kings and queens. Seven bloody fifty dollars an hour. I am telling you my brother is not been crying many of these tears when certain people who I shall not say their names lost half their fortunes. So big deal, he says to me, now these bastards only have got half a fortune. My kids, he says to me, are going to be really upset about that, I tell you. But these town, mate, like the brother-in-law he says, it is like the legacy of this madness, yeah. And it is complete mess, a hell of mess. Cricket! But I love it, you know. A beautiful city. I am fishing in the weekends."

The doily under the driver's head had been gradually worked out of position by movements that had grown increasingly frantic with each mention of the brother-in-law, and now it fell onto Healey's knee. For one moment Healey thought about putting the doily in his pocket—a souvenir.

"Here," Healey said, handing it back over the seat.

"Ah, this is from Greece, you know. But you are telling me Christchurch. Now this is a pretty town, yeah?"

"You've been?" said Healey.

"Me? No, no. I have a friend who goes to Christchurch six, seven years ago. I seen him last year. Said he is still driving with the same taxi, very same car as here. I think maybe Christchurch people is not so bothered with old car for taxis but he say is still going strong, no problem. No hills, he tells me. Only Port Hills, okay?"

"Yeah, but the hills," said Healey. "Don't you find the hills, you know, interesting?"

"Oh, hell's crumbs, mate, interesting!" The driver gave a snort. "I tell you. I not doing this business for interesting. Christ. New transmission, new gearbox this last month. You know what these little packages are affording to me? Three and a half. Thousand. This taxis is two years old, friend. My mechanic look at me and say, completely stripped it, mate. You maybe are hearing this pulling now? That is my new problem with this hills. These is interesting enough for me.''

Here in the city of paths, Healey was reminded of the sentence he had read in the city of wide American four-lane roads in which the writer who had choked on a different sentence was living: "The path is the fundamental existential symbol which concretizes time." In the American city, of course, walking was a sign only that you were without a car. Even the students who lived just off campus would drive to school in the cars they had been given by their parents. You could walk for some distance in any direction without coming across another pedestrian, which contributed to a certain level of paranoia, Healey growing to believe that the people in the passing cars were looking at him as if he were mad. He felt sure that one day he would be the cause of an accident with his solitary walking. And without such a network of walking routes, perhaps the Midwestern city had lacked a certain firmness or reality for him. Hadn't he tended to lose track of the days while at the same time spending much of the energy that should have gone into his study on calculating how many weeks and months would have to elapse before he could return home?

When they arrived, the driver pushed the button for the trunk and then reached between his knees for the cup once more. "Slow, slow, slow," he said. "Not a drop is dropped.''

Healey paid him and got out. Taking his case from the trunk, he looked up through the bushes toward his parents' house.

"You need a hand, mate?" the driver called from his window.

"I've got it," said Healey.

"Hernia city," said the driver. "I am telling you what my wife says when we visit this other brother, a young man. The steps, these are killers. These brothers was in the moving business here. Carrying, carrying, all the time. Up and down, up and down. No escaping. The back of this one brother is completely gone, you know. Kaput! Cannot pick up his very shoes. This wife of the brother has to go round behind him, always helping him, you know. Interesting you say to me? Ask her, I am telling you, she is bloody fascinated, I bet. This—what do you say?—*vertebrae* on this brother is popping like the first teeth come out on my little girl. Pop. Pop. Pop."

Then both of them were looking up the slope, Healey holding his suitcase, the driver his breakfast cup. They stayed motionless like this for several moments.

"You up there?" said the driver finally.

Healey nodded.

"Hi, Wellington," said the driver.

"Hi, Greece," said Healey.

3

The
King of
Mount Edgeware

ON THE MORNING AFTER THE FUNERAL HEALEY HAD RISEN early in a house already filled with aunts in dressing gowns. The uncles, too, he found to his annoyance, were up, although they had tended to accumulate in the living room while the women moved about in the kitchen.

In the evening the living room had belonged to the aunts, he thought, just as in the morning the kitchen was clearly their territory and the husbands might only approach for refills of tea. Only now, with the women in the kitchen, could the men venture into the living room, though they did so, he noticed, with a kind of exaggerated freedom—striding about, moving from chair to chair—as if the room had been theirs all along and they'd merely tolerated the wives' evening proprietorship. Here they were secretly brewing between them the game of golf that would shortly be announced in the kitchen as a *fait accompli*. This, Healey knew, was the game which would cause the uncles' mostly silent enmity to flourish for another year or until they could get together for what his father always called "a bit of a hit around." Soon, of course, the father would quietly remove himself to the patio from where the sounds of violent swings would issue as he tried to regain the form that had earned him his narrow, bitter victory on their last outing.

"Whoa, whoa, here's someone who'll show us up, us old fellahs," an uncle called out as Healey looked into the room. "Here's our man." Healey, however, quickly retreated, offering his apologies, recognizing in the invitation a sharpening of that combative tone that would find its fullest expression later that afternoon in the lifting of massive divots from the fairways of the Karori Golf Club. He explained that he was meeting an old friend.

The friend lived in the Aro Valley and now, as Healey rediscovered a flight of steps down an unmarked alleyway, which he believed was a shortcut to the house, he came across a street that was very familiar to him, though in a new way. It then struck him that he had taken this particular street in the Aro Valley many times before as a university student without recognizing it as the same one he and his mother had driven up to deliver a parcel to the cousin who had stood a little way away from the hugging at the funeral in his unfamiliar short, neat hair and dark suit. At the time of the delivery, perhaps seventeen or eighteen years before, the cousin had been a long-haired, barefoot drug addict and occasional construction worker.

In his second year as a university student, Healey had often toiled up this street, generally with his head down and feeling the prickly sensation of sweat breaking out over his back beneath his shirt and sweater and coat. He never remembered it as hot or sunny in this street but always as chilly and sweaty. There was the constant smell of rotting piles and floorboards, rusted drainpipes, drawn curtains behind which faces seemed to have just retreated, old and damp sofas decaying on high verandas weighted down with car tires and abandoned washing machines. From one of the windows, perhaps, a string on which a T-shirt or a row of plastic bags was drying. All this Healey could see most days without lifting his head while struggling up the steep, broken footpath and imagining the time when, shortly, he'd be sitting down with his coat off in the close atmosphere of a tutorial in which he would listen to the other students discussing the books of a writer who was no longer thought to have documented the ills of Victorian society but rather to have written out his own fantasy that sometimes coincided with what the writer saw when he walked around the streets of the city. Many of his readers now believed the city "belonged" to the writer, since they, too, whenever they thought of that city saw in their minds the images he had described.

Often Healey would think of opening his mouth, but whenever he actually succeeded in making a sound, the words came out heated and overwrought, as if he had been pondering the issues very intensely and secretly seething against the responses of the other students so that he found himself introducing a note of harshness totally out of proportion with the air of amiability in which the class was conducted. Healey longed to be able to speak as if he were thinking while he spoke and not as if he had lost all patience with everyone in the room, including himself, and could only utter sharp, brief comments in correction of what had already been said.

Healey sometimes thought that if he took a different route to the university on the morning of the tutorial, his problems with public speaking would vanish, since he always seemed to arrive agitated and with too many layers of clothing on from the struggle up through the Aro Valley. He believed that if he could enter the university buildings on the level, having walked on the flat, the breathless stabs of commentary that usually caused the other students to look at him would give way to the natural patterns of articulated thought, slightly hesitating, but flowing on and filling the tutorial room with the calm of a well-turned sensibility. But this was impossible. There was no other route, except by the longest method of walking into town and then catching the cable car or taking one of the lifts up through the James Cook Hotel, which linked the Quay with the Terrace. This would probably cause him to miss the tutorial or arrive so late that he would be the object of irritation as he opened the door of the small room, found a place to sit, took out his books, placed his coat on the back of the chair, and attempted to pick up the discussion that he had interrupted. And even by this route through the downtown buildings, still there was the hated upward climb toward Kelburn Parade.

The university had been built on a hill overlooking the city so that no idea could ever reach its walls. No mind could achieve the equanimity of knowledge, he thought, as he prepared his next tutorial outburst, because of the constant steps and slopes which first had to be negotiated. No meeting, lecture, or seminar could be attended where all the participants were evenly well disposed toward the matter in hand, because they were too aware either of the climb that had brought them there or of the descent or ascent that would follow. Still, he imagined the day when he would be able to speak at length and with intelligent ease and when what he said was not met with an awkward silence that the tutor then rushed to fill as if taking the last steps of an unbearable staircase.

In the years since Healey and his mother had delivered the parcel to the house no different from those Healey took in at a glance while sweating his way to the tutorial, the cousin had spent long periods of time in psychiatric hospitals because of fits of violence toward himself and his parents. Watching him from across the room after the funeral, Healey had the sense of someone extravagantly composed. The hair, the suit, the polished shoes existed almost exclusively as tokens of pure effort, he thought, so that he had difficulty recognizing in this figure the cousin who on the day of the parcel could barely lift himself out of bed to answer the door, even though it was afternoon, and could scarcely utter a sound for some time after he had taken the parcel in hands that were shaking uncontrollably. The parcel, containing clothes and food, had been sent first to Healey's parents' house, with a letter asking that it be delivered in person to the cousin. The cousin's parents needed to know that their son had been seen to receive the brown paper parcel and that the food that had originated in the kitchen he had known through childhood was now with him again, in the aunt's words, to "nourish and protect" him. "What's this?" he finally said, bringing the parcel to his ear. "A bomb or something?"

The cousin had earlier cut his parents off completely, writing to them to say he was never going back to that house and that town which had made him what he was. Besides, he wrote, living in Wellington, he worked when he had to, he had a place of his own, and there was no one behaving *like a sick martyr around him.*

The cousin lived in a second-floor bed-sit in a two-story clapboard house near the top of the street. To reach his door, which was at the rear of the house, close to the mossy bank into which the house seemed to be sinking, Healey and his mother had to climb the wooden steps of an old fire escape that shook as they went up. For once, the sun came out and Healey first felt the sensation of prickling sweat that in the future would be with him every time he entered this street. The sunlight was fierce on the veranda circling the upper story, yet there was no heat, only the brightness of the light, which seemed to have burst through the clouds for the sole purpose of blinding the cousin when finally he appeared at the door and asked who was there.

The cousin had always viewed Healey's side of the family

with a kind of affectionate envy, Healey thought on the morning after the funeral, since they were from the big city and had lived, in the cousin's opinion, which he had delivered on the day of the parcel, sophisticated lives under a limitless variety of stimuli, whereas he had grown up, he said, in a small town where there were only one or two things to keep the mind from turning in on itself in a violent and destructive way. When he had been living overseas and was on hallucinogens, the cousin had written not to his own parents but to Healey's, including drawings of himself stretched out on the decks of yachts and descriptions of those minutes he was living as he wrote, though he never described what had happened before or what was likely to happen after he put down the pen. He wrote as if Healey's parents could understand the stimuli under whose wild pressures he was now living his life in a big overseas city. His own parents, he said, could never understand, coming from that small town that had martyred itself in the cause of avoiding at all costs professing a faith in any sort of excitement or even reality.

More recently, the cousin had completed the university degree he had begun almost twenty years before, when on leaving the town of his childhood he had been the envy of his classmates, a very bright and even athletic student who everyone said was sure to do well in whatever field he tried. After the first year of his degree, in which he missed too many lectures and deadlines to maintain his bursary for the next year, he left to go overseas, where it was generally thought that, following the temporary aberration of a university that had not really suited his needs, he would regain the momentum that had made him so popular and successful at home, returning in the not-too-distant future the promise of youth realized.

The infantile drawings of the cousin on the sunlit decks of yachts, which Healey, as a boy, had laughed at when they arrived in the post, appeared now while Healey and his mother were climbing the fire escape as increasingly desperate bulletins from a life whose sole purpose had been to mock the aspirations others had for that life. The cousin had been so closely identified with these aspirations that he had attempted to disappear into the "wild" moments of letter writing and leave behind only a sick cartoon of his existence for people to puzzle over. And as the door of the house was being opened and the cousin stood with a towel around his waist, shielding his eyes from the reflected sunshine, Healey immediately thought of the shining veranda as the bright deck of the yacht on which the cousin had pictured himself, sailing breezily from one moment to the next.

A few years before the delivery of the parcel, Healey's parents had taken the children on holiday to the small North Island town of Edgeware in which the cousin had grown up. They were to stay in the house of the cousin's parents while Healey's father's sister and her husband were to live for three weeks in the Healey's place in Wellington. This house swapping was the most favored form of holidaying among certain branches of the family, since it was a model of economy and good sense for one family to be using something another family didn't need at the time. It was a scheme, Healey's father said, as good as the people who were in it, and naturally certain families, on the basis of past record, were politely excluded from the swap network.

One year, when it seemed that every other possibility had been exhausted, Healey's father had entered into the protracted business of persuading the Edgeware relatives—who had never really been involved in the network, theirs being among the least desirable locations—that three weeks in the big city would actually be a good break for them. Their only son, Healey's cousin, was by this time living overseas and supporting his drug habit by means of the "loans" his father kept sending, even after everyone had agreed that without this easy money he would soon come home and get a decent job. The father of the cousin wrote to Healey's parents that the boy was living in "a hellish vortex" in Sydney. If only they could get him back here! The father wrote that they didn't like to be away from the house for too long in case their son tried to make contact. He said this even though in two years the boy had never sent them so much as a letter or any communication except to say that he would not be returning, and this message had been scrawled on the back of a postcard showing a view of the Sydney Opera House from the water. The father also wrote that they preferred going north for their holidays, not south. He wrote that they'd always gone north for the warmer climate and because of his wife's lungs. "Breathing-wise," he wrote, "it's best we avoid the winds coming off Cook Strait."

When it seemed that they would never agree to come to Wellington and Healey's father had rung them one final time—

less to ask again if they wouldn't consider a swap than to inquire after his sister's "illness," which he had always expressed impatience over but which now, following his own recent "scare" with a gallstone, he seemed to consider if not serious at least not wholly imaginary—the Edgeware relatives suddenly agreed to the deal. They said they recognized the importance for the Healey children, especially, of a quieter, steadier environment. Healey's sister and brother, older than him by three and two years respectively, sank into a deep holiday despondency when they found out they would be going after all to the town from which their mad cousin came. An inland town. No beach! No cinema! No friends.

Healey himself expressed the same abject disappointment as his siblings so that they might produce what his sister called a "unified front" against their father. First, they thought, they would win over their mother, arguing that she could just as well sit in her own garden in Wellington reading her books as travel three hundred miles to sit in someone else's to do exactly the same thing. She was, however, noncommittal and told them it was "out of her hands." Whenever their mother used this phrase they knew their chances were almost gone, but with nothing left to lose, as the sister said, they approached their father. Having worked at the negotiations for months, however, to engineer a swap which he had originally been only half interested in pursuing, the father now clung to the idea of Edgeware as if to an inheritance that his family was trying to jealously prize away from him. There would be no arguments.

The Edgeware house was small and dull—an old people's

home filled with shelves displaying tiny porcelain figures, egg cups, pieces of crystal—an arrangement that forced them all to constantly check their movements and step lightly about the rooms for fear of dislodging what the father's sister had denoted in bold, black lettering in a long list she had fixed to the fridge door as "the valuables." There was also a large oak cabinet strategically placed in the already cramped hallway so that a decent walking speed could not be achieved; rather one had to edge along cautiously, constantly adjusting one's stride to the shiver of the aunt's objects. Even their father, who on first entering the house, eager to quell any rebelliousness, had loudly admired the piece for its grain, after a few days of banging his elbow on the cabinet's sharp edges, was heard to remark on its ugliness and its obstructiveness. This, as the aunt's inventory suggested, was where the "good" glasses were kept together with the silver, although there was no corresponding information as to the whereabouts of the key that might unlock these treasures. In the living room, an ancient television set had been built into a wooden wall unit and fixed in a certain position, which meant that not everyone in the room could watch the screen at the same time but that reports as to the goings on in important scenes had to be provided by the person occupying "the chair." Such was the burden of this narrating and the arguments it provoked, the television, which at first had seemed the children's only hope, came to lie mostly idle through the evenings.

The boys slept in the mad cousin's room, which had been left, Healey thought, as if its former occupant would shortly be coming back to town as the sporty, overachieving seventeen year old who had walked out years before. On his return he would be in need of the shelf with his trophies, a wall display of his certificates, and the framed, enlarged photos of himself crossing finish lines running barefoot, pushing his chest out in his white singlet toward the unbroken tape. All these images would remind him of himself when he returned from the vortex of Sydney to begin again, in his mother's words, with "a clean slate."

At the reception, while looking across the room in the direction of the composed figure of the cousin, Healey experienced again the odd sensation of sleeping in someone else's bed without their permission, without even their knowledge. And when he finally met the cousin's eye, for a moment it was as if he had been caught out, that the cousin had come across him studying his most private possessions, hunting through his drawers, as indeed Healey had, though he was always careful to follow at least the letter of the aunt's written directions to "leave as is." In this moment it was as if the cousin had made an unexpected return, entering his boyhood bedroom at the point when Healey had been looking too intently at one particular photograph prized above all for the truth it contained about the cousin. This photograph, Healey remembered while looking at the cousin, was framed and hung above the cousin's bed in the house where he had grown up and in which they'd spent those three weeks many summers ago. It was titled *The King of Mount Edgeware, 197–*.

Healey's parents now lived in a three-bedroom house on the top of a hill near the university. Nearly every room afforded spectacular harbor views so that at the reception much of the conversation had centered on the land and the water that had been "lain bare" like this at their feet, groups standing at the windows pointing out the features they recognized and those they wanted explained to them, and saying how beautiful the city looked, speaking always from a sense of surprise. "You could rent this to the Japanese for weekends," one uncle said. "You know, if this *revolved*." Healey, too, spent much of the time excusing himself from one party in front of one window to join another at the neighboring viewing post, before moving off into the adjoining room to complete the vista. On the streets below, the tiny roofs of cars moved too slowly while the sails of those few yachts braving the choppy conditions went around the container ships anchored in the middle of the harbor. It was only when his mother asked him why he was looking like that—was he worried about something?—that he realized this moving from window to window had caused him to become anxious. Healey had the feeling that in the moments he was away from the windows the city might somehow lose its beauty. Every time someone turned away from the window, he felt, ridiculously, that he needed to move to fill the vacant spot.

As a child, Healey had often thought that the result of any significant sports event—a cricket match or soccer game— was not fully present to him, or verified, unless he had been watching over it. He believed a result that he hadn't expected might well have been different had he been there at the time when it was decided. The English soccer scores, which came through early on Sunday morning, were particularly painful to listen to, since he always felt things had been going on behind his back and that his team had been playing, in effect, with ten men. In the same way, he believed he needed to verify the landscape as seen from his parents' house, a house that had first been the object of some displeasure among the guests because of the endless steps leading to the front door but was now envied for its "magisterial" location. The Auckland contingent, in particular, who had always considered the size and spread of their city to be a mark of superiority over this insular, self-contained city in the south, now saw how satisfying it was to take in a whole place almost in one sighting, since Wellington was not exhausted in a quick glance as they had previously imagined, but raised, as it were, to the eye for repeated inspection. Of course, the aunts had grown up in this city, and yet Healey felt that often this seemed to cause them to behave toward it in the same way a piece of slightly embarrassing juvenilia might be approached—dismissively, and with a degree of sentimentality that would always obscure true seeing.

When Healey recognized this impulse in himself toward the obsessive collecting and discarding of views and understood in his mother's question that his face was creased with a look of concern—the same look, he guessed, which had assembled across his features whenever he was about to speak out in the tutorial—he was annoyed and spoke more sharply than he intended in telling her that nothing at all was wrong.

On entering the harbor, the architect beside him catego-
rizing from the deck of the ferry what he saw to be the dom-
inant forms of the landscape, Healey had thought with
confidence of the phrase "a return home," believing the city
to be his with each word the architect uttered. Now, inside
the city and above it, in the fashionable hill suburb that he
had always had to climb to as a university student, with his
head down, he had no confidence and could only make his
peace by attempting to join together the landscapes framed in
his parents' windows by rushing from room to room, much
as a child runs through a quiet house early in the morning,
upset that he is the only one awake.

Each year the aunt and uncle's district held a competition for
the fastest ascent of Mount Edgeware, a large hill of about
two thousand feet that stood to the north of the town and
was the only feature on an otherwise flat horizon. A hundred
or so competitors of all ages took part from around the re-
gion, training for this one day, devising tactics, and imagining
the time when they would be standing on the summit looking
down on the houses in which they lived, trying to work out
which was their roof. When the Healeys arrived for their three-
week stay, they had already missed the annual event by a
month, although the posters advertising the race were still up
everywhere, pinned to lampposts, on noticeboards in the post
office and in the bank, in the windows of shops, confirming
in the children's minds the impression of a dead community
and a long, uneventful summer. His sister used this against
the town, making announcements each morning as to how

many days it was until next year's mountain race, and ignoring Healey's pleas that, if not a little dangerous, then certainly her goading had lost its freshness. "What is it?" she would say to the puzzled shopkeepers, "only three hundred and twenty-three to go?"

Studying the photographs and newspaper clippings in the cousin's room, Healey learned that the cousin, in the year before he left for university, had, in fact, won the junior section of the Mount Edgeware race, breaking the long-standing record and setting a mark which the newspaper reported to be "almost invincible." It was only when Healey was returning to Christchurch on the ferry and was reading from the scrapbook clipping about his grandfather's sporting achievements, having had the impression that he was leaving the city prematurely, that he remembered this exact phrase—just as later in the voyage it was only when he was listening to the veteran jogger's "three-hour barrier" on the poop deck while "considering" the American's "proposition," that he remembered the cousin's time of "forty-two minutes," which the paper said had "smashed the old fifty-minute barrier."

In the second week of their stay, Healey's father announced that they would set out in the morning to climb Mount Edgeware. Healey's mother said she would prefer to stay down on the flat that day and catch up on some reading, though she had spent every afternoon of the past week in her sister-in-law's back garden doing exactly that. Wherever she went, she was always pursued by a column of library books. She would often complain of having four or five on the go at one

time and refer to them in exasperation as though they had
chosen her from all the other library users, forcing them-
selves into her life and swallowing her spare time. It was
sometimes remarked upon by her sisters, partly in admiration
but also, Healey thought, in mild censure, that Angela could
read a book *in any situation*. In later years, Healey came to
understand that, just as when he had been a child he had
coveted the grandfather's knee, so in watching his mother
reading he had begun to see the page she was now turning,
which at first he had resented, since it took her away from
the family, as a kind of vantage point which he, too, might
one day reach toward.

"I won't be going myself," she said. "But it's an exciting
idea." Healey knew that whenever his mother used the word
idea, she meant that for her it would never have the firmness
of reality and that she had already put it out of her mind.
Healey's sister, seizing the opportunity, also said she would
prefer to stay at home, but the father informed her of the
necessity of climbing Mount Edgeware *as a family*, and Healey
knew that whenever his father used this phrase he meant that
because they were his children they had a duty to support
him in his whims and stand beside him for the whole world
to see in the public spectacle he often conceived of as father-
hood.

Healey's father had no idea as to which road would take
them to the bottom of the Mount so that they might begin
their climb. Nor in defeat did he ask any of the locals. In-
stead he pointed the car in the right direction and drove. It
was seven in the morning. They quickly found themselves on

back roads that turned into farm properties where barking dogs raced at the car, and despite the fact that the Mount was only ten minutes from the town, they drove for half an hour without appearing to get any closer. Every road they tried seemed to take them around the Mount at a certain distance so that it felt as if they were mapping the far circumference of the hill's influence without ever puncturing the inner circle. Healey watched the Mount through the side window; now it was to the west of them, now to the east, and still no road would let them nearer.

At first its changing position was something worth commenting on—"There it is!" he said, "I see it"—calls which were then picked up by his sister and mimicked with what Healey considered an unhealthy disregard for their father's worsening mood. "Hey, there she goes!" she yelled, pointing at the mountain which filled their view. The father, however, seemed scarcely to hear these useless reports, absorbed as he was in his own belief that there had to be an entrance to the National Park that surrounded the Mount. After a time, the children sank into a hostile silence, already looking forward to driving back to the town where they could finally escape the words "clean through the forest," which now issued from the father again and again, as if he had gone into a trance.

Finally, when they had been driving alongside a disused section of railway track, a clearing appeared and suddenly the Mount did seem a little closer. Healey's father stopped the car. "This is it, then," he announced. "We'll walk in from here."

"From where?" Healey's sister said.

There was no track, there was no possible opening in the bush that would lead them to the Mount, which was still a good distance away. But the father, already pulling on his pack, assured them it was "a light tramp." He was even beginning to walk away from the car that had failed to deliver them and that he was now not bothering to lock—almost as punishment, thought Healey, sensing in his father an urgency to overcome the failures of the immediate past with a throttling of the present—striding into the bush now, so that his children had to run, despite themselves, to catch up, while Healey was telling his brother under his breath, which still tasted of toothpaste, that next year he, the brother, would have his driver's license—wouldn't he—and they'd drive off—wouldn't they—and leave the silly bastard where they couldn't find him. "You'll be fifteen then," said Healey. "Then things will change." The brother heard him out sulkily but said nothing. He was in the first stages of a kind of retreat which he periodically fell into and from which Healey knew it was impossible to retrieve him.

For the next hour they wordlessly pushed through the dense vegetation, the father in the lead, hammering at branches with a large stick, the children, too, thrashing almost senselessly at the bush that had swallowed the Mount. Occasionally they came across a clearing, a grassy slope which the morning sun had filled with a translucent green, and they stood for a few moments looking up at the Mount before beginning again their surly path making.

On one of these grassy slopes, Healey's sister sat down

and started taking off her hiking boots—the father had outfitted them all with boots in a family shopping expedition—and as Healey and his brother watched her massage the toes of one socked foot, then the other, and waited for the father's words, the father himself had sat down nearby and was also working off his boots, saying, "Good, good, a nice place to rest a little." All of them lay back then on the shining grass of the clearing and closed their eyes. When eventually they pushed on toward the Mount there was talk among them and laughter, or at least a kind of delirium. Even when Healey asked why, when it had taken their cousin just forty-two minutes to get to the top, had they been going for more than two hours without even reaching the Mount, there was laughter and not, as would have been heard before his sister massaged her toes on the shining grass, the increased tempo of bush-beating.

As they struggled through the bush, Healey could not help thinking of the photograph titled *The King of Mount Edgeware, 197–,* in which the cousin was pictured at the summit in running shoes and a singlet—not outfitted in heavy boots and woolen bush shirts, but dressed lightly, as for exercise. Yet what Healey found remarkable was the expression on the winner's face, which was not one of jubilation but rather an odd indifference, a distance, as if the cousin had already begun moving away from the camera and from the town that now lay at his feet. It was only by reaching this height, Healey thought, and within a certain time that had never been matched that the cousin had been able to take his leave. In this way, his stunning victory was a culmination of everything that he had achieved in his life up to that point and also a revelation, perhaps, of the path ahead; but in neither of these, the look on his face said, could he take any comfort, since just as Healey, his brother, his sister, and their father had been affected by the grassy clearing under the Mount, so the cousin on the flat peak of the Mount had finally *come to his senses*.

When, at last, they reached the bottom of the Mount, Healey had already begun to think of the place as "belonging" to the cousin, so that climbing the wide, circling path which led to the top, he had the same feeling of trespassing as when he climbed into the top bunk in the cousin's bedroom.

As Healey caught the eye of the cousin at the funeral reception, he saw that the look which had been captured in the photograph was now hollowed out so that what remained, he thought, was distance without perception. A looking off without the corresponding act of recognition. Standing high above the city and not far from the street in which he had lived for several years and once received a brown paper parcel from Healey and his mother, the cousin, Healey believed, no longer knew where he was but only how he was feeling at this particular moment, and then again at the next, since when Healey actually went across and introduced himself, the cousin's conversation was built almost exclusively around such phrases as "I'm good now," "I'm quite thirsty," "I have a degree." It was not that he spoke unintelligently, but the relentless recording of the immediate present caused Healey to make an excuse for leaving the cousin who had run out on his parents beside a window, which, because of the sudden glare of sunshine breaking through the clouds, appeared momentarily blank.

Near the summit, they came across a small lake or volcanic pond, and the sight of the water after the hot climb made them quickly take off their clothes, put on their swimsuits, and run to the water's edge. At the first touch of water, the children cried out. The water was lukewarm and felt close as it gathered at their ankles like damp cloth. Healey's sister danced with high steps back to her clothes, shrieking that there were things in the pond. The water was almost black and, looking down at his feet, Healey saw that it was filled with the tiny, dark bodies of tadpoles, so thickly layered the bottom could not be seen. The father, meanwhile, had cruised out to the middle of the pond with his stiff breaststroke. "I don't want you putting your heads underwater," he called out. "Amoebas." The word darted back across the surface and stung the boys where they stood stationary up to their thighs in the dense, throbbing material. They couldn't move. In the hot pools of Rotorua people had died from this word; it had crawled into their ears and eaten through to nest in their skulls. After a brief show of hanging around and cooling off, they retreated. Then they sat in the grass and watched the father, with his ludicrous breaststroke and his proud head stuck high in the air above the amoebas, circling the dense, black pond.

Walking the short distance from the pond to the summit they saw ahead of them on the track a man in the brown uniform of the Forest Service, as if in camouflage, Healey thought, except for the white knee-length walking socks, which shone like small fluorescent tubes. "I'll do all the talking," the father whispered to them.

The moment the ranger was within earshot, the father began speaking very loudly and rapidly to him, telling him where they were from, how long they were staying—did he happen to know his sister who'd lived in the township for thirty years?—before launching into details about his own previous experience in tramping and climbing. The ranger, stepping back a little from this onslaught, said they had a beautiful day for it but that it was a shame they'd missed the great race, because then the people of the town really made a fuss over the Mount. Most of the year they forgot about it, he said, then at race time, well, naturally it caused some problems, that many folk on the Mount all at once and some folk just didn't know how to treat nature, had never cared or even thought about the Mount before this one day and after that it was business as usual for another year. "Wellington, you say," the ranger said.

"Not originally, of course," said the father. "Originally from the deep south."

"Wellington," the ranger repeated, shaking his head. "Me, I've never been to that neck of the woods. No, I never have. Not Wellington." Then he laughed and looked at the children. "These yours?"

"That's the tribe," said the father.

"Wellington," said the ranger.

When the ranger had finally walked off, the father told

the children that he hadn't wanted him to know about their little hike into the Mount because they might have been on land they shouldn't have and these forestry chaps, he said, had some odd opinions about sticking to the marked tracks, which was why he had told him about his previous experience in rough country. "These chaps," he said, "they hear you're from Wellington, see."

Soon they reached the summit, a flat treeless crown, but after their swim in the volcanic pond, a strange boredom had set in, as if they'd already reached a higher peak some time ago and this was just another lookout point. They walked around it a few times, not quite knowing what to do. It seemed so small. They bumped into each other. "This is the summit," their father said. But then he, too, fell silent. After a few minutes of this uncomfortable pacing they were ready to leave.

Their father was pointing out the views as if in a hurry— endless vistas of flat farmland and, to the south, a cluster of shining roofs, which was the town where their mother sat reading her books. Moving off the summit, they pulled from their packs the sandwiches she had prepared for them, eating quickly, almost violently, inspecting the cuts and scratches on their bare legs. Then they began to trot down the Mount, gaining speed as they went, surrendering themselves to the momentum of the slope. "If you kids fall—," the father was shouting from somewhere back on the path, beginning to break into a jog himself, though for two thousand giddy feet Healey felt that nothing was going to catch them.

———

While following the shortcut that took him down the street on which Healey now recognized the house his cousin had lived in, he thought of how it was that a cousin on the paternal side of the family had come to be at the funeral of Healey's maternal grandfather, which was, of course, why the cousin had stood mostly alone at the window while everyone else was embracing wildly and guessing at each other.

In the later years of his grandfather's life, when he had been living in the Auckland rest home, Healey's mother would periodically fly up from Wellington to visit him. On one such occasion, by chance, she met in the street the cousin, who at this time was in that city completing the university degree he had abandoned years before. The cousin had always found his aunt to be a sympathetic figure, coming as she did from a place he considered the exact opposite of his hometown. On the day of the parcel, the cousin, once he had overcome the initial shock of being visited and had woken up properly, acted as if he were very pleased to see them, and had attempted to get them a cup of tea, unsuccessfully, since it first appeared he was out of milk and then that he was out of tea and even finding three cups, he finally admitted, might have been difficult. Now, in Auckland, he urged Healey's mother to sit with him in a coffee shop while he explained some of the intricacies of psychology and sociology in which he was preparing to sit an exam.

When Healey's mother got up to leave for visiting hours at the rest home, the cousin followed her to the car, although by now he had grown silent, as if, she later told Healey, having given her the full benefit of all his tertiary learning, he expected something in return. She was forced to fill the silence by speaking about her father. "Your cousin made me nervous with that staring," she said. Next she had found herself driving her nephew to the home. This had not been her intention. She first asked whether she could drop him somewhere on the way, and he had accepted the invitation without specifying where exactly he wanted to go. Then, as they were driving along, he announced that his plans could wait—as if he were sacrificing *his* afternoon—and that he would accompany her to the rest home, though of course this had never been mentioned as a possibility.

Healey's grandfather, however, when they reached the home, said he was delighted to see not one visitor but two and a young person in a place where there were never any young people. When they had sat down in the communal lounge, the cousin immediately announced that he was thirsty, yet his aunt had just bought him several cups of coffee while he was talking on and on about his study schedule and, in the process, making them late for afternoon tea. The last trolley was being wheeled past them as they walked in. The cousin then said he would never be able to understand a place where you couldn't just go and make yourself a cup of tea whenever you wanted. Healey's grandfather had, apparently, laughed at this remark as if in approval, announcing that the cousin had something there, since he, too, he said, now felt thirsty even though afternoon tea had just concluded, which went to show, he said, that the human body was not simply a mechanism that you wound like a clock. Healey's mother was dispatched to find some tea while the pair of them, she said, carried on like old cell mates.

For the remainder of the visit the cousin had entertained the grandfather by saying, it seemed, the first thing that came into his head, speaking earnestly of all manner of mad schemes. "Mad schemes," Healey's mother interrupted herself. "I suppose I'm not allowed to say that, am I, but they were, you know, mad as a meat ax, really. Schemes of deer farming, of living on uninhabited islands, whatever. And all of it fascinating to his audience. Well, it wasn't exactly that your grandfather was interested in the details," she said. "I doubt if he actually heard the bulk of it. Whenever I said something he always asked me to repeat it, but never with your cousin. He just let him go on. Every now and then he'd turn to me and say, 'Listen to this chap talk, will you!' but, you know, you could tell he wasn't taking it in, not the sense. He liked the sound of it, I think. Then he'd occasionally find some little opening and start back at your cousin. I haven't seen him so animated in years, which is a good sign, isn't it? Not that your cousin was any more interested in what was being said to him, but he had to wait it out until his turn came around again. Both of them, I think, liked the battle, the contest of it. Me? Oh, they didn't bother about me. I wasn't there. I was the chauffeur. The tea lady."

After this, Healey's mother had learned from her Auckland sisters that the cousin had become a frequent visitor to the rest home, often arriving just after afternoon tea, never at quite the correct time, always managing to create a small fuss. He would sit with their father, they said, who always spoke highly of his new young friend and told the daughters that he had learned much that day about the id and the ego. The sisters, who knew the cousin's history, could never bring themselves to tell Daddy about his visitor, but quietly informed the staff that the young academically minded man sitting with Mr. Banks had once pulled a knife on his own father and had tried to use it on himself, although he was now deemed no longer a "nuisance."

When Healey heard about this unlikely friendship, he had thought the reason the cousin was going to the home was for the heat—the rooms were kept very warm all year-round—and for the food, and he had seen it as a piece of harmless opportunism. Yet he also experienced a prick of envy and guilt, too, picturing the old man indulging the cousin, who was not even a blood relation, while the real grandson sat eight hundred miles away and had only thought to visit the grandfather once or twice in all those years, despite the so-called, the so-thought sacred bond that existed between them. In the instant that he recognized who it was at the funeral reception in the dark suit and neat hair, standing off to one side, stupidly staring out the window, Healey had felt an intense irritation with the cousin, which he then transformed into a laugh—the same laugh he had used years before against the childish self-portraits of the cousin on yachts, and which he now understood had always issued from him whenever he had been forced to experience any deep emotion.

As he passed his cousin's old house in the Aro Valley and, looking at the veranda that circled the upper story, thought of the wide path up Mount Edgeware, the first tears came to his eyes. The first tears, the prickling of sweat, the chill. Not even at the graveside had he wept; only now the first tears came, he thought, not when you expect them at all, but on this street. Behind the curtains, he thought, he was being observed. In the dingy flats above the sounds of the television, they were talking about him, remarking on his state, secretly peeping at him, and forcing him to look away, to look at the broken lines of the footpath that he was now hurrying down.

4

Creek

HEALEY HAD ALWAYS KNOWN THE HOUSE BY SIGHT, BUT after two years away, as he came to the group of similar-looking houses that stood together toward the city end of the street, he experienced a moment of panic—was the friend's house blue? Were the windows trimmed in that green? Approaching one house, he turned away—this fence had recently been repaired. In another there was brick paving leading to the door. So much industry, the little gentrifying details—these threw him. He realized he had never known properly the number of the friend's house.

In the two years in Christchurch, having written and received countless letters through his job at the paper, he had neither written to nor received a letter from the friend, whose handwriting, anyway, he knew to be almost indecipherable. Nor could Healey imagine the friend sitting still for long enough to compose a page of sentences. The thought of using "Dear" and "Love," he knew, would be enough to put him off writing any letter which was not a business letter. It was not that the friend lacked feeling, Healey thought. Perhaps it could be said that he had cultivated a suspicion of the conventional forms of its expression, especially in writing, but Healey considered such suspicion misplaced and exaggerated, since he believed it had only grown in the years in which their friendship had assumed the character of their respective professions. As Healey had moved more toward books and what the friend always called the literary world, the friend had felt more and more constricted in this area, until even the most casual letter could hardly be written because of the pressure the friend felt to disown each sentence as it appeared, through humor or irony or mockery, with the result that little or nothing could now be said between them.

It was not until much later that Healey came to understand that the friend's letters, which had grown less and less frequent when Healey was living in America, were, in effect, copies of his own, or at least examples of a shared style, and that he, too, could not put down in writing anything that was not first "doctored" and altered beyond recognition. As he walked down Aro Street and could find no excuse in the wind, which was now at his back, for the stinging in his eyes, he believed the time was approaching when something might finally be said between them.

The friend had grown up fifteen kilometers to the north in the Hutt Valley, a flat expanse given shape by the river that ran through its middle and the hills that rose on either side. Healey could not resist the symmetry in supposing that it was, after all, natural for the friend to have bought his house on this particular street, which acted as the main artery through the Aro Valley and which was surrounded by a network of steep tributaries, as if, standing in his kitchen, the friend might imagine himself looking up at the hills from the bed of the Hutt River.

As he stood, hesitating between the houses, Healey thought of the journey that the friend in Lower Hutt had invited him on when they were boys. They were to walk the length of the creek system that threaded together many of the suburbs of Lower Hutt but that remained a mostly hidden dimension of the life of that city. For much of its length the creek was obscured by footpaths, low bridges, and the properties through which it ran. In all his previous visits to the friend's house, Healey had never suspected that beneath the driveway water was being carried in secret channels. On this journey, however, he remembered he'd become disoriented and had gone through a moment when he said to himself that he would never again visit Lower Hutt or his so-called friend, as he stood up to his knees in the dirty creek water, peering through branches at places which all looked alike.

The friend was now a lawyer, a profession whose training depended upon the forming in its aspirants' minds of the image of themselves in the posture of "the lawyer." Once this image was secure, the lawyer was admitted to the bar. The trick was, as Healey knew firsthand, to begin outlining in a voice of "discovery" some facts that were totally obvious, and to speak in sentences as if they were numbered and followed logically from one to another. He considered that in their training lawyers were told to test the strength of this word or that word, but never the right word—always, instead, the word which had a legal history and which other lawyers could instantly identify as belonging to them.

In his first year at university, prior to enrolling in English in his second year, Healey had taken law as his major subject. In lectures he sat beside the friend, who had now been so completely formed in the image of a lawyer that sometimes it was difficult for Healey to recognize in him the boy with whom he had spent those hundreds of hours, though he also believed that if he remembered clearly just a few of those hours, he might indeed see in his mind the boy and the man as one figure.

Still, it was almost physically painful to talk about books in the friend's house, since Healey sensed in every inquiry the friend made about a certain author or title the terrible weight of duty. Then, as Healey answered, a look of appraisal would come across the friend's face, though Healey felt that it was never the opinion itself being judged but the opinion as delivered by *a person in his field*.

"This guy," the friend would say, referring to some writer, "now what's all *that* about?"

Invariably, the friend would claim not to have read the work in question. He was always getting around to it or waiting on what he called "some solid advice from someone in the know." It had become so that he never claimed to have read a single work he mentioned, while his interest in what Healey had to say in reply to his tireless inquiries intensified on each meeting. It was not just that Healey felt himself to be humored; he also believed he was being tested in some way. For when Healey told him what he knew, the friend, as was his unnerving habit, would be studying Healey's face a little too intently. This is how a person in his position of intimacy with books answers such a question, Healey believed the friend was thinking while he spoke. And this appraising look often had a perverse effect. It would make Healey modify or alter in some way the opinion he would have given casually and straightforwardly. Sometimes he felt the pressure to change completely what he had been about to say, venturing an extreme view, distorting his own tastes which, in private, he guarded obsessively, just to see for one moment a look of confusion cloud his friend's composure.

Healey was annoyed that the friend could no longer see him as separate from his profession, when Healey himself had always considered the yoking to be accidental, even unfortunate. He thought how the description "literary editor" was used between Louise and himself only in sentences which had a teasing quality or which poked fun, and always with quotation marks around it. "Would a 'literary editor' do such a thing?" "After all, 'a literary editor' . . ." In the past two years, he had met so many literary editors that whenever someone introduced himself as a literary editor Healey thought only of a man *numbering sentences in which the wrong words were given emphasis.*

They entered the creek at a neighbor's house early one Saturday morning in waders and with backpacks in which they had stored provisions. The friend carried a flashlight and a stick sharpened to a point, which he called his eel rod. Though the creek appeared stagnant from above, once they stepped into it Healey could sense the slight pressure of a current and immediately felt relieved; they were to travel downstream.

They walked for a long time underground, passing through narrow tunnels whose sides, when the flashlight caught them, appeared coated in a glossy, dark green fungus. Up above was the square, his friend said, then it was this or that street, now they were beneath the school grounds. The smell in some places was such that they could go forward only by holding their noses and breathing through their mouths so that when they talked, weak cartoon voices echoed along the tunnel. Whenever the creek came out in someone's backyard, the boys were momentarily blinded and they staggered about until their eyes grew used to the daylight. This reopening of the eyes after the darkness of the tunnels was Healey's favorite part of the journey—it was as if they had spent a whole night under the streets of the city and now were coming into a new day, an experience which, as it was repeated again and again, had the effect of condensing into the few hours of their wading whole weeks of time. Here in the daylight, however, the friend warned, they might also be discovered trespassing, so they crept along, bent low to the creek, the straps from their backpacks dragging in the water.

In certain properties, the friend had promised, they would come across "sights." On one creek journey he had taken, he said, a middle-aged man in slippers and dressing gown had wandered down his backyard path smoking a cigarette and coughing. Then the man had removed the cigarette from his mouth, vomited violently into a bush, and immediately replaced the cigarette as he wandered back up toward the house. On another expedition, the friend said, a woman had appeared in a window, naked to the waist.

As they crept along, Healey only saw men pushing lawn mowers, a woman digging in her garden, a child in a sandbox, its tongue caught between its lips in concentration. There were no sights, only the pressure of the creek water against the sides of his rubber boots and the feeling of cold in his feet. Yet as he moved along the creek he began to watch more closely and to feel a curious excitement at these so-called ordinary images. His anxiety about the breasts, which he had imagined caressed by the early morning sunshine, subsided. In the back garden, people grew more vivid.

He saw a man mowing his lawn who at first seemed to stand for every other man who might take up this position— erect and dominant over his turf! But then, as Healey looked again, he saw poses he had never seen before, as if they had been forbidden—submission, a strange tenderness as the clippings fall through the air from the catcher onto the pile of cut grass, which the man, for no reason, touches with his hand, as if stroking someone's hair. The woman gardening, inspecting a nail on her finger, then biting it while staring right through Healey and the friend, who are crouched barely ten feet away. The child with sand around its mouth, spitting out long, viscous strands, which it plucks at like strings.

If he passed the house from the street, he thought, none of this would have happened to him; only by crouching down

low, submissively, behind the houses, in the secret waters of
Lower Hutt, were these images possible.

In later years, how often had Healey longed to have these
off-guard images of himself circulating in the minds of others,
and yet how horrified he had been when, by chance, he learned
that a certain image had indeed escaped—just as when the
woman gardening had finally seen the two boys crouching at
the bottom of her property and had become *the angry woman,*
or the child, discovering itself wrapped in the glistening ropes
of its own saliva had then, as was its habit, begun to cry out
for its mother.

In the law class at university, a seating plan was instituted in
the large lecture hall, and students were not allowed to sit
anywhere but in the seat that appeared as a box with their
name written inside it on the sheet that the lecturer always
opened on a desk in front of him before beginning the class.
Healey saw how this opening of the sheet that contained the
seating plan affected everyone in the room, fixing in their minds
the image of themselves answering a question when their name
was called, a name Healey always heard as if from very far
away and which he immediately thought of as not his own,
but the name of the person sitting a little way away from him.
The lawyers in the room were those who could fix themselves
in the image of their fathers, who were also lawyers, or who
could fix in their minds the sound of the voice of "discovery"
in which the class was conducted. Then, when they spoke,
they would have the correct emphasis and they would be
"recognized" by the lecturer so that in the future he would

not have to consult the seating plan to call upon them to speak—the name coming quickly to him as if they were old friends. Healey's name, and the names of the others in the room who had begun to feel it was impossible to fix in their minds anything but a mounting sense of dread, remained small and almost indecipherable, the letters squeezed tightly into the box that represented the seat to which they were forced to return twice a week for one-and-a-half hours over the eight-month term.

Healey could see that the friend who sat next to him in class, although he said that he also feared the so-called Socratic method, was really learning how to imagine himself five or even ten years from then, a trick which Healey himself could never master. He told the friend that he preferred to live from day to day. "I don't want to be hemmed in," Healey heard himself saying. "Careers, careers, careers. That's all this is about." He had once heard an English professor saying that the law school really had no business on a university campus, since all it was doing was accrediting members of a profession. "This accrediting of a profession," Healey said to the friend, "does it really belong on a university campus?"

In fact, this trick of imagining oneself in the future was something Healey had practiced again and again, without success, in an effort to make it come as naturally as it had seemed to for the friend. In short, Healey had begun to see his own options narrowing. Whenever he spoke to the friend about the deficiencies of law as a profession, he always thought as he spoke how constricted had grown the field which, in the unimaginable future, he might call his own. And when the friend spoke of the fearful second and third years of law, in which there were mock trials and endless opportunities to be called upon by name to act as a lawyer, saying how awful it all seemed, Healey saw the excitement in the friend's eyes and also the reflected image of himself in years to come, always trying to belittle lawyers, running them down for getting things exactly the wrong way around, just as the friend always said how he hated it all when he really meant it was the only thing for which he had a passion.

Eventually, they came out on the open stretch of creek behind the library where they sat on the sunlit grassy bank eating the lunches they had packed. The only sound came from behind the fence of the nearby bowling club, the wooden clack of bowls nudging each other. The adjoining playground was deserted; the cages of the municipal aviary were empty after a recent teenage arson had destroyed all the birds. There was no one else around. Healey tried to imagine the smell of burned feathers, the cries of alarm, the sound wings would make beating against the wire of the enclosure, but nothing came. It was as if the world existed only behind the fronts of the houses and when the two boys were moving low in the waters that cut paths through this forbidden territory. In later years, whenever Healey thought of that city or it was mentioned by someone, usually in connection with its dullness, its almost complete lack of interest, and its separateness from the capital city just to the south—that is, the way Lower Hutt was completely overshadowed by Wellington—he immediately thought of the creek system as a series of winding streets making their way at the bottom of valleys of sloping lawns, and he thought of the belief, which had come to him as he sat on the grassy bank eating his lunch and which he still held, that these were the only real streets in the city, the only places where people actually lived and became what they had previously become only when they imagined themselves acting in front of their perfect audience.

In addition to the law lecture, attendance was also required at a tutorial that met three times a week. Various options were available, and Healey chose the earliest—seven-thirty on the mornings before the lecture, which began at nine. This way, he figured, he would contain law to just three days. He failed to consider that soon he would be getting up in the dark to go to his convenient morning tutorial. He thought only of his free days, Tuesday and Thursday.

The tutorial was held in a small, dark room in the basement of one of the newer buildings, which was an exact copy of an office block in Auckland and, as such, was totally unsuited to the mass movement of students on the hour or to any aspect of university life. The corridors were too narrow, the rooms either too large or too small for teaching, the elevators hopelessly overworked, since the stairwells could only be negotiated in a painfully slow single file. Without double glazing, the rooms lost their heat in winter, while in summer, the constant noise from the construction (more office blocks), which the university often cited as part of "an ongoing commitment," made it impossible for the windows to be opened for adequate ventilation.

In the dark mornings of the middle months of the academic year, as Healey took the staircase—not wanting to meet anyone from his tutorial in the elevator—to the gloomy room to hear yet again the lawyers wooing each other with their odd noises, he thought of those who still wished to be let in on the secret signals, who still harbored the vain hope of being admitted to the team, complaining to the tutor about the speed of information, a complaint that really had to do with the speed at which their dreams were receding from them, a feeling not dissimilar from being shut out by a foreign language. Once the tutor had actually been asked to speak more slowly, as if the desperate nonlawyer who requested this and the tutor, who had a master's degree in law and always wore a different gloomy suit every second week lightened by a jazzy tie, were not both native English speakers. Before reaching the room, Healey would stop on the middle of the staircase and, using the railings, swing himself off the ground. In this moment of swinging, he would decide whether today was, in fact, a twenty-five percent day (seventy-five percent was the minimum attendance required of each student), in which case he would turn back and walk briskly from the building, or whether on this morning he would finally be able to bring himself to say something in the tutorial.

At several places along the way the creek split into two, and the friend's rule was to always take the left fork, since this, he said, would bring them homeward in a circle. Near the end of the journey, they arrived at a junction where the friend said he would take the right fork and Healey the left, since they ran almost parallel to each other, divided only by the thickness of the tunnel wall, and once inside their respective tunnels they should strike the wall, as if, the friend said, they were prisoners in adjoining cells. The sounds in the tunnel when this was done were, apparently, not to be missed and would go some way toward making up for the lack of sights they'd seen so far. Healey said that, since he didn't have a flashlight, perhaps it was best if he followed the friend into the tunnel on the right where the noises could just as easily be demonstrated. The friend, however, insisted that there had to be one on either side for the thing to work and even offered his light to Healey for a tunnel which, he said, now becoming annoyed, was quite short and not that dark anyway. Healey told the friend he could keep his light and waded quickly into the tunnel on the left, now carrying his own eel rod, although he had neither seen nor felt the promised eels but only passed families of alarmed ducks and ducklings.

The tunnel was no less dark than all the others and must have been shaped in a long curve, since no hole of light appeared at the far end. Immediately came the sound of blows reverberating through the wall, now in sharp cracks, now in hollow thuds, setting up a pattern of echoes that caused Healey to place his legs farther apart for fear of stumbling. Then he was also beating the darker shape of the wall with his stick, responding in like rhythm to the friend's blows, finding gaps in the noise and inserting his own "messages." He had once seen a film in which two inmates work out the details of an escape by the simplest taps of their knuckles through the concrete. He felt pieces of the fungus or moss flying from the wall, bits striking him on the ear, making him wince and close his eyes. But now the friend appeared to be thrashing the sides of the tunnel and Healey, too, was striking out wildly until there were no gaps or messages but only a constant ringing din. In these moments, he felt the same rage as he would later in the foothills of Mount Edgeware when their goal seemed unreachable, together with that same sense of excitement in unreflective action. It was not until after several moments that Healey realized the noises coming from the other side were reaching him as if from an increasing distance and were becoming fainter—the friend was moving rapidly to the end of his tunnel while Healey had barely entered his own!

Suddenly, he decided he no longer wanted to be in the tunnel, creeping around like this, unable to see ahead of him. The friend didn't know the tunnels as well as he said he did, or perhaps he had tried to trick Healey. Yes, that was it: deception. And this was the moment when Healey, looking for his lawyer friend's house, remembering the boys in the creek, thought that the lawyer and the friend might be one and the same. Retreating toward the daylight, he lifted himself onto the bank and began walking, upright, through the back gardens that he had previously only spied upon from a distance. Now, Healey thought, he would not only be able to move faster and beat the friend home, but he would also approach these vivid characters he had seen from the creek. Now he was part of their world of luminous gestures.

Whenever he thought he was about to speak in the tutorial, his breathing lost its regular pattern and he knew that it was all over until he could regain the control that would allow his words to come out evenly and without the rushed delivery that made him sound as if he were speaking after a short uphill sprint, the kind he would often make when climbing the last few yards of the steep path to the house in Miramar. Yet when everything was under control and a gap in the discussion appeared, Healey's first words would invariably be lost in the sound of someone else who had now claimed the moment. Then, if the tutor had heard Healey start to speak, he might ask if there wasn't someone else with something for the group, but by this time Healey's breathing would be out of control again and a brief silence would follow until a lawyer found the right word, which they could all then discover.

As the year went on and Healey lost virtually all power of speech within the vicinity of the office-block building, so that even in the few minutes before the tutorial started he could scarcely bring himself to say a few words to the person next to him—whereas on meeting the friend after class he could hear himself *lecturing* the friend on how dreadful law was—Healey began to find in written expression the only confidence he thought he would ever have, although, in the assignments, which on sufficient occasions he guessed correctly the legal word that needed to be tested, it seemed to make no difference as to the quality of the prose in which these words were discovered. Healey had seen the assignments of fellow students, and these were often written in numbered sentences against which the tutor had placed large red ticks. Still, each subsequent assignment for the almost-dumb Healey became an exercise in discovering or guessing the right legal word and then obscuring it by means of humor, irony, or mockery so that the tutor was often forced to pass the assignment while writing a brief sentence in which was expressed a muted hostility for its "puzzling presentation." When the assignments were handed back, Healey at first felt surprised that he had passed, then disappointed that he hadn't achieved a better mark, and finally a secret pride that he had outdone the tutor in his lawyer's outfit.

Only years later, when standing in front of the group of houses on Aro Street—searching for that something in any one of them which might lead him to the friend's front door and realizing that in the two years he had been in Christchurch he had never seen the friend's address written down— was it clear to him how, in the gloomy basement room in which the law tutorial was held, he had begun the journey away from himself in the pages of the assignments by which he hoped to defeat the tutor, and how only now, having received the phone call from his mother and sailed into the harbor, had he begun to retrace the steps of that journey.

Standing here, having heard from his aunts the night before the story of his grandfather, which had caused Lillian, grouped with her sisters on the sofa, to shed tears, a story about a character moving away, he began to believe, no matter how false the analogy immediately sounded in his own mind—as much a transparent act of force as his belief in a special relationship with his grandfather, or the need to discern in his life a rhythm, which would not seem wholly the result of accident but, on closer inspection, would yield a vast network of small corresponding noises—that his own story had the dimensions of the streets of the city in which he was standing and of all the cities he had moved through, including the underground creek city of Lower Hutt and the city with deserted pavements intersected by busy four-lane highways in the American Midwest: the evidence of himself, as it were, hopelessly dispersed across these innumerable landscapes. Perhaps it was only by retracing all the paths he had ever taken—an impossible task, a completely hopeless undertaking, a waste, a waste, as he repeated to himself—that Healey could begin to imagine what it was like for any other figure to move along the paths which sometimes intersected with his own.

We assemble these random movements, he said to himself, these left turns and right turns, and imagine ourselves symbolic navigators, first-time explorers, everlasting pioneers, and then we look at this beautiful map inside our heads and it is like no country that has ever existed, though we should not fool ourselves that we have invented any of this. If we look closely we see only the faint image of our own wishes pressed onto paper as flimsy as skin. It is the mere tattoo of our pattern mania. And still we cannot resist these relentless misreadings of our own situation, since it was not a "return" Healey told himself he was imagining, no more than by stepping out from the creek tunnels of Lower Hutt was he returning into the same daylight—each step was new, he believed, and had never been taken before.

But then, in front of the now anonymous sanded-down houses of Aro Street, he almost abandoned this impossible resolution. It was wearying that everything appeared at this

moment so unfamiliar and that the house he had walked
straight into on several occasions was hidden from him. In
this state of weakness, he felt a longing to be walking, with-
out thinking, through the door of his own house, although
he knew that when he was back in Christchurch he would
struggle to think of it as anything more than temporary and
"a trial location."

As he walked across the back gardens of the friend's near
neighbors, pushing through hedges and jumping fences, Healey
felt suddenly strong now that he was not moving the weight
of the creek with his feet. The grass of the lawns near the
creek was springy and returned each step to him with re-
newed vigor. Here was an elderly couple who waved to him.
The look of surprise on the little girl's face. Then, as he en-
tered another property, Healey heard shouting, which he in-
stantly thought of as some form of greeting. A large, middle-
aged man was coming toward him in a white singlet and shorts,
waving his arms, in which Healey now noticed, he was car-
rying a cricket bat. The red skin of the man's face was swing-
ing from side to side, and in that moment Healey also saw
how, when the man moved, his belly moved a fraction later.
Then Healey ran through a hedge into a neighbor's place where
he kept running down toward the creek, still hearing the man's
cries warning him that if he ever caught him again on his
property he would thrash the living daylights out of him.

Back in the water, crouching down, he forced his breath-
ing into its regular pattern and then began wading down-
stream again, taking the left forks at junctions and looking

out for the house near the spot where he and the friend had entered the creek several hours before. He realized with annoyance that he hadn't bothered to pay attention to the place in the morning, since he thought he would be returning there later with the friend. Now, as he searched for anything that might seem familiar in the back gardens he passed, Healey began to feel, quite wrongly, that this would be his last visit to Lower Hutt.

It was only when he was finally inside the right house, sitting down with the friend, that Healey began to understand how he himself had always seen the friend and his profession as one. The way in which the friend had suddenly appeared in the window of a house Healey had already ruled out—pulling back the curtains to look first one way then the other before checking his watch, completing the gestures without ever seeing the figure who was standing almost directly across from the house and who was the object of this search—caused Healey to think of a man who measured time in terms of money, impatient over a late appointment. And it came to him that while the friend had always seen Healey as "literary editor" and therefore likely to be tardy, Healey had always seen the friend as "lawyer," whose constant accounting and dividing of the day into fifteen-minute portions a literary editor might well enjoy disrupting. What he hated in the friend's presumptions had, of course, come easily to him also. The word *lawyer* had always seemed like the wrong word, just as the friend's decision to go on into the "terrible" second, third, fourth, and even fifth years of law had been enough for Healey to think of that friend as "lost" to him. For although they had maintained regular contact with each other up until the time Healey had moved south, the friendship had by then become nothing more than a series of mutual and affable misunderstandings in which each man had assigned the other to a box in which his name was written in tight, almost indecipherable lettering.

The interior of the house bore the mark of the friend's salary rise, which had finally come through, he told Healey, after "pretty much carrying the firm for the past year." The puffery here was mostly ruled out by its accompaniment: a laugh, a shrug of the shoulders. Moreover, in looking around and thinking of the friend's dedication as a law student, Healey imagined that this was in fact no idle boast; the friend would have put in the hours and projected himself niftily into the future where present grievances would find their proper redress. The old carpets had been pulled up and the hardwood floors, newly varnished, now sported rugs of Eastern design. The dowdy furniture the friend had carried with him through his student days, and for nearly a decade since graduation, was gone, and in its place cream-colored sofas, glass-topped coffee tables, halogen lamps, discreet shelving that housed the books that the friend said, the instant Healey's eye lighted on them, all belonged to his girlfriend. A large piece of almost-familiar New Zealand artwork hung above the tiled fireplace.

"Yes, even a painting!" the friend said, smiling.

Healey was suddenly ashamed that he had been caught looking from the painting to the friend and back again, as if in appraisal. He then understood that he'd never allowed the friend any taste except that dictated by his profession, and although he was now forced to admit the rooms had been elegantly done, Healey still could not lose the image that had first come to mind on entering the house: that of the hardwood floors, on social occasions, covered in the gloomy shoes of teams of lawyers competing with each other to be the first to discover that rare phenomenon, through whose power they might rise to the top of their profession and by which "a precedent" might be set, *the new legal word.* Yet, he suddenly thought, wasn't this something like what he himself was looking for!

"I didn't know him at all," Healey began to say, but just as he was on the point of telling the friend the story his aunts had told of their father the night before and about the cousin who'd once lived not far from where they were sitting, he realized that he was immediately back in his old habits and that in telling these stories he might make the friend laugh a little and cause him to think that this "interesting material" was what made a literary editor, but he could never achieve what he really longed for. The friend would never discover, while Healey spoke, certain off-guard images, such as those uncovered many years before when, bent low in the creeks of Lower Hutt, they had searched hopelessly for the new morning breasts of women in windows.

The friend's father had fallen from a ladder while clearing leaves from the gutters one Saturday morning and had cracked open his skull. He hadn't died but rather had instantly forgotten not only those hours surrounding the accident but large portions of other periods in his life. He was forced to lie in a darkened room for week-long intervals until he could again stand up without vomiting. Often when Healey was visiting the house "a code of silence" would be in effect, which meant that they could not make a sound in the vicinity of the curtained room where the father was lying. Even in the living room at the far end of the house, the boys found themselves whispering to each other. Once, Healey had seen the father, dressed in long pajamas, moving toward the kitchen by tenderly pushing himself off the sides of the passageway wall. It was summer, though the father's feet were gray. "He wants some water," the friend said, as the figure passed in the doorway.

"Shouldn't we get him some, then?" Healey asked.

"The doctor says it's good for him to be up and doing things for himself. Lying down all that time, he says, the heart forgets its job."

One day the friend took Healey to the Lower Hutt Public Library, where above the issues desk there was a large, wall-length mural depicting a group of about twenty or thirty life-size men, women, and children who in the early 1950s had been chosen from among the local population to model the range of Lower Hutt's citizens. The friend described how each figure had been dressed in the clothes of a certain occupation, then painted on a background of a plateau through which the Hutt River ran, bordered on the horizon by the hills of the valley. "It's sort of our Noah's ark," the friend said. Here was a doctor with his stethoscope, a Plunket nurse holding a baby, a group of engineers carrying spanners, schoolchildren, judges in wigs, sportsmen with rugby balls, scientists in white laboratory coats peering into microscopes, carpenters, businessmen shaking hands over a table, someone shoveling concrete, another writing a book, a string quartet, a man opening his mouth as if in full song. Every face was happy and earnest and depicted with eyes raised, as if looking upon a sight even more astounding than their own definitive company.

In one corner of the painting, standing with a group of servicemen and women, the friend pointed out a figure he said was his father. Nothing in the painted version corresponded with what Healey had seen in the passageway. Apparently, some twenty-five years before, the father had modeled in the uniform of the air force.

"I didn't know he was in the air force," Healey said.

"He wasn't," the friend said. "He was too young to go, but they wanted him for his pilot's jaw."

As Healey sat in the friend's house in Aro Street remembering looking into the face of the man dressed as a war pilot—there had even been some marks of grease across the forehead—he began to speak about his own uncle, who had been the right age for the war and whose periods of blackouts, when he would lie in a coma for days before waking without any memory of what had happened to him, seemed so strangely close to the friend's father's ordeal that the father and the uncle, both of whom had now died, appeared for the first time in Healey's mind as friends. By this route, which soon took in a view of the grandfather's time as an ambulance driver in France near the end of the First World War—about which virtually nothing was known, since the grandfather himself had never spoken of it—Healey hoped to suggest an end to the picture of the two friends sitting in the house in Aro Street, dressed as if to represent their respective professions.

"He kept things loose in his drawer," said Healey. "Some of the most important things he never filed away or put to one side but had them rattling around in the top drawer of his highboy along with whatever, medication, receipts, just the stuff he'd thrown in there."

"He let himself go, then," the friend said. "Same as my grandfather. We found a heap of money in his bedroom when he died. I mean, not a whole lot, but still enough—"

"No," Healey cut him off. "From what I can tell he was always a meticulous keeper of things. There's a scrapbook with old tram tickets, concert programs, clippings from newspapers, the lot. I have it. And that's what's odd. Here's a man, an engineer, who in his day had everything riding on how careful he was professionally, because if he said a bridge was safe and it wasn't, well. But then, for all those years, next to the old aspirin bottles and the barley sugars, there are pieces of what?—clues?"

"What sort of things? What do you mean clues?"

Healey felt he'd said too much already, or started it wrongly.

"Medals. Certificates. Letters," he went on. "Momentous letters, telling him how his son got wounded. Right next to the gas bill from last month. There's no order."

"He wanted them at hand, maybe."

"Maybe—but a scrapbook you'd think is at hand, too, and a safer place. These are things just lying around under other stuff. *Carelessly.* I once found a calling card there from Ettie Rout. Do you know Ettie Rout? I didn't know who she was. But the card was for this service she ran, recommending clean places for soldiers in Paris. He's eighteen, nineteen and off with Parisian prostitutes. My grandfather."

"But he wasn't your grandfather then. He was just some kid."

"Of course he was!" Healey felt his hand come down hard on the arm of the chair. "And when I picked it up from the drawer I was the same age as he was when he first touched the card—that was an odd sensation. But the thing was, I didn't feel any closer to him or anything; in fact, I felt that here was the person who knew me perhaps best of all, no, not knew, but understood me somehow and I didn't have a clue about him. But more than that"—now he was on the edge of his seat—"every little thing I found out about him, you know from my mother or from poking around in the drawer, which I'd suddenly thought of as mine—I'm not saying this very well—all these significant tokens, they pushed him further away from me."

Healey had finished talking and looked up at the friend. The friend looked away. He hadn't meant to go on like this, with an absurd kind of apostate's zeal. All his gestures had been too large, and his insistence had caused the friend to sit back in his chair, to rest his chin thoughtfully in his hands. After a moment of silence, as if in competition, the friend had begun to tell Healey about his own mother's father who'd cut several members of the family out of his will for no other reason than that he didn't much like them. "Old bugger settled some scores there!" he said. Now in several places in his own story the friend was laughing and Healey joined in the laughter, since he could see that the friend's story was being told, partly, to take Healey's mind off the grief which was clearly causing him to behave so oddly. That was it, surely, a sort of spillover from the funeral. And Healey, touched by this effort, suddenly discovered that he wanted to please the friend and make him think he was succeeding in bringing about what both of them knew was the wrong result.

As he listened, Healey was also thinking that, because they had grown up together as boys, there persisted the mutual belief that, although they had now gone their separate ways, they each could, in fact, have taken *either* path—that the friend could have easily become a literary editor and that Healey could have easily become a lawyer—with the result that there existed a kind of resentment at the heart of their adult relationship that Healey thought they might never rise above. In each other's company they were instantly returned to the underground creeks of Lower Hutt and, each of them feeling that this was the only time when the other had truly been himself, they were condemned to suffer under *the pretense of the present*. Now, for almost an hour, at an ease fully proportionate to the years of their friendship, they sat together in the comfortable living room, occasionally looking a little too intently at each other.

"Cut them out just like that, did he," Healey heard himself saying, though now he was thinking of the strange history of Ettie Rout's calling card and his grandfather's pursuit of the French language, which he loved above any other. There was never any talk of the War, and whenever someone brought up the subject of his ambulance driving, the grandfather would pretend not to hear, or he would announce in French a sentence describing a simple scene out the window or some catchphrase that they would all have to repeat several times over until the whole room had achieved the correct pronunciation: *"Je suis très fatigué."*

When Healey's brother was approaching high-school age, a period known as the French Terror was launched. Now the grandfather, restless with being a pupil of his French ladies— the women who ran the French Club to which he'd belonged for more than fifteen years following his retirement—sought his own students. Once a fortnight he would come to his daughter's house with his small blackboard, which he propped against the dining-room table, and his chalk, and he would proceed to write up those phrases and sentences that were to be said over and over again until the mouths of the children might arrive naturally at the shapes of this, the finest language. The vowels, he said, once the vowels are in place. *"Rose originale."* *"C'est difficile."*

In addition to the dining-room lessons, there was the morning phone call. Each weekday at eight o'clock it was understood that Healey's sister would answer the phone by saying in a loud voice, because the grandfather was by now quite deaf: *"Oui?"* She would then respond to questioning with the three or four phrases her grandfather had previously supplied. *"Maman est à la maison,"* she would shout into the receiver several times before the vowels had properly assembled, each time pulling a longer face and miming a strangulation scene for her brothers waiting their turn. The phone would then be handed to Healey's brother and the same phrases would ring out, so that by the time Healey was up, he knew by heart the correct sounds to make though he scarcely understood a word he was saying.

On his eleventh birthday, his grandfather gave Healey a book by the French author he said was his personal favorite, Victor Hugo. It was a heavy book, hardcover, brown with an elegant border of intricate gold curls whose design Healey liked to trace with a finger, his eyes closed. Inside, the pages were made of more than a thousand sheets of the finest tissue paper, though Healey could only verify this several days after receiving the book. When his grandfather presented him with the package and he first opened the book, Healey had been unable to tell anything about it, so anxious and muddled had he been on seeing that the title of this favorite French author's work embossed in gold lettering on the spine was in the language whose vowels he could place but whose sense he believed he would never fathom: *Les Misérables*. The Miserables, he said to himself, the Miserables, he repeated again and again, searching for an adequate translation. Now, he thought, he would be uncovered for the fake he was. Of course, the book was in English, only its title had remained as the author had written it, but Healey, on first looking at the words in the grip of this French-panic, failed to recognize any of them. It was all he could do to close the book and

admire the gold design against the brown while his grandfa-
ther, luckily, began to rehearse those details of Victor Hugo's
life that had led him to hold that artist in the highest regard—
his unstable childhood; his political idealism; his gloriously
productive exile; the death of his sons; the insanity of his
daughter; the treachery of his friend Saint-Beuve in stealing
his wife; the epic obstacles overcome along the way, until
there was now a street in every French town bearing that
great name.

A number of years after, Healey had come across the card—
whose significance his mother had explained to him before
putting it not with the things that were to travel with the
grandfather to Auckland, but with those items that she said
she would keep an eye on herself—a newspaper advertise-
ment appeared asking for any material or information to as-
sist in the writing of a biography of Ettie Rout. Having seen
the advertisement, Healey asked his mother whether she might
not volunteer her father as a source. The woman writing the
biography was also asking for anyone willing to be inter-
viewed to come forward. His mother, it turned out, had al-
ready sent the card to the biographer and given details of how
it had come into her possession. Since her father had never
talked about the matter, and it was not something she felt she
could ever bring up, she herself, she wrote, had nothing to
offer except the enclosed card. And while she could not vouch
for the extent of her father's knowledge or memory, the biog-
rapher could be assured of a warm welcome at the rest home,
since any visitor was greatly appreciated.

Several weeks later, Healey's mother received a reply from the biographer. She thanked her for her kindness in sending the card and wrote that she would keep her father's name on file. Regrettably, she said, there was not sufficient funding available for her to make all the trips she wanted and so her resource pool would at this stage remain around the central region. She had been overwhelmed by the response so far, but if she did find herself in the Auckland area she would, with the kind consent of all parties, be sure to pay a visit to Healey's grandfather. The letter concluded by asking whether the card should be returned. "I would be grateful if it could remain in my possession at least a little while longer," the biographer wrote, "because it is itself a fascinating document." Healey's mother had instantly agreed, sending back a note to that effect, and somehow over the course of time, a period in which Healey's parents moved, the card had never found its way back to her. When Healey brought it up again, his mother said it was too long ago and too insignificant a matter to bother the biographer with. Besides, she told him, the card was perhaps in its rightful home now.

While sitting with the lawyer friend in the Aro Valley and hearing the word *intestate,* Healey recalled that when the biography of Ettie Rout had finally been published a few years before to very good reviews, he had searched its pages hopelessly for any mention of his grandfather. He had looked in the index, without success, for his grandfather's name. And he thought how, from that date onward, he believed that whenever the name Ettie Rout was mentioned, people were operating on only a partial truth, that they did not know the full story, and that the absence of his grandfather's name from a collection of sentences which had as its subject Ettie Rout marked the singular failure of that enterprise.

5

Beehive

From the friend's house in Aro Street, Healey turned down Willis Street and walked toward Lambton Quay. The wind had come up and was pushing at his back, causing his feet to leave the ground for a fraction longer than normal. Soon he was bouncing along under its pressure. This, he remembered, had often been his Palmerston North aunt's excuse for the bulkiness of her purchases, that she had needed something to anchor her down in the streets.

Suddenly, the wind was blowing across him, forcing him sideways. Passing a man and his dog, he saw how the wind had given them both the same slightly lopsided canine walk. In Christchurch, on days when he heard that the next weather system would be coming in from the north—fast-moving cloud cover with the chance of rain—he would catch himself looking at the sky, as if awaiting the delivery of some important mail, or word from Wellington. Yet invariably he was disappointed, since when the weather did arrive, it would hang too low, or be too sluggish, or be defective in some way as to earn itself the label "Christchurch weather."

Then, by chance—although the compact city restricted the usefulness of that phrase—he recognized coming toward him a woman he hadn't seen in years. She had been on the radio a few times, and once he'd caught her on television. He knew that she had some job high up in government, a job in which it was said she had been "advanced beyond her years." A so-called highflier, she had attracted, in the words of a colleague Healey had once met, envy and a certain amount of ill will, so that some people were apparently waiting for her to fall and asking whether she could last the distance.

On television, Healey had watched her answering a reporter's question on some matter of a Cabinet Minister's schedule. The moment of confusion he suffered as he tried to place her had caused him to miss what she was saying. He had been thinking of her as she was fifteen years before, and none of the language she used on television seemed to fit with the old image. All her words were marked with that note of professional ease and control, whereas when he had known her—or rather, known of her, since most of his contact had been secondhand—she had appeared, and not just in his mother's words, "a little flighty." He also remembered his sister, around the time this woman had dropped from their view, making some odd comment about "desperate females," though Healey had tended to ascribe this to the spirit of rivalry that was then infecting all his sister's judgments.

Still, the confusion of these conflicting impressions returned to his mind on Willis Street, and Healey might have hurried past her if she herself had not stopped him. This immediately, however, provoked another silly awkwardness in him, since he was forced to act as if he had just seen her and to pretend that he hadn't recognized her from a distance and decided that she was lost to him. But did he really believe, Healey asked himself, that a person in her position would not stop a person in his position for a chat? Or that a person in his position was above stopping someone like her on the pretext that they had known each other a little in the past? She would hardly have reacted to him—that was now obvious— as yet another distant acquaintance trying to take advantage of some spurious connection to pester her about who and what she knew.

Nevertheless, this had been his fear on first seeing her, a reaction sponsored, in good part, by exactly those elements of his job from which the funeral had imposed this useful exile. For in his dealings with other literary editors he always had to be on guard against such false notes of sycophancy and crawling. One witnessed daily the shameless exploitation of even the most fleeting acquaintance with a certain name that perhaps then had currency but that would soon fade and be viciously abandoned. Whenever literary editors were gathered together with other members of the so-called literary world they began to let things slip, never talking about books but only about "the trade," never about the quality of a work but only about certain "problems" attached to certain names.

Though, finally, it was not the others, Healey thought, that he should be concerned about, but himself, since it was at these gatherings that he sometimes recognized his own tendency toward adopting the voice of the profession, with its pretense of candor and discretion, while dealing largely in gossip and lies.

Since, day to day, most of his dealings at the newspaper were with management or with his stable of book reviewers, Healey, generally, had little opportunity to use what he had come to know about certain names. Louise might listen for a time to these pieces of information he had uncovered, but there would gradually come into her eyes a look, not of boredom, but restlessness, as if to say, "These stories have nothing to do with *you*." Healey would, in turn, become frustrated on seeing that what he had thought of as detachment was, in fact, a kind of hiding in the senseless details of others' names.

On Willis Street, the woman took him by surprise by actually stopping him and beginning to talk to him.

"Dear me!" she said, placing her hand on his arm. "This is one from way back, isn't it."

"Yes," said Healey. "A voice from—"

"The vaults," she said.

They stayed like this for a few moments. The wind had dropped off once more. And here it was again—the stillness about her which had so thrown him and which he'd accredited to the artificial framing of the television. In the old days, he thought, she had been all movement and anxious energy.

"You sound like him, you know," she finally said. "Your brother. I never noticed that before. Maybe it wasn't true then."

The woman, whose name was Claire, had been the girl-friend of Healey's brother's best friend. It seemed hardly a connection at all when he announced it to himself like this, though at the time the three of them—Healey's brother, his friend, and Claire—had formed a very tight group that had often convened at the Healeys' place to plot their weekends; it was unthinkable that the couple should do anything without their third member. Healey's brother didn't have a girlfriend through this period. He had Claire and her boyfriend, for which he earned the contempt of his sister, who referred to him as their little mascot, their eunuch. This couple had been going out together for years, all through high school and beyond. Then one year, without warning, they split up and the boy-friend had quickly married someone whom no one knew, moving north, while Claire was left with a group of friends—mostly his—who'd only known her as part of a couple, or a threesome. That is, she was left mainly with Healey's brother, or, as the sister used to say, with her third leg.

When she'd been with his friend, Healey's brother had always acted around Claire as if they were good mates. After the split, Healey had sensed a wariness in his brother when-ever Claire was mentioned and a nervousness in her com-pany. Claire's recklessness, her loudness, seemed to have found solid ground in the brother's natural reserve. But it was exactly this new freedom between them that made the brother uneasy. "She tells me everything," he once confided to Healey.

"And what do you do?" said Healey.

"I listen," said the brother. "Then sometimes I feel I have to tell her things. Fair trade."

"And do you?"

"I make them up," he said. "Her stuff is always, you know, *better* than mine."

His sister, seizing on these new circumstances, warned the brother about a woman on the rebound. "She has that look," she said. "You can hear it in her voice. Desperation."

Healey never knew what had really happened, if anything, between the two of them, or, as his sister intimated cheerfully, between the *three* of them, but finally, his brother stopped mentioning Claire. Now Claire was asking about his brother and speaking of the days when she would receive in the mail jars of honey from the bee farm on which the brother had once worked. "Is he still an *apiarist?*" she asked, laughing over the word and causing Healey to join in the laughter, so that it might have appeared to a passerby that the two were, indeed, good friends. This pleased Healey and gave him the confidence to talk more freely about his brother, who was now working in the south of England in a remote research station, studying not bees, as he understood it, but skinks.

Growing up, the brother had exhibited no particular affinity for animals, or plants, or any aspect of the natural world, and when he enrolled for his first year at university it was as an engineering student. Just as Healey had entered as a law student, so the brother before him had entered the wrong field. For a brief time, then, the brother had come under the wing of their grandfather, who, at his retirement, had risen to the position of Chief Regional Inspector of Bridges for the Central North Island. The grandfather would demand to know of the brother what area he was now studying and whether they had reached a certain point in class that was concerned with— and then the grandfather would begin to speak in the language of engineers, making a point of its difficulty by lowering his voice so that only the other engineer in the room could hear him. Whenever this happened, Healey thought not of becoming an engineer but of being initiated into some other secret society, so that he, too, might be allowed these private conferences in rooms in which the excluded sat straining their ears to catch something in the strange talk.

In the summer holidays following his completion of the intermediate year of engineering, when he was deciding at which university he would continue his studies, the brother went down south to earn some money. Several of his friends had jobs picking fruit, and this had been his plan too. The farmer, however, needed only a certain number of pickers that season because of the weather, which had attacked his trees. There was a neighbor, though, who needed help with his beehives, and Healey's brother, who had imagined life in the fruit pickers' huts with his friends—late-night drinking, dope, finding girls—now found himself sleeping alone in the room of the beekeeper's fourteen-year-old daughter, who was away for the summer. The walls of the bedroom were covered with posters of horses, the windows smothered in lace, and even going through the drawers of the girl's dresser late at night failed to make up for the humiliation he felt. Each morning he had to pull on the full-body suit, the strange helmet with its heavy gauze visor, and the white canvas gloves and walk into the hot sunshine to check the trays of honeycomb.

The farmer had around five hundred hives spread in distant corners of his dairy farm. What had started as a hobby was now a profitable sideline, although the size of the honey crop varied greatly according to the weather and to the bees themselves—from thirty tons some seasons to just five in others. At first the brother hated the work, which involved handling hundreds of forty-pound boxes of honeycomb to be sent off for extracting. Despite the protective clothing, he would receive anywhere from ten to thirty or more bee stings each day. When the bees swarmed, the farmer had told him to stand perfectly still. "Even though every muscle in your body is crying out 'Run!' ignore it, lad. Let them do their little dances on you. Here's the trick I learned—act *interested,* not scared. I'm not saying they have brains or anything, but they seem to, you know, almost respect that."

When the brother met his friends on the weekends, they were tanned and full of the apples and peaches and plums that had become their diet along with the beer that they spoke of drinking in excessive quantities every evening. He only had the sickly, sweet taste of the honeycomb in his mouth and in his nostrils and his hair and could barely remember the bitterness of the one glass of home-brewed beer he was occasionally invited to have with the farmer when, in the farmer's estimation, it had been "a good day."

Yet as the weeks went by, the brother's postcards home began to suggest an interest not only in the money he was now earning but in the details of the life of the farm and especially in the life of the bees. Amid the usual details of weather and meals, a sentence would fall into the text, almost by accident. "I saw a queen today so fat she kept falling over." Nor would anything be made of it by the writer; they were presented as casual observations. "I think they know me now, I'm learning their different dances." At this time, also, jars of honey would arrive in the mail, though it was only when Healey heard from Claire that she, too, had received these gifts, which came as a surprise to him, since they had always believed themselves to be the only ones so favored, that he begin to understand that the jars of honey had been the brother's signal of intent, a kind of warning or preparing of his family and friends so that they would not be too surprised or think the change too sudden or ill-advised—as had the parents of a certain cousin when she announced she had been "born again"—when he returned from the south with his mind made up.

In his second year at university, Healey's brother enrolled in zoology, biology, and botany. The grandfather was forced to retreat and no longer talked about systems of suspension. Now, in his summer holidays the brother would choose to travel to remote areas to work for little money, collecting data on endangered species, tracking birds, counting the numbers in colonies unreachable by any conventional means of communication. Every now and then he might return to the city and suddenly it would be like having the old brother back again. He seemed at first to show no outward signs of the person he had become at some point on his daily trips to and from the beehives, or the figure his family imagined he had become—the solitary and meticulous diarist of nature. His demeanor was almost one of apology, as if he, too, could hardly believe the direction in which he had turned. After a time, however, he would feel the sudden need to go back into the bush. Another project would come up, and he'd be gone without warning.

Gradually he did assume these outward markings, but it was almost as if he was comforting his family in this, putting on the bush clothes to reassure them of his seriousness— green shirt, brown corduroys, and boots—growing the full beard which was expected of his type. Now he could not be doubted. Whenever he was home, he was careful not to disappoint expectations. He would tramp through the streets of the city in full garb, content to appear oversized and quite out of place. When Healey told him he looked like a real yokel, the brother only smiled with a kind of satisfaction. In the city he was amused by most things; only in the remote areas of distant National Parks, Healey imagined, was his brother now serious.

Shortly after Healey's brother graduated, and when he was at the height of his amusement with everything outside his work, the best friend split up with Claire. The discomfort this caused the brother was noticeable if only because of what otherwise surrounded it—the good-natured, cheery disposition that enveloped everything in a calm whose source was located, Healey imagined, somewhere in those long treks through remote bushlands. Was it this calm, finally, which had allowed him to abandon her? Or that had driven her away? It seemed likely that such a calm might not depend on other people, that it had cured the brother of the need for company. As Healey talked to Claire on Willis Street about the brother, he also began to feel a certain discomfort. Was it possible that he, too, would soon abandon her? Immediately, however, he realized how silly this was. She was the one with the power; it was she who had appeared on national television, speaking about matters of state in a voice of absolute control.

The month before he was to go down to Christchurch to marry Louise and begin work as literary editor on the newspaper, Healey visited his brother, who was then living by himself in a prefabricated unit on the grounds of a trout park up north called Rainbow Springs. It was a recreational reserve where the public could walk around a series of winding paths bordered by ponds and streams stocked with trout. In the clear water, shaded by overhanging trees and mossy banks, large rainbow and brown trout could be seen swimming near the surface and rising to take the food which the employees, including Healey's brother, tossed to them at regular intervals. "We feed them a little less because of the junk food people throw in when we're not looking," the brother said. "I've seen trout eating potato chips."

There was also an indoor aquarium on the site, as well as

an aviary. Occasionally, Healey's brother had to clean cages or be on path duty, which meant stopping the kids from throwing things at the trout or from entering the ponds. But his main occupation, for which he received, in addition to his earnings from part-time policing of the reserve, a small bursary from the university, was his continued work on a doctorate involving the breeding patterns of tropical lizards.

Near the prefab in which he lived, there was a small fenced-off grassy area containing four or five young trees enclosed in fine wire mesh boxes. These trees were the control area of his experiments. When Healey was shown them, it hardly seemed possible that the small, almost invisible creatures hiding against the glossy leaves had occupied the brother for a number of years already. And although he knew that he was supposed to feel admiration for this activity—and, indeed, he had initially registered the stirrings of such a feeling as he watched his brother open the little cage door and pull back a leaf with the end of his pencil—Healey began to be annoyed at the whole setup: the prefab with the sight of the unmade bed immediately apparent on opening the door, the caged trees, the tourists, the trout, there for the taking, swimming slowly, as if drugged, around the clear, shaded ponds. And he understood that his brother's calm had often caused him, Healey, to become irritable and sometimes had filled him with the desire to shake his brother from his mindless amusement.

It was not until later in the day, when he watched the brother sprinkling a bucket of purifying crystals into one of the ponds, the purple spreading quickly through the water, that Healey began to notice, in even the smallest gestures the brother made, a certain physical grace that in the city could not be seen. What was ungainly in the city was just right in Rainbow Springs.

That evening, after a dinner of fried pork chops—cooked on the little stove that smoked out the prefab, forcing them to open all the windows and the door even though it was bitterly cold outside—the brother took Healey to meet the young couple who ran the park and with whom the brother said he had become good friends. When they were sitting in the living room of the couple's house, the man had begun talking about the brother, though not directing the remarks at Healey but rather at the brother and occasionally at the woman. "This bloke here—," the man began, looking squarely at Healey's brother.

After the initial introductions, Healey himself had not been asked any questions by which he might have been able to further enter the conversation. Everything had been directed at the brother. Sitting in the far corner of the room, he had the sense that his presence was scarcely noticed, although it had been the cue for the man's almost continuous speech about the brother. While the man was saying, as a sort of joke, what a "terrible" worker the brother was and making numerous references to things that had apparently happened in the past and of which Healey had no knowledge, mentioning this practical joke or that instance of the brother's "laziness," the brother and the woman had exchanged only the briefest conspiratorial look which, nevertheless, caused Healey to imagine a story of the brother's life at Rainbow Springs far different from the one he had previously imagined while looking into the transparent waters of the trout ponds. He had imagined a life of detachment, of celibacy, of dedication and scholarship. He had imagined the skinks on the undersides of the glossy leaves and the trout cruising in the congested pools to be living the brother's life for him, and only skink desires, only trout desires imparting urgency to this sleepy place.

Then, in the opposite corner of the room, above the chair in which the woman was sitting, Healey saw movement and suddenly realized that perched on the top of the chair was a large black hawk. How could he have missed it before? Why hadn't anyone said anything about it? At that moment, while the man talked on about the brother's "misdeeds," which the brother smiled at, and as the woman had also begun to talk, about technical matters arising from the heating system in the aquarium, Healey believed that he should now leave the room quietly so as not to alert the hawk to his movement. He would slip outside and get some fresh air. But the brother had seen that Healey had noticed the bird, or "Handsome," as he called it, and had begun to talk not to Healey but to Handsome, while the bird shifted its head to fix the brother in its eye.

"Can Handsome fly?" the brother said. "Is Handsome a lazy, spoilt bird?" he said.

"Don't taunt it!" the man said suddenly.

The woman now turned to Handsome. "Handsome's just had dinner," she told him. "Aren't you a stuffed bird, yes you are."

"You baby him," said the man. For the first time since shaking hands, the man now looked directly at Healey. There was color in his cheeks. "That's wrong, you know. He'll get really screwed up if you don't talk to him properly." He turned back to the bird. "What does Handsome think of our guest?" he said.

When they were finally back in the prefab, Healey and the brother drank some more beer before it was announced that they had to set the lines. Because of trouble in the past with poachers, now each night a complex series of tripwires had to be set up along certain key stretches of the paths. These wires—actually lengths of strong twine—were not hooked up to any alarm system, but were, the brother said, a good disincentive for anyone who decided to walk around in the dark. Even with a flashlight, the lines were difficult to see, since they crossed each other in such a way that there were only certain footholes that allowed safe passage.

Just off the path, concealed at the base of tree trunks or under large rocks, were the brackets over which the brother hooked the twine. It was cold, and the surrounding bush intensified the darkness. The brother had also drunk a large amount of beer, together with several glasses of wine at the couple's house. Yet he worked without stumbling or complaining, crossing and recrossing the tripwires, ensuring they were taut, never searching about for the hidden brackets, but going straight to them, moving nimbly through the footholes, while Healey held the flashlight. "Usually," the brother said, "I do this by myself, so it's a real bonus to have someone else helping out."

"I'm not doing anything," said Healey. "I can't even move." Off the path, the sounds of the trout breaking the surface of the water could be heard. "You ever been tempted to just reach in?" he asked his brother.

"Hey!" he said. "They're like family. Those are our children you're talking about."

"Oh," said Healey.

"But the guy before me . . ."

"Yes?"

"Well, he went into town with the boss once to do the grocery shopping. He buys tartar sauce, no fish apparently, just bottles of the sauce. They watch his rubbish. Fish heads, trout skeletons."

"He was eating his children."

"Everyone was shocked," the brother said. " I'm on best behavior, we all are."

While they'd been drinking beer, the brother said that he supposed, as the older one, he should be offering Healey some sort of advice about going into marriage and making all these important "life decisions," as he called them, adding that he had, in fact, been thinking about these issues himself quite a lot recently, since the "situation with Susan," the woman with the hawk, had developed to the stage where he said he would soon be leaving Rainbow Springs and most likely heading overseas somewhere. This was the first time the brother had mentioned Susan or leaving the country, though he spoke as if Healey knew the full story and announced his intention to leave as if such a major change in his situation could only be accomplished suddenly and presented as a *fait accompli*.

"You know, whenever I thought about my future," the

brother said, "I always imagined the life cycle of this or that specimen—when he reaches maturity, I said of this gecko, then I'll move back to the city. Imagine it! The thing was, Brett, it was always quite comforting, because far from neglecting to look ahead—as some people always thought—I was carefully recording and plotting in my notebooks more or less exactly when I would be able to achieve something. I even had graphs of the thing. Though this sort of worried me too, since it was never pure research I was doing—I was always aware of transferring too much of myself onto the data. It was Susan who gave me insight into what it might be like to reach directly to my subject—her work in hawks was a revelation, Brett—and now this happened and suddenly I don't even know what my subject is anymore."

While shining the light on the brother as he moved skillfully about the paths, Healey thought that, since meeting Louise, he, too, no longer knew what his subject was, but whereas the brother, in his own words, was going to "put some distance" between himself and what had caused these "questions" to surface, Healey felt as though he were finally closing the distance. As his brother spoke in the prefab for the first time about the things that really mattered to him, Healey could only make weak, consoling noises while struggling against a mounting impatience. This, he recognized as they walked the dark paths of Rainbow Springs, was the impatience the recently sick and now recovered person might have for those still, unaccountably, ill.

On Willis Street, talking to Claire not about that night but about the brother's current project in England, Healey thought that perhaps rather than being ahead of the brother as he imagined that night in the prefab, he had, in fact, been behind him in the level of attentiveness with which he went about things, further behind even than at the moment he tripped and fell on the path which led through the black trout ponds, a fall which he blamed on the beer and the wine and the smoke he had inhaled from the burned pork chops. "That bird!" he had said, while his brother helped him up. "That spoilt fucking Handsome!"

The night of the funeral, Healey had slept on the sofa, which was still warm from his aunts. They had fussed over sheets and blankets, and Lillian had demanded that she and not Brett should be the outcast in the living room, since it was her foolishness that had kept them all up so late. "But I've worn a place for myself there," she was whispering loudly as Margaret and Angela finally led her from the room. "That poor boy has done nothing to deserve those lumpy cushions—no offense, Ange."

Lying in the dark, Healey listened to the murmur of voices, the occasional giggle. For all his exhaustion, he realized he had gone to bed too early. Some delayed effect of the ferry ride in combination with the day's events, the food and drink, forced him to get up and walk to the window. The surrounding hills were black, punctuated in odd places by lights that failed to give shape to the ridges and gullies, while the harbor itself was only suggested by a series of dim flashes given off, Healey supposed, by the container ship he had seen earlier that day. Somewhere in a downtown nightclub, a gang of

Korean sailors would be trying, through an alcoholic fog, to catch a glimpse or even ahold of the breasts of the New Zealand women they'd paid to dance on their table.

From his parents' bedroom window, looking over in the direction of the suburb where his grandparents had lived, he might have seen the lights from the airport. As a boy, staying overnight at Miramar, he had trained his father's opera glasses on the runways beneath the illuminated wind sock and hoped for some mild disaster with which to wake the entire household.

He crept into the passageway, terrified of being grabbed in the dark by some sleepwalking relative, took the phone from its table and brought it into the living room.

Louise's voice, slowed by sleep, immediately helped Healey's breathing. He saw her standing in the kitchen in her bare feet, with the gradual chill from the hardwood floor making her move from one foot to the other. This slow hopping appeared in his mind as the correct accompaniment to her words, which were also showing signs of both irritation and indulgence. He wouldn't keep her long, but it was deeply comforting and he felt a childlike satisfaction that someone might suffer this inconvenience for him.

He had asked about her army piece and she was saying that it had been settled, that the trouble with the photos was all fixed. "How fixed?" Healey heard himself whisper, wanting the delicate, hopping connection to last a little longer still.

"Well," Louise explained, "it turned out that one of the soldiers photographed was now facing a court martial."

"For being photographed?" Healey asked.

"Not for being photographed," Louise told him. "He was running a book. Taking money off the other boys in his unit. For gambling. Turns out he was doubling his pay most weeks. That is until he lost big and couldn't meet the payouts. So someone dobbed him in. Sore losers. Anyway, they didn't think he was such a good advertisement. But what about the funeral, Brett? You've had the funeral."

While listening to Louise, Healey had been thinking of what he wanted to say. He wanted to tell her about sailing into the harbor that morning. It was somehow important that she know exactly what this moment had meant to him and that he should find a language that was not technical, or brash, or pushy, that had no trace of the Nelson architect who had stood beside him on the ferry. He did not want the phrases to sound, as indeed he heard them sound now in his head, hollow, overrehearsed, and theatrical in the hushed sibilance of his delivery. Then he would have to tell her about the Greek taxi driver, the father-in-law and brothers-in-law, the way the driver had held the cup between his knees, his analysis of the capital. And still Healey felt that he hadn't yet found the right approach. What was it he truly wanted? For Louise to drop everything and come up here? For good? Had he come to Wellington for good? He didn't think so. What about the hardwood floors of their flat, the newspaper office with its low ceiling?

The idea of moving once again, the idea of leaving his job and returning to his hometown—as he often promised himself he would and which he had often discussed with Louise, who was herself not hostile to the idea—had come to figure

as a thoroughly workable option. Yet this idea also seemed
to be receding and to be doing so even when its likelihood
was strongest, much in the way, he thought, what is inevi-
table, precisely because it has the feel of a sure future, tends
to be indefinitely delayed and put off. Perhaps the recognition
of the need to change is itself a sort of change, he thought,
though can it be said, therefore, that our desire never finds a
voice and that we are doomed never to act? Perhaps inaction
itself comprises a rich scale of nuance, the sounding of which
in our own minds is as delectable and invigorating as the sphere
of change. Healey was exhausted. His thinking had grown
rushed and full of these countermovements. Louise was ask-
ing again about the funeral.

"Lighter, love," said Healey. "He was lighter."

"Who was?" said Louise.

"Daddy."

"You mean—"

"It's Aunt Lillian's story. She told it to me. If you want
to hear it, you can. You will. But—"

"But not now, Brett."

"No."

Yet within the exhaustion there was still this velocity. Aunt
Lillian's story could wait, but there were others whose ur-
gency he now felt himself giving in to.

"Did I ever tell you about Russkie?" said Healey.

"Who? He's a cousin? I'm sorry. It's late, honey."

"I know. This won't take a minute. There were three
brothers. Russkie—we called him that. His real name was
Peter, and Dimmy and Alex, the eldest one."

"You never told me about any of these people. When you get back—"

"Sure, but this will help us sleep," said Healey. "This is a bedtime story, hon. Only maybe it's a 'when the bough breaks' type. Not meant to scare you."

"Scare me?"

"Anyway, calamity, especially when it's not quite yours, can be a great calmer, don't you think?"

But now he had really begun, speaking rapidly, convinced he had only a certain time in which to get it all out, that Louise would soon stop moving from foot to foot and simply stand there, both feet planted firmly, thereby announcing that their night talk was at an end. He was telling her about the war-gaming club, the Auckland visit, the parakeets, the guns, the invitation to dinner. There were noises of protest—*she* wanted *him* slowed down now—until mainly there was silence from her end, and it was finally this silence that made him stop. Was she still there?

"Lou?" he inquired into the phone. "I never went back there for dinner, Lou. I was scared, I think. I know I was scared, Lou."

"Brett?"

"Scared of where people end up. Is that what I'm scared of? What happened to those boys? That's what I was saying to myself over and over the night I was supposed to go round their house again for dinner. What happened there?"

He was remembering thinking, as he listened to Peter on that long-ago visit, that he should run for the door. Was there a clear passage? Yet he also wanted to know all the details, to go on listening. Even as he was heading for the door, he kept hoping Peter would come up with something else, some final piece to bring it together. These people are crazy, he kept telling himself. Don't get tangled up here. No one was going to believe this, he kept saying. No one is going to believe these three parakeets, one per brother. Still he couldn't get away.

"I don't follow any of this, Brett," said Louise. "Am I supposed to?"

"Well, it was what he said at the end about my brother, when I was thinking of escape. He knew."

"I was in bed just now, Brett. My head was on the pillow. It's cold. Is it cold up there?"

"All right," said Healey. "What time is it?"

"Late."

"All right."

"You're sure?"

"Sure," he said.

"Call me in the morning."

"Yes."

"Go to sleep."

"Yes."

"I'm going back to bed now. Soon we'll both be in bed. Thinking of each other."

"All right."

Healey sat in the dark, thinking of the moment when he realized Peter had known all along about the soldiers he had pocketed on the war-gaming afternoons. Dimmy hadn't even needed to tell on him. Each figure had its own compartment.

Peter could easily search his brothers' rooms, and neither Monk nor Healey's brother would have done such a thing. There was a battlefield etiquette. So it was Healey. And when Peter was talking about Healey's brother being crazy, he was really saying that he knew about Healey, too; that they were somehow in it together, the brothers; that they had been understood and recognized and identified; that nothing escaped Peter's attention. Peter had waited all those years to confront the thief and still he wouldn't give Healey the satisfaction of being uncovered. They simply stood there and Peter invited Healey once again to come for dinner, making him promise that he would, and both of them knowing that Healey would never come, even as they were both nodding their heads in agreement and, as the final humiliation, Peter had stuck out his hand and they were shaking on the deal.

After leaving Rainbow Springs, Healey's brother had lived for a time in a remote mining town in Western Australia, before going to England, where, bypassing London, he headed straight for one of the southernmost counties to work in a research station, again studying *skinks,* which word, when pronounced by Healey, caused both him and Claire to laugh.

"It sounds like your brother," said Claire.

"I think I've worked out the pattern," said Healey. "He never lives anywhere with an address. There's never a street or house number but only a district code and the name of some larger location—a farm or a reserve or something so big that you couldn't imagine a front door or even a mailbox, so that sending him any mail is always more of an act of faith.

I was going through my address book recently and I came across the page of his old so-called addresses, none of which were real locations but only kind of rough guides."

They had been chatting about the brother for several minutes on Willis Street, the other pedestrians stepping around them, and even when Healey and Claire stood to one side of the pavement, they still caused a difference in the flow, which excited Healey, since it now appeared as though their friendship was a permanent fixture around which the rest of Willis Street arranged itself. Yet as he felt the time approaching when he would soon run out of information about the brother, having brought Claire fully up to date with all he knew of his movements, it struck Healey that the relationship between Claire and himself was not sufficiently close to allow them to ask about each other's movements. He had always been the little brother, she irretrievably the older figure, and this was the longest time they had ever spent talking together. There were things, he felt, that were just put out of reach, and he resented these strictures.

He had the sudden desire to give her something, some token—the letter. If only he had thought to bring his grandfather's letter from John A. Lee, he might have passed it across now. She worked in government, perhaps this way the letter might finally come to be on the public record where it seemed to belong. It would be accorded its rightful historical value. Though more than this, he wanted to pass on the secret of his theft, to place that between them, to give her the scene of the bedroom and tell once again the story of his grandfather's top drawer, the story he had tried to tell without success in the Aro Street house of his friend the lawyer not an hour before. He wanted to come clean. And in return she might well have told him what had happened between herself and his brother fifteen years ago. In what way was he like his brother? Yet even the idea of mentioning his grandfather's funeral was ridiculous. Nor could Healey say how disappointed he was that his brother had not come back for the funeral, and how much he missed him. They could only talk and laugh about the brother. Soon they would leave each other, having used only a language that turned on certain words that struck them as odd and so characterized the odd brother— *apiarist, skinks.*

At the beginning of the conversation, Claire had raised her briefcase to her chest and cradled it between her arms. Now, as Healey approached the end of the story of the brother, she let her briefcase return to its "walking position." And although he wanted to tell her about seeing her on television and feeling at that moment that she could do anything she desired, that he did not envy her or wish her to fall from her position, he also began to move sideways, as if to get around her in a narrow passageway without any part of their clothing touching. He also wanted her to know about the hawk called Handsome and about the brother's physical grace in setting the lines, but then he thought that this might only seem again odd and push the brother still further away.

"Well," she said with a concluding sigh. "He always had, you know—"

"What?" said Healey.

"He was driven your brother, wasn't he."

"Ah."

"I mean it was lovely, the honey and everything."

"It was good honey."

"No, I mean, of course." Claire seemed, for just a moment, flustered. She tapped the side of her briefcase with her heel. "But the wrapping, the packaging, that was quite phenomenal."

Healey didn't remember the packaging.

"He must have really put in the time there, really worked on it," she said. "That's what I mean by driven. I mean, labored beautifully."

It excited him to hear this. The phrase was curious. Not a Willis Street phrase at all. She too had sensed the ridiculous bind they were in. She was trying to get past the old obstructions. It was a kind of gift, this "beautifully." Healey didn't quite know how to make more of her sudden opening. He was struggling to find the words with which her gesture might be acknowledged, returned in kind.

"Good with his hands," he said.

"Yes and more!" she said. "Are you that way too?" She kicked the case. "Stupid question, how idiotic!"

"Can't tie a knot," he said.

"That's what he'd say, so there you go."

"Seriously," said Healey. "I can't make a paper plane."

"You and him!" she said with a laugh. "I don't know."

He realized with disappointment that they had come back, after all, to their respective and companionable roles and when he next spoke it was once more as the school friend's younger brother. He asked where she was on her way to.

"Eventually to work," she said.

"On a Saturday morning?" he said.

"Oh, someone has to run the country, I suppose."

As he watched Claire walk off down Willis Street, Healey had the sudden urge to call out to her. There was something he had forgotten. Imagine that, he wanted to say, you in the *Beehive*! But she was already gone and he began to think, not of the winding paths through the shady ponds where the large, soft bodies of rainbow and brown trout occasionally broke the surface of the invisible waters, but of the hive shape of the building in which Claire worked, whose model in miniature the brother had once observed each summer morning for a period of several weeks, through the heavy gauze of the visor on his bee suit, while imagining in a neighboring valley his friends drinking beer in the fruit pickers' huts.

6

Cable

IN HEALEY'S MIND, THE CHARACTER OF THE WELLINGTON cable car had always owed less to the steep incline of its tracks and the harbor views it afforded than to the stern Eastern European demeanor of the men who took the tickets and drove the car dourly up the hill to Kelburn. These were faces lacking not only the inclination toward lightness, but also, Healey believed, the ability to show anything more than a vague annoyance at handling the fares, answering inquiries, waiting for the passengers, sounding the warning bell, until even the act of opening the doors seemed to be done begrudgingly. It often appeared they would have far preferred to lock the terminal gates and sit together in the dark, muttering punch lines to the jokes that occasionally made them bark alarmingly behind the glass of the booth. For some reason, Healey found himself attracted to these bleak figures and he often wondered about the paths they had taken that had led them to their positions in the glass boxes where they now spent their working lives.

Of course he saw that the good humor of these men was not improved by the fact that each day they had to ride the same half mile of straight track again and again, watching people enter and exit and make the same gestures, the same mistakes, the same noises repeating themselves—the sound of the cable spinning, the bell, the doors closing, the shoes skidding across the tiled floor and the helpless cries of "Wait!"—so that perhaps it was not surprising that there was often the feeling among those who had managed to secure a seat that a team of sour and mildly hypnotized drivers had control of the machines, which moved in odd patterns of jerkiness at an angle of almost forty-five degrees. Nor should it have surprised him, as always it did, that this team regularly engineered it so that the cable car was out of service due to some mechanical fault every third or fourth time Healey went to take the shortcut from town to the campus.

On several occasions as a student, Healey had been forced to join the other passengers in a climb up the tracks, their car having come to a halt halfway up the hill. In such cases, the driver would refuse to give out any information about why they had been stationary for the previous ten minutes. Instead, he would slide shut the door to his compartment and engage in difficult discussions over the radio with the Eastern European driver of the car that sat ahead of them. Sometimes the car would suddenly start moving again, and again this would happen without explanation or apology. Or else the doors would open after a suitable time had elapsed, by which the driver gave the passengers to understand that he wasn't going anywhere in a hurry, and if they wanted to get some place they would have to help each other down onto the tracks and walk the rest of the way. He would only utter the words "Cable! Cable!" which immediately took on the significance of a curse.

As those who could began the trek up the hill—the students and the commuters, the housewives, and the doctors who had their rooms on Upland Road, the elderly residents of Kelburn and the bemused, hysterical tourists—moving through the ill-lit tunnels and slipping on the loose stones between the tracks, careful to avoid the cable, which might at any moment return to life, Healey imagined a slight look of triumph crossing the driver's face as he spread open the newspaper on the control panel in his compartment and began in on the emergency sandwich that always made the journey up and down and was employed to stave off hunger until the engineers should arrive to rescue him.

After Claire left him on Willis Street, Healey had turned into Lambton Quay and then, while passing Cable Car Lane, although he had no desire to return yet to his parents' house, where several sets of relations still lingered, and believing anyway that the cable car would be out of service, he found himself paying his money to a man he recognized from years before as one of the drivers who had sat alone in his cable car halfway up the hill and who had caused Healey to be late for a tutorial in which American attitudes toward issues of censorship and sexuality in the 1950s and 1960s were being discussed. On that afternoon, the long climb up the loose stones of the track had filled his mind, not with the questions raised by the essays he was supposed to have prepared for the tutorial, but with the memory of another climb that had seemed endless.

After the holiday house-swap network had been exhausted, Healey's father began taking the family on camping trips. Remoteness and hardship became the twin indices by which he measured the success of each summer. He would say that it was necessary to get away from Wellington, that a man bound to his desk was half a man, and that the blood never reached the brain without a fellow moving his legs. Circulation and ascension, these were guarantees of both physical and mental freshness. In vigorous climbing there was also a kind of moral exercise. Healey's father had always loved a good stiff tramp, although now something other than personal gratification was driving him. A clique had formed at work to get the department shifted into more suitable premises. The present location was archaic, hopelessly outmoded. According to Healey's father, the extent of this claim lay in the fact that certain people didn't like walking up a few flights of stairs. It was the smokers' lobby and nothing more. Blaming the building for the state of their own lungs. The strength of his opposition, however, seemed more apparent and operated with greater force in the maneuvers he encouraged in his own family than those he tried among his colleagues. They at least—his children—would set an example.

One summer they ended up in a tent on the grounds of a

disused chalet on the western side of Mount Egmont. The chalet was open only in winter, which, of course, was the only time people came to that part of the country. Still, there was some excitement, though it was not acknowledged by the children, in approaching the chalet from the tree-lined sweep of driveway and imagining for a moment that this many-windowed place was their summer residence. Whereas, in fact, the father had turned off the engine so as not to attract attention and the car had silently coasted around the grounds, stopping perhaps twenty yards short of a group of trees and making it necessary for the family to get out and push the car under the branches. Then they had pitched their tent behind the generously proportioned buildings, so as to be hidden from the road and from the owners or management who might have misconstrued the little settlement at the rear of their property. The chalet, indeed, quickly became a kind of elaborately constructed torment for the children, especially when it rained and they were forced to spend the night in the car while dreaming of being inside the cozy rooms that waited empty beside them by the hundreds. How cruel the gleaming bathrooms seemed while they were squatting down in the bushes, holding the roll of toilet paper above the prickling, dewy grass. Yet there was the mountain rising directly above them and, at over eight thousand feet, it was, as the brother said "a real mountain." In the winter, when the chalet was full, the snow-covered peak would kill several people per season. In the summer, all but the snow in the summit crater was gone, and Healey's father said they would one day go up it for the view.

At this time, Healey's sister had developed what her parents called "a mind of her own" and she now simply refused to ascend to eight thousand feet to look out on Taranaki, a region which could only be a painful reminder of all that lay beyond the mountains to the south—notably, her circle of friends. There was also the shadowy figure of a boyfriend, although it would not be for several months after they returned home that Healey learned that, while they were up the mountain, the sister had been absent for the night from the chalet grounds and had been picked up at the end of the driveway and taken twenty miles to the north, to the city of New Plymouth.

Having dropped law and while gradually moving to the almost exclusive study of literature, Healey had continued with history, believing it to be a more solid backup than either classics or one of the social sciences, though the latter had seemed attractive from a distance, if only for the number of women students who gathered in the library to talk, often tearfully, sometimes excitedly, about their experiments with mice. If he, too, joined the psych lab, Healey imagined he might be able to console these women students and weaken the attachments they had formed to the pitiful animals inside their mazes and light chambers.

In his second year, at the time of the cable-car breakdown, he was taking a course in American social history. The lecturer was a bearded man in his late thirties, who had taken part in antiwar marches while studying in America in the 1960s. For this and for his comparative youthfulness and easygoing teaching style, he was universally admired among the students. Part of the way through the course, the lecturer, who was also Healey's tutor, shaved off his beard, causing the students in the large lecture hall to burst into spontaneous applause. "With a chin," someone beside Healey said, "he looks even younger!"

On the day he had to climb most of the way up the cablecar tracks, Healey entered the tutorial room ten minutes late. The room was on one of the upper floors of the library building and it always seemed overly bright under the fluorescent lights and too warm. At first, as he found a place and began taking out his books with exaggerated care, Healey had thought the lecturer was talking to the tutorial about a historical character, or speaking in the voice of one of the authors of an essay that had been set for class. Then he realized that the lecturer was talking about himself. He was saying that when his sex life was good, other areas went well also, and these were areas, he said, which we'd normally think had perhaps nothing to do with sex. "I find I can drive my car better," he said. "My parallel parking is suddenly astonishing!" The lecturer looked at the students. "But when things in the bedroom are not so hot," he said "I notice a corresponding falling off in other areas."

He said he was interested, then, in the relationship between sex and our so-called public lives, since the essays he had set for that week's reading were also, in effect, talking about the places where sex and society meet.

The lecturer spoke so naturally it was impossible to believe that he was even listening to himself and certainly, Healey believed, he was not listening to the way his words had settled in the room, since they had effected a quite unnatural silence. The other students were either looking directly at the lecturer while he spoke, as if in an attempt to outstare him and to suggest that they could handle this type of approach, or studying their notes with heads down, hoping not to be called on to respond. Healey found himself looking from the course notes on the table in front of him to the lecturer and then back again. Now the lecturer was talking more about his wife's responses to these same issues, saying that he didn't think this was necessarily a male thing and wondering whether there were people in the group who felt similarly about their own sex lives. And again Healey had the impression, when the lecturer used the words *wife* or *group,* that he was referring to purely historical figures whom he had perhaps come across in the course of some research.

It then struck Healey that the quiet in the room was, in fact, natural. After all, the lecturer's questions had provoked in him not an inquiry into his own "sex life" but a kind of rightful stubborn silence that gripped the entire tutorial. It was fitting that silence should meet the lecturer's "frankness," his prurience, and, Healey thought as a student of history, his *goading.* Yet he knew that at this moment of defiance someone was preparing to speak, one of the older students, the so-called "mature students," a man in his late thirties who often hijacked the tutorial by demonstrating a certain long-windedness and obtuseness that masqueraded as "experience," speaking as a contemporary of the lecturer's, and always beginning any statement, no matter what the historical context, with the words *In my experience*. Everyone knew when the mature student was about to say something, since he always moved his chair back away from the table, as if putting a distance between himself and what was being said at the time.

"In my experience," the man said, with a scrape of his chair, "sometimes, yes, good sex equals good life. A confidence thing, I can see that working. But other times, say I've been separated from my partner for a while, when I'm away or she's off somewhere, and it's happened to me quite recently, I feel I can channel those energies, those sexual energies into other areas. Into history essays, or whatever you like. I'm not distracted by the one, so I can think about the other in greater depth. If I don't have a sex life, sometimes I discover I have a better *other life*—no sex, better results—isn't that what the sports coaches say? Anyway I'd like to feed that into the group, perhaps other people—"

The tutorial then erupted, as it often did after the mature student had spoken, and several students began speaking at the same time, some in prim defense, others in heated attack, while the lecturer moved his chair a little away from the tutorial table.

Healey did not speak. He was thinking of the girl in the previous year with whom he had sometimes slept. He counted three or four times, four if lying down beside her until it was morning was to be included under the phrase "sleeping with." And he thought of his dream of involving her in a criminal scheme.

For several months of the year, as a law student, he would

regularly go downtown at lunchtime and steal one or two or sometimes three books from a large bookshop on Lambton Quay. He never thought at the time of stealing about the consequences of getting caught. Once he was inside the bookshop, he thought only of the books that were now on the shelves on Lambton Quay and of the inches they would soon occupy on the shelves in the bedroom of his Aro Valley flat. The only moments he thought about getting caught were those in which he approached the exit of the bookshop with his one or two or, if they were small volumes, his three books—he always carried the books in one hand low at his side—and even in these most exciting moments, he never considered the consequences exactly, but simply imagined the feel of the hand on his shoulder, or the sound of a raised voice, or, out on the street, footsteps running behind him. Just as years later on the poop deck when he had been weighing up the American's proposition of perjuring himself for monetary gain, Healey felt curiously distanced from the notion of "consequence" and thought only of how this particular piece might be fitted to what had gone before.

In the newspaper there were, periodically, reports of law students convicted of petty crimes. He remembered, in particular, the case of one female student who was said to be in her fourth year and one of the most promising students in her class. She was found guilty of shoplifting, despite a psychiatric profile that identified contributory and extenuating causes. The judge, in handing down the small fine, which would nevertheless debar her from her chosen profession, had spoken of the defendant "throwing away four years of her life with a few rash acts.'' He'd used the word *rash* even though during the hearing it had come out that, since the time of an unspecified family tragedy, the student had compulsively shoplifted items for which she had no possible use nor even desire, since it was also admitted in her defense that she immediately threw away everything she stole, sometimes dropping the merchandise into trash cans directly outside the shop. Nor did she have any memory of these incidents, except when prompted under therapy. The case had become something of a scandal among law students and their professors, but the lesson for anyone who broke the law, one senior lecturer said, was there for all to see.

When he read of this case, Healey imagined himself in court on similar charges, unable to name any contributory or extenuating causes, speaking only in breathless stabs, of those places on his bedroom shelves in whose empty inches he had imagined the spines of certain essential books. "I didn't pinch just anything, your honor," he heard himself saying. First he stole Russian literature from the nineteenth century, then twentieth-century French; in one go he stole the three books that Katherine Mansfield published in her lifetime; he stole American poetry and the selected letters of a German writer; he stole the black-colored Penguin paperback editions of Greek and Roman authors; he stole anthologies; he walked out with folktales, journals, and autobiographies; he stole several feet of the pale-lime color in which the Penguin Modern Classics were wrapped. And as the collection took shape, sometimes he was excited with the find of an essential book in a red jacket, which he pictured nicely breaking up the line of black, or with a white-spined classic to interrupt the run of green.

The girl who had constituted his sex life of the previous year was called Joanna. She was an English student. When finally Joanna had agreed to visit his flat, a few weeks after they had slept beside each other for several hours, she had immediately begun rearranging his shelves, so that they might appear as in a bookshop or library. Healey had never followed alphabetical order or any order except that of color and occasionally he would put beside a certain author another author in whose company he believed there might be some mutual pleasure. But he had never been systematic in any of this and as he allowed Joanna to alter the look of these precious inches, he grew more determined to finally bring it about that they would have sex together, if not that very night, then the next or the one after that—but soon, he promised himself.

It was a miracle, he thought, that Joanna had appeared at the door of his flat alone, since she was usually accompanied by a group of girlfriends and whenever he spoke to her, surrounded like this, Healey was forced to think not only of his image in her eyes but also of his image, or images, in the eyes of all her girlfriends, under whose appraising look the business of trying to bring it about that one night they might have sex together had to be conducted as if in committee. Now they were finally alone; did this mean the committee had okayed the deal?

"This is completely hopeless," Joanna said, taking two

books by one of the Russians from the space that had existed as a block of black and was now occupied by the various shades of the *C*'s, and letting them hang low by her side as she faced Healey. "You need a librarian or someone."

This was the moment—he remembered in the American social history tutorial, which he was remembering as he went up in the cable car—that he dreamed of involving Joanna in his shoplifting scheme. The way she held the books! But then he decided that they would first need to have sex fully and properly for a whole night and be lying naked side by side before he could begin to tell her how the books she had touched in his bedroom had come to be there. To tell her now, he thought, would have risked ruining forever his chances. He would have thrown away many hours, he told himself, with one rash act.

They set out up Egmont after lunch one fine day and by late afternoon reached the hut at five thousand feet. This first stage was on well-maintained paths through sparse bush, and only once had they become disoriented before another hiker put them right. After a dinner of baked beans, followed by canned peaches for dessert, Healey and the brother went to bed while the father carried on talking to some fellow climbers about routes to the summit, the weather patterns of the mountain, and the number of lives that had been claimed the previous winter.

The sleeping room, which they shared with four or five others, consisted of a joined bunk arrangement, with an upper and lower level stretching from one wall to another. There were no separate beds and during the night, Healey, on the bottom level, was occasionally woken by a neighbor's foot or by the sounds of hikers snoring and coughing. He heard his father above him cry out in his sleep and thought of him falling onto the floor in the middle of the night.

In the morning they rejoined the same path, though after a while the father led them off to one side, saying that he'd been put on to a good thing by a bloke in the hut and this route would save them time. Now, instead of solid ground, they were walking on loose rock, which the father said would soon give way to something firmer a little higher up. After an hour, the rock had become soft shingle into which they sank up to a foot before they could move off. Now there was little vegetation, and as the sun came around they found themselves on a bare and exposed face of the mountain, forced to track sideways rather than upwards just to escape this shortcut. It then struck Healey that, just as they had traced the circumference of Mount Edgeware a few summers before, so they were now circling the summit of Mount Egmont, never appearing to come any closer and, in fact, sometimes moving farther away.

Just as he had become almost mute in the law tutorial and spoken only rarely in the English tutorial and then never as he wished to be heard, so in the history tutorial he could only bring himself occasionally to read aloud a sentence or two from one of the required readings in answering the lecturer's questions. He could never trust himself to formulate a sentence of his own without running out of breath.

When researching a topic in the library by using the books that were deemed "essential" and that were invariably put on closed reserve so that every student might have the opportunity to refer to them, Healey was often weighted down by the history of the book itself. He would become ridiculously distracted by its appearance—by how it had suffered and been through so many students' hands over the years that its cover was in a state of disrepair and its original text almost completely buried beneath the notational markings, doodlings, and crossings-out of years of history students attempting to find what was essential in its pages. In his allotted two hours with the book, he found he could read only those paragraphs which had remained relatively intact and from which the essence had not been removed again and again, as the juice is squeezed from a lemon. And such passages, of course, were more or less useless for his purposes.

While slipping about on the exposed face of Mount Egmont, Healey thought that they would become the first father-and-sons team to lose their lives to the mountain in summertime. When they rested, there was nowhere to sit except in the soft shingle they had been struggling through for hours. The sun was shining in a clear blue sky and yet at five thousand feet they had to put on their jackets. At "base camp," Healey knew his mother would be removing her shoulder straps while sitting on the sunny veranda of the empty chalet reading her book.

His father now seemed concerned and gave up the lead to walk behind the boys, making sure they got up when they fell by supporting them with his arm. And this supporting was not done hurriedly, but gently, the father waiting with patience until everyone felt like going on. He kept speaking about the bloke at the hut the night before who'd put them wrong, and he seemed hurt, not that they were suffering, but that another climber could offer such bad information to *one of his own kind,* as if it were only a matter of protocol; Healey kept thinking through the tears, which now came freely to his eyes, that they were to become summer's first victims.

The brother, who was in the lead, then gave a shout and pointed ahead. Twenty yards away, a line of tourists, with cameras swinging from their necks, was sauntering up the side of the mountain. The party was moving swiftly up the same track that they themselves had abandoned hours before. At first his father acted as if he hadn't seen the tourists and their jaunty flight. Then, as Healey began shouting to them, he was silenced, his father telling him in almost a whisper to conserve his energy, though the boy saw in the father's face, mixed with relief, a momentary flush of shame. Finally reaching the track, stepping up on to its firm surface, Healey had the sensation of being plucked from water. Quietly, almost sheepishly, they tagged on to the end of the line of tourists.

At the end of the social history course, Healey failed a "conversation" with the lecturer on the early history of the American film industry. This had been the topic of his essay, which the lecturer, in awarding an average mark, had described as "a literate precis of the source material." The so-called conversation was worth ten percent of the final grade, and Healey had been awarded four percent. Since then, when "talking" to the lecturer—a situation Healey did everything to avoid— he felt that each sentence he uttered was worth a little less than half its possible value. Whereas, with other people, he believed he sometimes had conversations that might rate an eight or even nine and that many hovered around the six or seven mark, he knew that he would never reach such a standard with the lecturer.

On meeting him at a social engagement several years after the film conversation, when Healey was sure the lecturer did not remember him, he listened to him talk of his days in America in the 1960s, just as when he was a student he had listened to him lecture on the 1960s peace movement. It was a luncheon, a few weeks before Healey was to leave for America. The lecturer had been a consultant on the board that had given Healey a travel grant for his studies. He listened to the lecturer talk of the time when he had simply left his books behind, in those first few weeks of fall, and gone up to Vermont to watch the leaves turn. "This," he said, "is something everyone just has to do." As he spoke, Healey could not help but think of the lecturer's sex life and whether he and his wife gave each other marks out of ten, and also whether the turning trees in the Vermont fall might not be worth *a perfect score*. And he began to understand, even as he tried to picture the fall leaves of Vermont and rid himself of these old thoughts, how he had feared this man with whom he had once tried to have a "little chat" about film in that office on whose wall was a large poster of the Marx brothers. He remembered that even as the lecturer talked about Harpo in a certain favorite scene, and Healey, recognizing that this was supposedly the icebreaker, had smiled back at him, he could not help thinking *How am I doing? I should say something now; there's a gap for me* and all the time busily trying to lift a cup of coffee to his lips without the whole thing flying out of his tense grip and ending up against the walls of the office.

One winter night several weeks after he had promised himself that he would wait no longer for Joanna, Healey found himself again surrounded by her girlfriends, in the cold, dank living room of the flat where she lived, seemingly with all the girlfriends, on the side of a ridge high up in Kelburn. He had already had perhaps five or six cups of tea, and when he protested that he didn't want to drink the house dry, one of the girlfriends assured him that it was okay, since every cup had been brewed *from the same tea bag.* "Our record," she told him, "is thirteen cups from one bag—it's criminal how people throw them away after just one!" (Years later, when he came across one of Louise's used tea bags waiting in a cup for a second dunking, he would remember the face of the girlfriend with its look of boastfulness and he would take inordinate delight in throwing the bag away.)

He was now feeling bloated and slightly ill from the milky water, which, for want of conversation, he had heard himself repeatedly agreeing to. Earlier in the evening, the bottle of wine he'd brought had been divided up among the girlfriends and when equal shares had been poured, the alcohol, with which he had hoped to induce a certain receptivity in Joanna as well as a degree of boldness in himself, scarcely reached the halfway mark in the teacup that he was forced to share with another of the girlfriends, since Joanna had taken up her position in a chair on the other side of the room.

The girlfriends were all "alternative" types of varying convictions and while describing the course of his study, Healey let it be known that books were really his thing and that as a law student he had quietly seized the opportunity to act as a kind of *irritant to the system.* Joanna did little to confirm this status, but agreed that he had a lot of books, perhaps even too many, a comment that made the girlfriends nod their heads, as if *they had all had dealings with the sort of boy who had too many books.* She said that she doubted whether he was the type of person who took easily to organizing material and that this probably accounted for what she called his "problems with law." As Healey suffered a moment when he firmly believed he was in the wrong room and began summoning the effort needed to explain in his now constricted breathing that it was not just a case of organizing material, but rather that he was profoundly opposed to certain tenets of the profession and especially to its methods of deciding membership, one of the girlfriends cut him off by saying that she, too, like Healey, couldn't handle "all those weekly assignments."

The tea had begun to press painfully against his bladder, yet the toilet was right beside the living room and had periodically, through the loudness of its reports, given the impression of actually being inside the room. He couldn't bear to imagine the sound of his urinating into the bowl filling the living room and being appraised by the girlfriends, though equally unbearable was the thought of contriving his relief so that there was no noise, by which they might think him, somehow, prudish or unnatural. It was only when a group of clearly drunk male students arrived, "friends of the flat," as Joanna announced them, two of whom Healey recognized as law students whose names the lecturer did not have to look up in the seating plan and who now caused the girlfriends and Joanna to become quite lively, that he finally went to the bathroom. By this stage, he no longer cared how he sounded and purposefully neglected to lift the seat, nor did he bother to wash his hands afterward, but spent some time scouting around in the medicine cabinet, examining all the bottles and prescribed lotions that bore the names of the girlfriends who were sitting behind the paper-thin walls, shrieking at the lawyers' jokes.

When he had become almost speechless in the cold living room and was imagining the walk home down the steep streets in the rain, Joanna led him, unexpectedly, since she had been engaged in earnest conversation for some time with one of the law students, to her bedroom where she said she was now tired and had to lie down. She kicked off her shoes. "Everybody wants me," she told him, closing her eyes. "Before, no one wanted me and now there's you and—" Drunk with the tea and the crushing success of the young lawyers in the living room, Healey fell against her. He could not bear to hear about all these others. He had her now, and that was what mattered. He wanted her mouth. "My neck," she sighed. "My neck's the place." He bit into the skin beneath her ear. "Don't mark me," she told him. He pressed his open mouth hard against her throat. "I don't know who I am," she said. "They always go for the neck." Healey continued to nuzzle. He could taste the tea in his breath. "Don't suck," she said. "Sucking marks."

They collapsed onto the bed, a mattress on the floor beneath a window facing the "wrong" direction, since it looked away from the harbor and caught, full on, the force of the southerly storm that had come up quickly in the evening and was causing the window to rattle so fiercely that it was difficult to hear without speaking in a normal voice, whereas Healey had imagined lying beside her and speaking only in *the voice of shadowy bedrooms*. This window was to blame. She pushed him off her and lay still. She wanted one sentence. Words were what she wanted, all strung together in the right order and accompanied by a kind of music in whose rhythm they could be joined. But with the window banging he grew more fearful that, speaking in his normal voice to make himself heard, he would lose everything.

He lay beside her for a time. "So," he started finally, "how do you know those guys?" And it struck him then, in the time it took those terrible words to form in his sour-tasting mouth, that the moment in which he might have told Joanna about the criminal lunch hours of her bookish law student and his dream of the two of them becoming a double act in the aisles of the downtown bookshops was gone forever.

When he was rising above the city in the cable car, moving away from Lambton Quay, the scene of his life as a petty thief—a thief hardly resembling those who, driven by social necessity, ran through the books of his grandfather's favorite New Zealand author with such giddy energy, yet connected to these soiled figures all the same—he realized that he had never told anyone, not even Louise, about these most exciting moments in the year he had entered the wrong field. When he had phoned Louise the previous night and woken her up with his senseless rambling about the Russkies, had he not been moving toward such a confession? But of course he had chosen the wrong forum. Nothing was possible on the telephone. He should have known that. It was only when their heads were close together, when their elbows were almost touching on the table, when they were separated by only two small bottles of beer, he thought to himself—was it only then that he could truly say something? Only in Wellington, he said to himself. We always say the timing is wrong, he told himself in the cable car, the conditions, the location, something in the atmosphere, the height of a ceiling, there's always something. What hope we place in these poor incidentals! How lovingly we contrive these small setbacks to keep us from that real failure which at any time might take us by the elbow.

When the tourist party reached the end of the easy path and there began a period of moderate rock climbing, which involved finding a way up some large, rounded boulders, Healey's father signaled that their team should now make its move. Excusing themselves, they pushed through the tourists and hurried up the boulders, as if they had been kept back for a time by the slow crowd ahead and were now taking things into their own hands. As they passed the guide who was leading the party, Healey saw his father give the man a commiserating look, as if to say "You poor bugger, having this lot on your hands!"

In the sunlight, the untouched snow of the empty crater hurt their eyes, but they clambered to the topmost ridge of the bowl-shaped summit and then, while their father urged them to take in the views, Healey and his brother crouched on their haunches and tobogganed down the icy curve, using the ice picks, which Healey had thought ridiculous on the way up, like rudders to steer themselves. Then they climbed back up and repeated it. Now the father, tired of pointing with his arm to various landmarks visible in the distance, joined them, and they let themselves go faster, shrieking as they careered almost out of control, so that when the tourists appeared on the summit, they, too, believing it to be, Healey supposed, a local custom, wanted to slide down the sides of the crater. Soon the formerly deserted place they had discovered as if for the first time was swamped with the bodies of inexpert tobogganers rolling about the crater like marbles on a saucer, causing Healey to feel that the experience of Mount Egmont was now over and that they should return to tent by the chalet.

Healey's sister said she had gone to a nightclub in New Plymouth. While the rest of them had been in their long bunk at five thousand feet, smelling each other, she said, she was at sea level, drinking and dancing. This was the year in which the sister "emerged." She had left school and started working as a receptionist and dogsbody at a graphic design studio, earning the money with which she could afford to refuse offers to walk for hours without getting anywhere on the exposed sides of mountains. The work had also allowed her, after a few years, to give up on New Zealand, as she put it, and go to London where she was still living. On the rare occasions that Healey had heard her voice on the phone, she apologized for sounding "like a real pom" before adding that she couldn't get over how bad *his* accent sounded.

Inside the nightclub, she said, there had been a large fish tank stocked with tropical fish. It was not enclosed, but open at the top. "Can you believe that," she said. "An open fish tank in the middle of a nightclub!" Nor was the fish tank set in a corner away from danger; it occupied pride of place, being close to the dance floor and to the booth of the deejay, who, between songs, kept alerting patrons to the fact of the tank and warning certain "wild" dancers over the sound system that they were getting a little close. Apparently the tank was a recent addition to the club, a novelty item to entice outsiders. However, the locals, the sister said, had grown protective of it and were policing the area around the tank. Some bitter words had been exchanged between the outsiders who had been tapping on the glass and what she called "the fish patrol." While the outsiders danced and tried to have a good time, she said, the locals watched closely from the sides.

As the evening went on, one of the sister's party—though she would not specify who constituted this group—had become a little drunk and, while dancing, had thrown an empty beer bottle into the fish tank. People had rushed from all sides, she said, to rescue the bottle; dozens of pairs of hands had been thrust into the water, even reaching it before it settled on the bottom. Meanwhile, the bottle tosser had been quickly escorted from the club, almost for his own safety, the sister said, such was the hostility aroused by his offense. Now, when any member of their party tried to order a drink he was refused, so that after a short time they were all forced to leave. Outside the nightclub, they were chased down the main street by some locals and only escaped, the sister said, when one of their pursuers twisted his ankle, the others stopping to gather around him. Afterward, she said, running over the phrase as if it meant nothing, she had "spent the night" with a member of her party. Around this time she was fond of telling Healey's brother at a particularly vicious moment in any argument that all his problems would come into perspective once he was no longer a virgin.

Years later, as he was climbing the cable car tracks toward the tutorial, and ever since then, whenever Healey thought of the city of New Plymouth, it was as if he were recalling a purely historical city that the sister had once come across in the course of some research she was doing on the places where sex and society meet.

As Healey went up in the cable car and could hear the inevitable conversations about the old cable car and its superiority over the present model, since passengers had formerly been able to sit on the outside and jump on and off as they pleased instead of bruising their shoulders on doors that closed inopportunely—instead of sitting in this malevolent little box, as he'd once heard a woman tell her companion—he remembered that there had been one set of circumstances under which the sternness of the drivers lightened sufficiently for even a smile to enter those small compartments. It took a child of a certain age, perhaps between the years of three and seven, and a certain child's face, not too open, but guarded, a little suspicious. This certain child, he pictured, knows that the man sitting by himself in the front of the car, fingering the lighted buttons, has a kind of secret life, is involved in some deeply private game with another man, dressed in the same manner, who, even as the child watches, is approaching from above them in his own cable car. The child swings casually on the door and the moment he catches the man's eye, the child has looked away up the hill in the direction of the other man. Soon the driver will take the child on his knee, from which vantage point the child may cast a brief conquering look over one shoulder at the ordinary, seated passengers, and when the other car passes them on the only part of the track where there are suddenly two lines instead of one, the passengers traveling down to the city will see transposed onto those dour Eastern European features in the driver's compartment the smiling face of a child.

Toward the end of the funeral reception, a family friend, who had contracted polio as a child and now walked with difficulty, each step throwing her body to one side, had said that she would be leaving but that she was not looking forward to the steps down to the road from Healey's parents' house. "I might have to be carried down!'' she said. Everyone had laughed at this remark and agreed that in ten years or so the only way that the Healeys would be able to eat would be to have food delivered by air, and that the sooner they installed that hydraulic lift they'd been talking about, the better their social life would be. ''What good was a view,'' someone said, ''if it killed you getting it.''

Then Healey's father, whose pride in the house could be pricked by the smallest remark, had begun to speak earnestly, although everyone was laughing, about reaching certain summits and of ''effort rewarded,'' grabbing Healey and setting his hands on his son's shoulders while pushing him in front of the group. ''Brett here will tell you,'' he said. ''Mount Edgeware! Mount Egmont! Oh, this house is nothing to the Healeys. This is only a mound. A molehill. This keeps us fit. It's only a ridge, but it might just be our lifeline. You can feel your heart going by the time you reach our front door. That pounding is music to my ears!'' He went on like this until he, too, began to laugh.

Meanwhile, the family friend had not, as expected, moved toward the door but was standing up and looking pained and slightly guilty. It became clear that, because of the glasses of wine she'd had, which, she joked earlier in the afternoon, had gone straight to her legs, the family friend would indeed require assistance in reaching her car on the road below. Healey's father was then first to move, offering her his arm in helping her down the flight of steps to the lower level of the house.

The father and the friend, making their way with difficulty down the stairs, found themselves at the head of a long procession of mourners who had all been drinking for several hours and now wished to offer their advice and assistance to the family friend on the best way to proceed down to the road and what sort of grip the father should be using, since it was also now clear that Healey's father had drunk several glasses of beer and wine and was showing signs of an unsteadiness of his own.

"Careful! Careful with her!" Lillian was calling out.

The organist was saying that he could pick out something on the piano to accompany them on their way down, maybe a little Mendelssohn, though he didn't have his music with him.

"Keep back!" the father was shouting behind him. "Everybody back or there's going to be an accident."

"Well at least we're dressed for it," someone shouted.

"Maybe the priest does discounts for group bookings!"

"Blasphemy!"

"Business!"

On reaching the front door, Healey found that the hysterical note he had heard in its various stages since the graveside—of thirst, expansiveness, fun—had now, evidently, reached a kind of apex in the crowd gathered at the top of the steps. When he arrived at the scene, having had to push through to find out what was happening, he saw that a rope had been wrapped around the woman's waist and, while several of the men present prepared themselves to take the strain at the top, the father, assisted by a group of cousins, was half carrying her and half letting her fall down each step. On

everyone's face was a look of intense concentration and se-
riousness, occasionally broken by fits of giggling and the odd
voice of dissent, which was immediately shouted down, since
what had been finally settled on was the idea of teamwork.

The woman herself, who appeared at times to be abseil-
ing, was giving slight cries each time she left the earth and
blowing her cheeks out with huge satisfaction each time she
returned, so that it was not certain whether it was terror that
finally got her down or the ingenious management of the fa-
ther's pulley system.

7

Farmer's Tan

WHEN THE CABLE CAR REACHED THE TOP OF ITS RUN, HEALEY didn't turn left to go back to his parents' house but right to enter the Botanical Gardens where, he remembered, he had once come on a school trip to visit the Kelburn Meteorological Office. The trip was memorable not because of the weather-measuring instruments nor the explanations offered by the guide, an elderly volunteer whose nose ran constantly and who had difficulty hearing the children's questions, but by the slide show which followed the tour. And even here it was not the succession of images of different types of clouds, nor shots of weather balloons that created the excitement in the darkened room, but a close-up, black-and-white photograph of a boy who had been struck by lightning.

The elderly guide, while hurrying over the slide, sniffing, said that although some people might be shocked by what they saw, it had been decided to leave the boy in the presentation as a warning about the power of nature, which, he said, should never be underestimated. The boy, the guide said, had climbed up a tree to better see the lightning. The sudden silence of the room was broken only by the guide running the back of his hand across his nose, though now the sniffing had an eerie appropriateness, as if the old man was paying tribute to the poor boy who lay before them. Several girls were reaching for their tissues. Even the teacher, Healey noticed, had dabbed quickly at her nose. After a time, the slide was replaced by airy, white clouds, yet Healey saw superimposed here the strangely blackened body of the lightning boy, lying as though on a bed of pillows.

As the cable car took the class down, the talk was about lightning. It was said that in a particularly bad storm the cable car itself, because it went so high and was a good conductor, had been struck by a bolt, and many of the people traveling inside at the time had the clothes burned off their bodies. The teacher, buttoning her coat, said this was absolute rubbish. Now the talk turned to other horrible pictures. Though only a few people had ever seen it, it was well known that in the locked medicine cabinet in the woodwork room at school there was a photo of a woodwork accident, a palm pierced through by a chisel. It was said that the woodwork teacher showed the photo to anyone who'd hurt himself—which the teacher always referred to as "the height of stupidity"—to scare them from their supposed pain.

One time, Healey had been at a literary awards ceremony when a picture book on weather watching had won the book-production category, and as he turned the pages of the winning volume, for once in approval of the judges' decision, it struck him that the curious disappointment he felt in flicking through the beautifully designed book was due to a hopeless search he had unconsciously embarked on for the black-and-white image of the lightning boy in the clouds.

There was no lightning today, but a gray drizzle that forced Healey to return to the cable car. He had decided to see more of the city. For the downward journey, he had to stand, since all the seats were taken by a party of elderly American tourists in whose talk he thought he would invariably hear the words *San Francisco*. He'd often been engaged in conversations with these women and their baseball-capped men, and over the years had learned a good deal about the sons and daughters of the medical schools and business academies of the states of Florida, Arizona, California, New York. And just as he felt attracted to the dark, brooding manners of the drivers, so he believed that a certain correct balance had been achieved when the seats of the cable car were filled with the luminous pastels of the tourists' leisure wear and their open, tanned faces. He could not dislike for long the lavishness of their gestures, nor finally resent the easy group formation in which they moved. Today, as he watched them, dressed in their weatherproof tracksuits, busily pointing and passing on with great excitement the new information they had learned from their neighbors about what they were looking at, the rustling sounds of their constant movements began communicating itself to him as a kind of electricity, a bright charge in the gray atmosphere.

In his early teenage years, Healey had coveted the expensive tracksuits of other boys. These were made of a shimmering dark blue material, with three white stripes down the sides. There was also a zipper at the ankle that allowed the wearer to slip in and out of it without first taking off his shoes. The tracksuit Healey had been given, when he had specifically requested three stripes, was the more common two-stripe variety in a dull green material that clung to the body and very quickly attracted small tufts, as might accumulate on old sweaters, so that he was constantly picking at himself. The three stripes against the shimmering dark blue were like lightning in a summer sky, whereas his two stripes seemed as slow as grass and as dull as the painted lines on a rugby field.

It was not when he was actually playing or competing that this mattered, since he could run faster than most his age and was, in the coach's words, a thinking halfback who could general his team. But rather he felt it when he was approaching the field and preparing to play, or when he was leaving the grounds after the game, or simply when he was walking around the streets of his neighborhood. It was then that he believed insufficient sign of his skill was exhibited and, in fact, that his true worth had been sabotaged by his parents' budget choice of tracksuit.

On one of their regular Sunday visits to his grandparents' house, Healey happened to be wearing the top half of his two-stripe tracksuit. This was shortly after he was given to understand by his mother, who had finally lost patience with his complaints, that no second tracksuit would be making an appearance. His grandfather had remarked on its general "smartness," and as Healey had begun to suggest that it wasn't quite what he'd wanted, his mother cut him off. "Do you think your grandfather had all manner of fancy clothes just to run around in?" she said. "Have you seen the outfit he wore?" She clapped her hands and stood up. "I just wonder."

Healey had noticed earlier, on returning to the house with his bottle of Coke, that instead of the regulation one small bottle of beer in the kitchen, the adults each had two bottles in front of them, and that when they'd all moved into the living room, a third bottle had been suggested and accepted, with the result that everyone was talking in slightly louder voices and their gestures had grown looser and less accurate; his father had dropped himself into his accustomed chair from a slightly greater height than normal, settling amid a small cloud of dust, which so alarmed Healey's grandmother that she was now threatening to give the whole place a good vacuum. His mother, meanwhile, had gone into his grandfather's bedroom and after several minutes of searching noises had emerged with an old cardboard box that she held above her head and shook, as if in triumph.

"Goodness," his grandfather said. "You've not found all that old stuff have you, Angela?"

She opened the box and snatched from between the layers of tissue paper a large piece of fragile-looking cloth that she unfolded roughly into a pair of oversized silk running shorts of a luminous purple with a yellow stripe down each side, saying as she did so, without looking at what she had uncovered, "That's all he had—there! A university rep!" But as she waved them at Healey she was also beginning to feel the cloth, and Healey, too, reached out to touch the shorts.

"They're not so shoddy, Angela," Healey's father observed from behind his newspaper.

"Of course, they had silk in those days," his mother began to say uncertainly. "It was less expensive then, and they didn't have all the new fibers we have."

Healey's sister had entered the room and had taken the shorts from her mother and was trying them on over her jeans, laughing as she stepped into them. "Hey, these I like!" she said. "So sexy."

"Go easy," his father said. "Go easy with those."

"Here," the grandfather said, beckoning for Healey's sister to come nearer so that he could inspect the material. "Well I never. You say I wore these? Heavens."

Finally Nana had said that although it was a very long time ago she remembered him telling her they were the most comfortable things he had ever worn, and that they had been kept because, she believed, at one time there had been plans for making them into a nice pair of summer pajamas.

"How astonishing," the grandfather said. "Summer pajamas."

Healey's mother now approached her daughter, her hand seeking out the material with a look on her face as if she had discovered stolen property. "Let me see," she was saying. "Hold still." Finally, she turned to her father in accusation. "These are almost heirlooms."

Years later, after Nana's death, when Healey and his

mother had the job of packing the grandfather's belongings before his move to the Auckland rest home and Healey had removed the letter signed by John A. Lee, he had also been tempted by another article. It was not the silk running shorts, but the medal engraved with his grandfather's name as New Zealand Universities Triple Jump Champion for the year 1915—a bronze star-shaped medal decorated with a crest showing four stars and, in the center, an open book inscribed with the motto *sapere aude*. Healey, forgetting his school Latin and recalling his grandfather's most persistent piece of advice to anyone about to engage in physical activity, immediately translated the phrase as "Stretch wisely." This, of course, wasn't its meaning at all, and yet in the time it took to travel these three syllables, he imagined the hop, skip, and jump by which the medal had been won and the phrase stuck in his head.

His grandfather had remained an active sportsman through his membership at the Miramar Golf Club, where he would play a midweek nine and, on Saturdays, the full eighteen. He was also a keen follower of other codes. Any sport was worthy of attention, the more removed from his own experience the better. When Healey's brother took up basketball, the grandfather was immediately fascinated by the technical aspects of a game, which, he said, struck him as quite outrageous. He then began, through a series of taxing questions, to track down every permutation, all the nuances of this strange activity, an interrogative process which often made his source feel that in the future caution in announcing how one spent one's free time would be best. "So how long does this *dribbling* last?"

At the core of these delights remained the grandfather's devotion to rugby. He was a season ticket holder in the Millard Stand at Athletic Park. The Millard Stand was the largest stand in the park, its steeply tiered seating towering over the playing field. In bad weather, patrons in the upper levels were said to be exposed to subalpine conditions. The grandfather sat in one of the middle sections, although from there the players appeared far away. There was also the fear, when Healey and his brother were occasionally treated to a provincial game or even a test match, that the upper levels would prove too much for the spindly looking metal girders and, in these middle seats, they would be caught horribly in the sandwiching of tiers. For this reason Healey sometimes preferred the quieter moments of a game. He would feel himself tensing when a promising play developed and the home team brought the crowd to its feet. Above him, he could hear the roar of hundreds of fans and he could feel the vibrations as the huge Millard Stand began to shake with their collective excitement. On other occasions, he would act recklessly, shouting and stamping his feet like everybody else, carried off by the game. As he got out of his seat to catch the run of a winger in the near corner, he would feel the tricky wind of the park, which had defeated the world's best goal kickers, swirling about his ears. In these moments, he believed he truly understood a phrase he had sometimes heard teachers use and which his parents had once used when talking about his brother, "he has his head in the clouds."

The pie cart was underneath the stands, and buying the longed-for Coke with the money the grandfather had slipped them involved missing a sizable portion of the game. As he jogged down the steps, Healey sometimes hoped that in the time he was away a try might be scored, so that when he returned to his seat the terrible vibrations would have settled down. Every time he left Wellington, even as an adult, a voice inside him said, "Maybe they'll have that big earthquake while you're away." Traveling to America, he had thought to himself that living in a more or less flat state there would be no problems. Yet he arrived to discover that he had simply left one fault line for another and that a man who was said to have correctly predicted the recent San Francisco earthquake was predicting *the big one* for the city Healey had imagined as completely calm.

As a boy high in the Millard Stand he could take some comfort in listening to the conversations his grandfather always had with the spectators around him. Clearly, these men were discussing the game and not the imminent collapse of the tiered seating hanging above them. In their passionate talk about key players' performances, refereeing decisions, the rules of the code, Healey found a certain peace, which in later life, when similar pressures fell on him, he would try to coax from a different set of words, though now the words had to do with *deadlines* and *copy* and *space*.

The grandfather would also check regularly with a man

who always occupied the seat behind him and who always watched the entire game with a small radio pressed to one ear. When he looked closely, Healey saw that there were several such men in the stands, straining against the noise of the crowd to catch something on their little radios. Through their looks of annoyance they would periodically inform everyone around them of something that had just come through. By the tone in which they spoke, he could tell they were proud of having got to the news first.

"What's happening?" the grandfather would say to the man behind him. And the man would shoot out his hand as if in warning, straining even harder to hear, pushing the radio tightly against the side of his head. After a certain time had elapsed, the man would give out the required information; there always had to be these moments of waiting. The grandfather, in this manner, would get the progress scores from other provinces and also the results of horse races. "You have the fourth in yet?" he would say. And the man would again hold his hand out, as if silencing the forty thousand while he picked up details of the dividends on the two-inch speaker wedged inside his ear.

The grandfather was mainly an off-track bettor. Trentham Race Course was an hour away by train and he went only five or six times a season. Occasionally, however, at Healey's mother's suggestion, they would collect him from Miramar and drive up for a day at the races. Once they arrived, the grandfather, who had "connections" with one of the breeders through his old job on the bridges, would disappear in the direction of the Members' enclosure and only reappear perhaps twice in the course of the whole afternoon—first to pass on to his daughter a few tips that had been whispered in his ear; and second, of course, to give the children a little too much money with which, in Healey's mother's words, "they would make themselves sick." In this setting, however, she said these familiar words only halfheartedly. She had other things on her mind.

When the grandfather had left them, if it was a chilly day, Healey's mother would head up into the stands to find a place to read the race book. This she would do quite thoroughly, consulting the racing pages of the day's newspapers, cross-checking all the information, and jotting down a list of names and figures. On warm, sunny days she would sit down on the grass in front of the stands and begin the complicated business of choosing a horse on which to place her regulation two dollars. Meanwhile, Healey's father, who had little patience for such careful systems when he regarded the whole affair a mixture of "flagrant fixing" and "pure luck," would sit in the stands or on the grass, but always finally drifting off by himself, ending up in the public bar underneath the stands from where he would occasionally emerge with a half can of beer for his wife.

The children would also split up for long periods during the afternoon. Healey might catch sight of the other two through the crowd—his sister, resting her mouth against the rail, looking at the horses parading before the race; his brother inspecting betting slips that had been thrown away, perhaps, he hoped, in error. Coming across the figures of his brother and sister like this, it sometimes took Healey a few moments to recognize who it was he had been staring at, as if he were seeing their faces for the first time. They had arrived as a group, Healey thought, and the moment they entered the gates of the race track, each had gone his or her own way, so that whenever he thought about Trentham he didn't picture an eliptical-shaped track around which groups of horses ran again and again, but rather a series of interweaving paths carrying people in different directions, until one path intersected with another, allowing a fleeting glimpse of a face that had previously been thought lost.

He saw a jockey spit into the wind. He watched the small, fat old man dressed like a butler, who went behind the horses scooping up their droppings with a silver pan. There was paper everywhere; by the end of the day it almost completely covered the grass. It fell constantly through the air from the stands, as in a movie wedding. He noticed how people didn't care where they threw their losing tickets. Sometimes, as they were watching the horses enter the home stretch, they tore them up and let the pieces trickle through their fingers. Or they tossed them hard onto the ground in anger, as if there would be a loud noise when the paper landed on the grass.

Among the crowd, he caught a glimpse of his sister picking her nose, his brother staring off into space. Unobserved, he followed his father to the toilets behind the stands and watched him search for a safe place to put his can of beer (under the rosebush) before entering. He saw a man leave his hand under a woman's bottom when they sat down together on the grass. Some men were wearing slippers; others had the tops of their underpants showing above their trousers. As he wandered around, he grew to believe that there was something about an erect horse tail and the steaming turds that followed which allowed everyone at Trentham to go his or her own way.

Only once had he managed to spy his grandfather and only then with the aid of his father's opera glasses, which he'd taken without permission for the express purpose of identifying the path by which the grandfather had escaped from them. He spotted him in the middle of the Members' Stand where, just as in the Millard Stand, the grandfather was involved in animated discussions with the people around him. From beneath his racing hat, strands of his long hair, which Healey's mother trimmed every third Sunday, flashed silver in the sunlight as he turned to talk to the woman seated behind him, who was laughing and having to hold on to her own large feathered headgear. How Healey had wished for the woman's ridiculous hat to fly off, just as he'd once seen a man lose his cap to the winds that swirled in the heights of the Millard Stand. Why wasn't the grandfather telling his own daughter the things which so tickled the woman in the hat? Then the grandfather had turned back and stared directly at Healey, as if, with the opera glasses trained in reverse on the eyes of the boy looking up from the public enclosure, he could now see magnified the image of his grandson spying on him, causing Healey to suddenly look away.

As the cable car, on its downward journey, passed through the series of small tunnels, Healey remembered the shadow that had fallen across his father's opera glasses when his grandfather had looked straight through him, a shadow that had failed to lift even when he had looked away but that had remained, he now saw, a shadowy imprint on the edges of his vision, as if someone had left his fingers on the lenses.

Healey's other grandfather, his father's father, had been killed in one of the first fatal motor accidents in the small town down south where he had an interest in thoroughbreds. An infant when it happened, Healey's father had never known the figure who, he said, appeared to him now *as an ear, the back of a neck, a hand,* but never as a whole person. For sixty years, it was believed by the family that, after ''a few too many at the track,'' a group of friends had driven too fast back to town and had failed to stop at an intersection. The father, who had been driving, was killed instantly as was the man in the front passenger seat, while the three friends in the back all had ''fortunate escapes.'' For sixty years, Healey's father's mother had lived with the phrase ''a few too many'' and the thought that her husband had killed not only himself but the husband of a friend who, from that day, could never bring herself to call on her for fear, as she wrote in a letter when they were both old women, that she might have torn the hair from Healey's grandmother's head. ''An irresponsible rage with the world is what I felt,'' she wrote.

It was not until all the men who'd been in the car had died that the widow of one of the men who escaped wrote to the widows of the men in the front seat to say that Healey's paternal grandfather was not drunk at the time of the accident, since as everyone knew he never drank when his horses won, as indeed they had that fateful day. The accident had been caused not by his negligence, she wrote, but by her own husband and the two other men who'd been treated to several drinks by the day's winner. They had been fooling around in the back and forced the driver to turn his head at the crucial time. The widow had heard this story from her husband on his deathbed and, she wrote, for the first time in her presence, he had wept. He had described the cowardly fears that paralyzed them and made them mute at the inquest, even when the driver was found to have been responsible for his own death and for the death of his friend. They had thought it would be the end of their careers if they came forward and told the truth. One of the lads was in insurance, another taught at the local primary school, and her own had been a publican. All of them with young families. Now, the widow wrote, she was clearing the air, though she understood that no amount of apologizing could make up for sixty years of wrongful hurt. At some point in the future, she wrote, she hoped they might be blessed and find it in themselves to forgive what had been done to them, just as she prayed that she might one day be so blessed as to be able to forgive herself and to forgive the man with whom she now realized she had spent a lifetime in a kind of darkness.

After his first year at university, Healey got a holiday job at a halfway house for psychiatric outpatients. He had taken the job for the money and because he thought it would be easy work, but also, he now understood, because he hoped occasionally to be able to tell a story or two about something that had happened in the halfway house involving the patients and himself. He was aware that cousins such as the one who had appeared at the funeral the day before seemed only pathetic and uneventful when he tried to talk about them to friends. He also thought that people might be surprised and think him callous to be talking about his own family in this way.

Healey had somehow convinced himself that it was true, when he heard it said repeatedly of his taking the job, that it would be "a real experience," although he had no interest in the mentally unstable, nor in pursuing the social sciences. There would, apparently, be some work in preparing the backyard for the patients to walk around in and this seemed a little more promising, especially as a small putting circuit was being planned. The things that interested him finally, then, were the money and the golf.

Healey had never played golf on a proper course, though for several years he had been a regular putter. Behind his grandparents' house in Miramar, a square of land had been leveled from the hillside, grass planted and a six-hole putting course put in. On the Sundays when they visited, after the Cokes and beers had been consumed, Healey and the brother would accompany the men out to the lawn where a best-of-three-rounds contest would be played. Often the grandfather, with his steady stroke and his local knowledge, would emerge the winner, though the father, always attacking the hole in a style which caused the grandfather to say of his son-in-law that "he was never shy, never afraid, always there or thereabouts," might sometimes defeat his more consistent opponent by a string of aggressive holes in one. Owing to the difficulty of having four balls in play at the same time on the small surface—it was a one-stroke penalty against the hitter should another's ball be struck—Healey and the brother would usually act as spectators and have a turn themselves only once the main event was concluded. On special occasions, however, they would play as teams, taking alternate strokes. Now Healey discovered that he didn't want to be on the grandfather's team. He hoped, instead, that by playing against him he would come more under his notice. Of course, it was necessary to weigh this view against the prospect of actually combining with the grandfather, of hitting the same ball the grandfather had so recently stroked, of finishing off what the grandfather had started, or of making it easy for the grandfather with a good approach putt. But generally he preferred to go head-to-head against the grandfather.

Healey was to work at the halfway house with another student who, he discovered, was interested only in the money. Their supervisor, a woman who had worked as a counselor before taking time off to think about things and to have a baby, and who was a friend of the woman who directed the program, was interested mostly in the well-being of her new child. She would sit in the kitchen, drinking tea and breast-feeding the baby, and Healey would try to look at the baby without looking at the breast of the supervisor. He would try to think about something else, but his mind would always return to the schoolboyish idea that the baby was not drinking milk but rather some weaker version of the tea that its mother was guzzling constantly, so that, despite himself, he began to imagine her nipple as the spout on a teapot.

The house had just recently been established and so for several weeks only one or two patients would come each day. No one else seemed to know about it. "We have a public relations thing—" said the supervisor, before adding the word with which she finished the majority of her sentences, "*problem.*" The house was about three miles from the other, larger center for social activities in the area and most of the patients seemed to prefer going there. None of them had cars, and there was a general distrust, if not fear, of public transportation.

Most of the hours of these days Healey spent outside, practicing his putting stroke on the circuit they had cut into the back lawn. The times when a foursome would be convened on the back lawn at Miramar were, of course, distant now, though he could still replay in his head certain holes crucial to some match, or catch the slightly beery smell of breath as, bending to retrieve his ball, the grandfather would let out a little puff of effort. When the patients came to the house, however, they could not be persuaded to take part in the golf, nor could they enter the kitchen to make themselves some tea, since the supervisor was breast-feeding her baby.

Sometimes Healey and the other student worker persuaded the patients to sit in the living room on the chairs set in the depressing around-the-walls formation that the director said was "the most conducive to group interaction"; upon entering the room there was the immediate sensation of being surrounded, so that, quickly finding a seat, one was aware of moving to the far edge of a hole that threatened to swallow everything. The huge expanse of carpet revealed by pushing all the chairs against the walls seemed ugly and oppressive. There, sitting awkwardly beside one another, or at far points of the circumference of the room, the student workers would attempt to play games or otherwise "entertain" the one or two patients, or kill time until the visitors felt they could leave the house without giving offense to the staff.

Standing in the crowded cable car, a feeling of resentment came back to him; how strongly Healey had wished there to be no patients at all, no fellow worker, no supervisor, no baby, no director, but only himself in the summer afternoons over his putter in the smell of lawn clippings.

After a time, when it was clear that the halfway house was a disaster, the supervisor said, "We need a darkroom! We'll convert the laundry room into a darkroom and teach them photography!" The supervisor herself was an amateur photographer and developed her own prints in her own darkroom at home. The morning after she had mentioned this plan of the darkroom, she brought along an envelope of large-size photos of herself, taken when she was pregnant. In the photos, she was naked. The supervisor showed these to Healey as they drank morning tea in the kitchen, where she was breastfeeding her baby. When he was looking at the photos, he tried not to look from the supervisor back to the photos. That afternoon, the student workers, under instructions called from the kitchen, made the laundry room into a darkroom by taping newspaper to the windows, and as they worked Healey thought that all the photos that would be developed in the darkroom would have superimposed over them, as it were, the shadowy lines of images of the supervisor naked and pregnant; that no photo would be clear and sharply defined, but that every one would suffer this same ghostly distortion.

The following day he overheard the supervisor telling the one or two patients about the darkroom. "Always knock before you enter here," she said. "And even then, *John, Helena,*"—using their first names with a revolting emphasis— "wait until the person inside has said come in or opened the door for you. If you let the light into that room all the photos will be ruined." Then she pushed through the door, told them to come in as they stood hesitating on the threshold, and started explaining the developing process, holding up the bottles of fluids in one hand, while in the other she balanced her baby. When she was finished, John asked, "So can we get to the backyard through the laundry room anymore, or do we have to walk right round the house?"

"John," said the supervisor, "this is now a darkroom! If you try to open that door you'll rip up the paper we've put down there to stop the light from ruining our photos!" The supervisor then turned to Helena, who at least had not failed her yet that day, and asked whether she owned a camera. No, Helena said, she had never owned a camera and hated herself in photos anyway. She, Helena, would obey the supervisor and, she said, never even approach the door of this terrible darkroom.

Although the supervisor said this was just Helena's thing— *problem*—none of the patients seemed remotely interested in entering the darkroom, or even knocking on the door to see what would happen. After a few weeks, everyone was so sick of walking right around the house to get to the backyard, the student workers, under instructions, ripped down the newspaper and threw open the doors, as if they had all been imprisoned by the idea of the darkroom and had finally broken free.

When it was clear that the house was at a critical distance from the other center and that this was discouraging the patients and ex-patients from visiting, the supervisor suggested that the staff might take some steps to bring them there themselves. This was not going to be coercion, she told them, but simply a form of assisted guidance. "Under their own steam, it's hopeless," she said. "We'll get out there and we'll hustle!" Neither Healey nor his fellow student worker said anything. "We can't sit on our backsides all day long," said the supervisor. "You two are getting damn good money. You're university students! And I'm always the one who has to come up with the ideas." Healey knew that the previous day the director had come to the house, and that she and the supervisor had a long shouting match in the kitchen, during which the baby had to be taken from the breast and put on the cot in the spare room.

The idea was that, if the students were coming to work by bus anyway, they should arrange to meet patients at the bus station and bring them to the house at eight-thirty in the morning, despite the fact that most of the patients said they didn't get out of bed until ten-thirty or eleven because of the medication they were on. When Healey said this to the supervisor, she clapped her hands and said, "Hustle, Brett, hustle, hustle, hustle! Listen, the only reason they don't get out of bed is because they think there's nothing to get up for—we'll give them something!"

Because Healey had no desire to drag someone out of bed and force them onto a bus to come and sit in a house that was now full of shouting and surliness and spurious "frankness," and also because he didn't want to sit next to a person who had recently undergone treatment for psychiatric problems and to pretend to that person that they could be friends or that he was helping them in any way by taking them on this bus at this time in the morning, he lied about how he got to work and by what route he came. Even though he'd always caught the bus from the central bus station, he said that he got on at different stops along the way, depending on who he happened to be staying with, since he also said that he was looking after the house of some friends, then staying with relatives, that he was constantly on the move during the summer. At other times, when questioned by the supervisor, Healey said he was catching a ride with someone who dropped him off at a certain distant corner and he would be walking the rest of the way to work, because the morning air was so good.

In fact, he still caught the same bus he always caught from the central bus station, though sometimes he deliberately got off early and walked to the house, so that if the supervisor was driving past in her car (which she never once suggested giving up so that she herself might catch a bus or so that it might be used to bring the patients to the house) she would see that his story was true. As with all previous ideas, the busing plan soon fell by the wayside.

The final scheme of the summer was suggested not by the supervisor, nor by the students, but by a woman who lived next door to the house. The neighbor was a horticulturalist, who sometimes gave them advice about planting in the back garden and who often talked over the fence to the patients, gaining such a popularity among them that on entering the halfway house, the patients' first question was whether the horticulturalist had been seen that day. The horticulturalist said that there was a way for the patients to make some money of their own by selling compost by the bag door-to-door. She herself, along with some friends in a charity group, had done it a few years ago and people loved the stuff—they couldn't keep up with the orders.

Healey had instantly formed a liking for the woman because she never used the words "it would be good for them" or talked of getting them "out and about" but spoke only of the patients "making some money of their own."

The compost was to be in the form of horse manure, which the groundsman at the local racetrack would donate to anyone willing to dig it out of the mounds behind the stables and haul it away themselves. They could have "as much as they could shift, or stand!" the horticulturalist said.

When Healey told the supervisor about the horticulturalist's plan, a look of total skepticism crossed her face, even as she said "Good." Then she added that at least it would get him out of the house.

The afternoon they had arranged to go to the racetrack

was very hot, and as they drove in the horticulturalist's car—
Healey, the horticulturalist, and three ex-patients (two men
and one woman), with their shovels and plastic sacks in the
trunk—Healey could feel the backs of his legs sticking to the
car seat. The female ex-patient was in her thirties and had
come because she enjoyed the company of the horticultural-
ist, who was in her forties. The two male ex-patients were
friends in their fifties who said they hadn't been to a race-
track in years and were looking forward to the prospect of
coming back from the horses not emptyhanded but, for once,
with "a sure-fire thing!" Healey, too, had not been to the
Trentham racetrack since spying on his grandfather in the
Members' Stand through his father's opera glasses.

Even though this was, thankfully, Healey thought, the last
week of work, and even though he'd had enough of "helping
people," as they approached the stables he felt an unaccount-
able sense of excitement for the job ahead. Clambering up
the mounds, he stuck his shovel in the top, as if planting a
flag. Finally, he thought, after the days in the kitchen with
the tea-soaked baby, after the weeks of inventing every ex-
cuse for not sitting in the terrible around-the-walls living room,
and after knocking the golf ball mindlessly about the little
course while a few patients looked on from the back step and
said that they would caddy for him but could never attempt
what he was obviously so skilled at, finally he was doing
something.

When the digging began and went on in the heat—the
two male ex-patients taking off their shirts to reveal white
singlets and arms brown to the elbow, the female ex-patient

standing a little way off because of the smell, or sometimes coming over with more sacks from the car, holding her nose and talking in a blocked voice to the horticulturalist, who was also digging—Healey felt the work had acquired its own rhythm in which rested a certain calm.

"Hey, you two!" the horticulturalist called out to the men. "You have real farmer's tans there!"

Healey now understood that he had always been anxious in the radius of the supervisor, his breathing had always become shallow, and even when he talked about her behind her back and laughed at her, there was a pressure against his chest that was not always comfortable. Her very name dug its heels into his sides. This anxiety had lifted once they reached Trentham. He recognized the new feeling as similar to the one he had experienced on those rare occasions in the Millard Stand when his grandfather, through engaging with those around him, had made them all of a piece with the surrounding action. Nothing was out of place behind the stables at Trentham, Healey thought, though they themselves could shift around, swap tasks, put their chins on the handles of their shovels, light cigarettes, and joke about the smell and the woman talking while holding her nose. In the distance, there was even a horse being walked by a tiny figure in whose outline could be seen the slightly ballooning pants.

Standing in the cable car under the drizzling skies of Wellington, Healey then realized that whenever he tried to tell the story of that afternoon to friends, he was, somehow, never able to be true to the sensation of calm that lasted perhaps twenty or thirty minutes, but always tripped up on the words *manure* or *psychiatric patients* until all that was left was a feeling of the absurdity of their quest, which was not how he felt in that moment, nor how he felt whenever he remembered the word *racetrack,* or the letters stretched across the elastic of the underpants of the men who had stood watching the horses of years before, or those of the men who were shoveling the manure alongside him, the word poking above their trousers—*Jockey.*

8

Cabin Fever

HE FOUND HIMSELF ON THE NEWLY RENOVATED WATER-front and looking across the harbor toward the bays of East-bourne; Healey remembered the afternoons of three years before, when he sat on a veranda looking across the water in the direction of the spot on which he now stood, though then it had not been covered in grassy mounds and walking paths but piles of stone and dirt.

After studying in the American Midwest—a name which implied a kind of prevaricating, a hovering, neither one thing nor the other—Healey had returned to Wellington with his two-years-toward-a-doctorate. In these two years he would meet periodically with the writer whose work he had intended to focus on and they would discuss the thesis-in-progress, always spending the majority of the time, however, at the unspoken wish of the writer, speaking about anything but the thesis.

Upon his return he suffered familiar feelings of rejection—against which he'd been warned repeatedly by other people who had gone away and then come back—detecting in old friends an inadequate welcoming spirit and, foolishly, the sense that he should move off again, that he had returned prematurely. He had left at the beginning of a recession and returned in the middle of a recession, though only now was it being reviewed as a time when there had been anything more than a "downturn." He had some idea of going into publishing, but most of the industry was based in Auckland and he had no desire to live there. Finally, he found a job not as literary editor but as sub-editor on a newspaper. Nor was the job in Wellington; it was in Lower Hutt.

Every morning of the eight months he had the job Healey would take the train those fifteen kilometers along the edge of the motorway that skirted the harbor, having first pushed his way through the morning commuters at the Wellington Railway Station who were all heading into the capital, having come from Lower Hutt. Hardly anyone took these early morning trains out to Lower Hutt, although the incoming units were always full. At first he thought it was a backward step, but then he began to enjoy the almost-empty carriages taking him in virtual privacy around the water.

When his semi-deserted carriage passed a full commuter carriage traveling in the opposite direction, he sometimes caught the accusing and envious look on a face staring back at him. Healey took an odd kind of strength from this look, since it instantly made him feel as if he were unemployed, or, somehow, sneaking away, as the child playing truant is looked upon by his fellow pupil passing him in the school bus. And this, too, gave him strength. It was difficult for him to believe, and this softened the actuality, that he was indeed off to work.

In applying for the position of sub-editor, Healey left off from his application the two years Ph.D. experience. At previous interviews, although the interviewer had often expressed interest in his American studies, Healey discerned a type of suspicion entering the questions. Several employers suggested that he was perhaps overqualified. Behind this, however, Healey felt a deeper accusation—that as an academic he would be difficult to work with and would probably leave after a short time once something better came along. Just as you dropped everything and went off to America, the thought was, so you'll drop us as soon as you can. The lie he told the Lower Hutt paper—that the last two years had been mainly spent traveling, though with the steady interruption of work on small magazines—was not a large one. Now, he said, he was looking to settle.

To supplement his income from the newspaper in Lower Hutt, where he worked mornings, Healey also offered his services as a free-lance editor and in this capacity received a call from a man announcing himself as Pickering from Eastbourne.

Pickering spoke in a vaguely Irish-American accent, the vagueness a sign of a wider indeterminacy clinging to this, Healey's first and only client. Pickering did a lot of talking, and what Healey presumed to be the man's deafness caused many of Healey's questions to go unanswered. The man said he was putting together a kind of memoir—part biography, part social document, part something else that he couldn't identify—which was why, he said, he needed someone like Healey to come and tell him exactly what he had, though he knew he had something "quite real."

Healey wanted more exact details on the scope of the project, but Pickering again just failed to hear him. He told Healey that he needn't worry, a good working relationship was already assured. He was a fine judge of people, he said, and he could tell Healey was a good listener. "I need some-one such as yourself," Pickering said, "to *recognize* my book."

In the past, whenever he received such offers from any quarter, Healey had always made agreeable noises before backing out with some excuse. On placing his free-lance advertisement in the paper, however, he promised himself that he would say yes to everything. Even as he agreed to a meeting with Pickering, when the only evidence from the phone call suggested that the man was slightly crazy and his project was of little interest to those outside his own family, Healey felt that at least he would be, as a certain uncle liked to say of the only people he deemed worthy of admiration, out there and earning.

At midday, having finished work at the newspaper, Healey didn't walk to the railway station but rather to the bus station where he caught the Eastbourne bus. Pickering lived in one of the smaller bays. Healey had only a sketchy idea of the geography of the place, having come once or twice with his family on picnics to Days Bay in the summer, then later he'd accompanied the friend who now lived on Aro Street on a bicycle tour of the bays, from which the friend had suffered mild sunstroke. He could recall these occasions in only the vaguest detail, and as he found the correct mailbox and began the climb up to Pickering's house, he believed that his memories of previous visits to the area had been obscured by what had happened to him the last time he was here.

In the final weeks of high school, Healey and some friends had gone to a barbecue at the house of a girl whose mother lived in Eastbourne. They scarcely knew the girl, but such was the mood of those last weeks—a kind of sentimental attachment had sprung up for even those things which throughout the five years of schooling had seemed unbearable—that the girl, on seeing this group of boys, uninvited, in her mother's backyard, greeted them as old friends, or at least as fellow sufferers with whom she had gone through a particularly bitter campaign. She ran to them and actually hooked her arms through theirs, leading them toward the barbecue and forcing plates on them. "Fill up, fill up," she said, before running off. Healey knew her as part of a set of girls who would weep at college rugby games and in whose eyes his own failure to follow through on what was strictly moderate sporting promise had caused him to become invisible; she had exchanged perhaps five sentences with him in five years and most of these had been in mild hostility.

There was one girl at the barbecue, however, whose quota

of sentences—although really no larger than that of the girl who had greeted them as old friends—was not a true indication of what Healey, at least, had come to think of as their relationship and whom he placed a little above all the others. Healey had known the girl, he supposed, for years, but only in the way he had known countless others with whom he had shared high-school classrooms—as faces, names, as bodies that changed without notice. It was odd, then, but as he stood in the backyard on a warm evening occasionally interrupted by brief showers of rain—the rain padding lightly into the sandy grass, gently dousing the barbecue, the smell of fat from the chops on the grill mixing with the whiff of the nearby sea, releasing into the air the odors of salt, ketchup, damp wood, wet sand—and he looked around at these figures with whom he had spent so many hours, days, years, confined in rooms smelling closely of sweat, socks, wool, chalk, he found that he could recognize them only with the greatest difficulty.

He saw, now that they were out of uniform—often the source of complaints by so-called liberal parents and their children because, they said, uniforms denied individuality and cramped personal style—*everyone looked the same*. Finally in their own clothes, he suddenly thought, they might have been anyone. And they moved quickly across the background, as it were, like extras, while in the foreground, he believed, he was only truly seeing the girl whom he had often dreamed of having beside him and who was now talking to a group nearby about how pretty it was coming across from the city on the new ferry.

"It really felt like the olden days," she said. "All the

lights. Like when Katherine Mansfield used to take the steamer across the harbor to come here for holidays. Of course, she wasn't Mansfield then," the girl corrected herself, "she was Kathleen Beauchamp, and a pain in the neck, and her father, Harold B., was Chairman of the Bank of New Zealand and all naughty Kathie wanted to do was to go back to London and start living. Stuff this country, she thought. Couldn't stand it." The girl laughed—an odd yelp, which came from the back of her throat. It was the kind of thing, Healey imagined, a child might cultivate, having been told it was cute and, keeping on with it until she's grown-up, find that it was then too late, that she is now helpless against a sound that only embarrasses her friends, who whisper about the unfortunate flaw in her makeup, though by this time she herself no longer realizes what it is she's doing. She went on: "The Beauchamp cottage used to sit on land quite close to here. I think they're putting up a plaque or something. *Mum's* involved in it."

When she said "Mum," the girl had rolled her eyes so that everyone should know she was using the word ironically; she was proud of her mother, but not too proud. Healey, listening in, couldn't imagine a time when he would be able to mention his mother in front of so many people and get away with it.

He had been noticing the girl only in the last months, although he didn't think of this as a sentimental attachment of the type which had caused the others to mistakenly see those around them as old friends. Rather, he believed he was at last seeing her for herself and, recognizing her as someone who would soon be lost to him, he felt a pressure to record clearly how she appeared from moment to moment. Despite the affectations, he discovered he liked the speeches she gave, the oddly loose pedantry. He was interested also in the weird laugh, which, at the point when she thought herself most clever and powerful, dragged her down, he thought, to a level almost of freakishness. He wasn't sure whether she knew as much as she hinted at knowing, but her hinting was so richly suggestive, almost a form of knowledge in itself, that no one really questioned it. (Occasionally, though, he noted, across her face, a worried look, as if it had been "a near thing" and she had almost been caught out. Yet this only increased her attractiveness.) In class, because of her voice, she was often called on to read aloud, and although he thought her renderings too precious in that speech-lessons manner, she at least didn't stumble on words and maul the sense, as did most of those who were singled out.

Her name was Karen, pronounced—after being plain, short-voweled Karen for four years of high school—now, in the fifth and final year, with a long *a,* which she insisted on so vehemently that whenever someone said it wrongly the affectation was quickly obscured by the performance it had engendered, making the difficulty of the long *a* seem simply part of the drama of her personality, her Karen-ness. After a time no one could get it wrong; the transformation was fixed in everyone's mind. How could she have been the other Karen? Healey at first resisted the change, but finally decided he admired the power that lay behind it—the impulse toward self-definition. And in the muted evening light he also discovered he admired the shading that sketched her pear-shaped calf muscles and ran a strong line up her neck, the sinews of which surprised him with their soft elastic.

In the few sentences they had spoken to each other over the years, Healey knew that he had never managed *to give himself away,* as he sometimes imagined himself doing while whispering to a girl in the half-light of bedrooms, and now, when he believed this was perhaps his last chance to do so, he struggled to come up with a topic under whose cover he might show to Karen this true self he had been keeping in reserve. They had nothing in common. The only thing he could think of to talk about was her laugh and the abandonment by her friends at its peak. But he didn't trust himself to explain this to her without giving offense. He had already caused one girl at the barbecue to tell him, without provocation, that he was the type of person who—but she'd been unable to finish the statement, because someone had come up to them, forcing her to leave Healey with a look of undisguised hatred. The girl had been chatting up a friend of his when the friend had made some excuse and walked off, so the girl was left standing beside Healey. When the friend had been there, she'd been polite and interested; she had even laughed at something Healey had said. When they were alone she had rounded on him and used the phrase *your type,* which made him for a moment almost physically ill.

The only thing he could possibly talk about with Karen was Katherine Mansfield. What had she thought about the play? There had been a class trip into town the previous week to see a one-woman show based on the diaries of the writer. Healey now went through the play in his head, working out an opinion he could present. This was a difficulty. He never had an opinion about something that he had not worked up beforehand, fashioning it with lengthy care. Then, if his breathing was good, he might give his opinion as if he were formulating it while he spoke. He did not lack spontaneity, but he believed that an unconsidered response was not to be confused with what one really felt, which was to be arrived at only after long deliberation. It distressed him that he thought this way, and he often attributed the almost complete lack of girlfriends among his group to their refuge in long-distance thinking and their total inability to say what they really thought or felt about anything at any given time. Perhaps this was what the girl had meant by *your type*.

In his mind he saw the actress as Mansfield sitting at a desk, composing sentences out loud, then flinging pages into the air, falling over and writhing on the floor, hugging her knees to her chest. When she got up she was calm. "At the Bay," she wrote aloud, "I am never bored! And this, given my youthfulness, my terrible youthfulness, is nothing short of a miracle." The actress smoothed her dress, brushed at her cardigan, and returned to the chair and the desk. "The reason I am never bored here," she went on, "is because I never feel *safe* at the Bay. Not like the others. Not like my father, who has safety sewn into his pin-striped suit like a name tag. God, that numbs me! But, oh, how the sea, the sky, the dark hills—they do frighten me into life! They whisper to me, anything can happen!" At this point, the actress looked up and, it seemed, stared directly at Healey sitting in the audience, but he also saw that she was looking through him in that trained way. "And I, Kathleen, am ready!" Then she'd leaped up again, spun herself around the edge of the stage, her arms flying out so that, sitting in the front row, he felt the push of air against his eyes and could have almost bitten the fingers of the actress as they came past. It had occurred to him to nip at her then, not to prove to himself that she really existed and thus to destroy what the teacher had been constantly telling them was "the illusion of the theater," but rather to prove to her that *he* existed and that she could not look through him in that way any longer.

Healey had been restless the entire performance, focused for one moment, then losing it the next, working up his opinion of the first act while the second was in progress. He dreaded most being asked by the woman teacher on the way home in the minibus what he had thought of the production and, surrounded on one side by the hills and on the other by the sea, not being able to respond with anything but weak-sounding noises of approval.

The thing about one-person plays, he had been thinking in the half darkness of the theater, was that they tried to make an audience forget that. They try to make you see a crowd, he said to himself. All the effort is directed toward alleviating the longing an audience has for someone else, another character, to push onto the stage and finally engage in conversation the one-person, whose voice has become like a drill. To divert this wish, he noticed, the one-person will use all reaches of the stage, just as the gymnast must touch all four corners of the mat in the course of a floor exercise, imitating a crowd. But at the center there must be stillness. There must be arrested motion. (There must be a girl and her calves set against the anonymous flux of her classmates.) And here it was. He had lost sight of all the women of this one-woman show—just as all the bodies of the gymnast are lost at the peak of the velocity of their tumbling and attain an impossible single suspension—so that, in the very midst of the actress's rushing and declaiming from all parts of the stage, something was frozen for him, and he was left with one perfect frame of Katherine Mansfield, as durable as a blink—just as now, at the barbecue, the girl had laughed and been abandoned by everyone but him. At that still point in the play, chiming in agreement when the words came out from the half-light, Healey almost said aloud, "I'm ready!" feeling himself lift dangerously off his seat then come down again just in time.

When Pickering appeared at the top of his path—a man in his sixties, wearing shorts, a large straw sun hat and a singlet made of netting material through which could be seen a sagging brown chest—Healey had a sudden image from a recurring midwestern dream.

In the Midwest, for two years, Healey had lived a celibate life, preferring to believe, on certain nights, the voice of the mature student from his American history tutorial telling him that he was usefully channeling these energies into other areas. Occasionally, during the American winter, he had gone with a group of Ph.D. students to the local bowling alley. While handing over his own shoes and putting on the special bowling shoes, which everyone was wearing, Healey had the impression that finally he had arrived. Then, as he found "his" ball from among the racks of balls, testing the weight and the fit of the fingers, he thought, in the tremendous noise of the alleys, that he had managed to slip into the community of bowlers unnoticed and even that he was part of it. Suddenly—with the sight of the amiable Ph.D.s jumpy in their bowling shoes, the group of middle-aged women next to them hooting at each other in their matching shirts with red piping, the curling blue script of a company logo on their backs, the row of flickering overhead color television screens monitoring scores—Healey believed, somehow correctly, in the five steps he took before delivering his first ball, that soon all the pins at the far end of the lane would be lying on their sides. In these five steps he saw clearly for the first time the posture of self-containment in which he had been living and felt the shell of this old existence falling away. None of the work he had done since coming to this country had the clean strength of these five steps in his laced, thin-soled shoes nor the release he felt in letting the ball go. How the women beside him seemed to cheer!

Then the Ph.D.s, whom he had assured of his lack of skill on the way there through the snow-covered streets— they would be seeing mostly gutter balls whenever it was his turn to bowl, he'd said—were calling out their congratulations, and a huge sense of accomplishment came over him as he sat down among them. And yet, Healey could see in their faces, even as they joked about him having set the standard, a determination to better him, which instantly caused Healey to feel a renewed homesickness. In subsequent efforts with the ball, which now felt too heavy and in which his fingers stuck, he returned to mediocrity. It was clear to him that his exaggerated reactions were the direct result of keeping to himself, holing up in his one-bedroom apartment, trying to persuade himself that the words of the mature student had weight. He had been suffering from a kind of cabin fever.

In the dream, he kept on bowling strikes. The women in the red piping shirts are now cheering him on to a perfect game. Somehow, his bowling shoes are enormous, and with each step he is brought ridiculously close to the pins so that he cannot possibly miss. He has the vague feeling each time he lines up that all this attention is undeserved, since with these shoes, he thinks, anyone could bowl a perfect game. Yet no one seems to notice the unfair advantage he has been given. It is only after releasing the final ball that he catches sight of one of the women in red piping, who looks familiar and on whose face there is a look of disapproval, as if she is about to uncover him as a fraud.

As the last set of pins, predictably, crashes down, the familiar-looking woman leaps to her feet and in the process loses several buttons on her bowling shirt. When she bends down to gather them, Healey sees, behind the cloth, the un-mistakable shape of a man's chest and he realizes that this woman bowler is the writer on whose work he is composing a thesis.

One of the Ph.D. students, in discussing the writer, had once told Healey that he, personally, would have difficulty working with someone "of that body shape." While drinking the beer that helped him to sleep on those certain nights when Healey heard the words of the mature student from several years before, he had begun to think that this might, after all, account for the problems he was having with his work. He had not prepared himself for the *body* of the writer, so that having seen only head-and-shoulders photographs, he was shocked to discover *the breasts*. They were small breasts, he supposed, but given the writer's extraordinary round belly, his small stature, and the style of sweater he always wore, the breasts often appeared in relief, as it were, pert even, and on cold mornings capped by clearly visible nipples. This was exactly the chest he saw revealed in the dream of the bowling women.

When Pickering appeared to him on the path all at once, then, in his netting singlet, without anything held back, as it were, Healey felt an odd relief and even began to believe Pickering's words about a good working relationship.

While he was thinking about the actress looking through him, the girl he had imagined having beside him now suggested to the group he had sidled up to that they should all climb the path behind the property from where, she had heard, they could look out on the whole area. Healey had found himself, still carrying his can of beer, tagging along on the end of this party, as if he were naturally included in the activities of a group which for five years he had laughed at. Among their number were several long-term couples who had encouraged each other in the business of being "born again," renouncing alcohol, sex, and swearing, and signaling their disapproval of most aspects of high-school life by withdrawing into each other's company. Here they found support from seeing

reflected the same looks of dreamy incomprehension and cen-
sure with which they greeted the world.

Karen was not, strictly speaking, part of this group. She
was retained by the couples, rather, as a kind of mascot, a
"wild spirit" whom they hoped one day to tame, but also
whom they secretly enjoyed having along, since she provided
the group with just that touch of the unrespectable that, for
all their piety, Healey believed, they still craved; it was pres-
ent in their "spontaneous" decision to accompany Karen on
her "mad" expedition, and he could hear it in their constant
giggling as they set off up the hillside.

As he climbed the steps, which were lit by small lamps
planted in the ground every few yards, he wondered how, at
the tail, he could manage somehow to make it through the
line of born-again couples to be walking just behind Karen at
the head, from where he would begin to talk about Katherine
Mansfield, thereby revealing himself as someone she might
one day walk alongside. After a short time, however, there
were no more lights, and the couples started tripping on the
steps and banging into one another. Now the giggling had be-
come hysterical. The pace of the ascent slowed until Healey
was forced to stop altogether while those in front found a
way up. "My night vision," someone called out. "My night
vision is hopeless! I've lost a lens. Where are you all?"

The couple immediately in front of Healey had, appar-
ently, fallen on top of each other, and he heard the girl whis-
pering that she wasn't going any farther on the path, which
she now believed to be evil. As he stepped around the couple
in the dark, the girl screamed, but clearly they had lost con-

tact with the main party, since all that came in response was the sound of distant laughter. Healey could see virtually nothing ahead of him, but he had found the measure of the steps in his stride and was making good time. He paused to drink the last of his beer, tossing the can far into the bush.

Higher up, he stood on someone's hand. Now there was sobbing. "Who's there?" a male voice said. "Who is it?" He pushed past more couples, some of them leaping at his touch from the path into the bush, giving him the not unpleasant sensation of clearing a way. In none of the voices, however, did he recognize Karen, so he carried on still farther at the same unvarying pace.

Then he did hear something familiar, though it seemed to be coming from off the path. Healey stopped and listened. It was the same odd kind of yelp he had heard at the barbecue, the same sound that had caused all her friends to abandon Karen for that moment, leaving only Healey to recognize and accept her for what she was. This was what had earned him the right to join their expedition. And how necessary his presence now seemed, since all her so-called friends had fallen by the way, whereas he alone stood ready to do anything for her. Without thinking, he pushed his legs out in the same long stride, although not up the path this time but off the path in the direction of the noise that was calling to him.

As he fell, rolling through the bush on the side of the path, he thought of landing in the water, which would be the color of peacocks in the year 1907, a date he remembered from the play. He would enter the sea close to the beach on which the girl, recently returned to the "wild country" from boarding school in Harley Street, London, was taking the afternoon summer sun. She is lying face down. She has no boots or stockings on. Her pink dress has ridden up over the backs of her knees, which are off-white, like paper. (The legs he sees are not those of the famous writer, except perhaps by accident. They belong, of course, to Karen. Healey recognizes the tight, pretty bulbs of the calves, spotted with freckles.) A panama hat with a large red bow covers her head and the back of her neck. A parasol gives shade. She is thinking of her million lives—she doesn't have just one—and how she must get on with it, somehow! I'm ready, she says into the sand. But for now, she thinks, I will lie here just a little longer by the water the color of peacocks.

Opening his eyes, he found he was lying face down in a pile of leaves from which came the powerful smell of decaying vegetation. He was having difficulty breathing and was forced to turn his head to take in clean air, as if swimming in the compost. This wasn't easy, since occasionally a light gusting of equally polluted air was blown into his mouth from above, so that he found he had to spit as well as inhale. It was only after several minutes that Healey realized someone was above him and that this blowing was coming from a body, causing him to say aloud: "I'm being breathed on!"

He turned his head farther around and one small, yellow eye stared back, close enough for Healey to see the muck floating over the liqueous cornea, reminding him of the flecks in an egg. A flick of the head above him and a second eye just like the first, looked down, unblinking. Beneath these fevered, dripping eyes appeared a pair of pink nostrils crystalled with fine snot and then a mouth set in a half smile over thin cords of saliva, which were falling down a muddied wool front, attaching its chin to its hoof.

The sheep sighed into Healey's face.

Hey, hey, he whispered into its eye. "There, there," he said to the other eye, stretching the vowel sounds until they shook slightly. The sheep had caught itself in a barbed wire fence—which was what had halted Healey's own fall—its head and front legs were through, but the wire had disappeared into the thick fleece around its middle, stranding the sheep's rear. There were pellets all around, and none looked fresh. Even in the rain—which had almost stopped—they had not been softened but gleamed like shiny black pebbles. The sheep had shat itself dry.

Healey knew little about sheep. He had visited his aunt May's farm a few times and chased the lambs his cousins kept as pets. After a bad run of frosts, when the men had to work through meals to clear the sheep carcasses, his cousin had driven down to the back paddocks with the Sunday roast. Healey, along with the other younger cousins, had been in the back of the truck with a plate balanced on each knee, trying not to lose them. "Let the peas run with the gravy, that's okay," his aunt had told him. "And if a potato goes, just dust it off and put it back on. They won't know." When they arrived, all the roast potatoes had to be collected from the end of the truck.

Now he showed the animal his hand, turning his palm out, and slowly began to lift himself from the ground, always keeping his open palm in front of the sheep's eyes. Thirteen years later, in the bar of the ferry, he would remember this moment when the American turned his palms out as if to say he had nothing to hide. "Hey, hey," Healey was saying. Calming noises. "Hoo, hoo, hoo." Softly, Healey bleated. But as the hand got nearer, the sheep started tossing its head from side to side and bucking violently against the barbed wire, its front hooves kicking up leaves and dirt, deepening the furrows, which had been its work over however many hours, days, perhaps, the fence had refused to give. Healey lowered his hand.

In its terror, the sheep had twisted itself so that the back half of its body was parallel to the fence, its rear hooves now within grabbing distance. It was staring ahead, turning regularly to check on Healey, who had pulled himself into a crouch alongside the fence, just behind the animal. He could see the back of the sheep, the dags fouling the wool, the flanks twitching. They stayed like this for several minutes, almost, Healey thought, like old friends. Then the sheep was absolutely still—posed—the constant shuffling of its back hooves ceased, with not even the constricted rise of its breathing discernible. It looked straight ahead. It had lost interest in Healey. It had had enough. And seeing the sheep set itself stiff in resignation, Healey had the sudden desire not simply to escape, as had been his first thought, believing that the animal might, somehow, hurt him, but rather to help it from the predicament, which he now felt shamed them both in the eyes of the wild spirit hovering somewhere on the path above.

He took a quick breath and tackled the animal. He still remembered how to do this from the rugby days when he had not yet become invisible to the set of girls who now regarded him as a type. He thrust both his arms between the wire of the fence and grabbed the hindquarters, bundling them in his hold, scooping them off the ground and pulling. Away they came, the whole package suddenly hugged to his chest. The weight, however, was a surprise; it caught him off balance and he was tipped forward onto his knees. It then struck him that although he had watched the sheep closely, looked into its eyes, listened to its pitiful noises, seen its excrement, he had not understood until this moment that the animal was really a living thing. Even though he had, in a sense, been drawn to the animal and had gone out of his way on its account, or at least on account of the cries, which he had believed were Karen's, he now understood that he had really thought only of himself and never considered the animal, nor the couple he had stepped on, nor even Karen, as anything but an object to which he might or might not pay attention.

The powerful muscles of the sheep's legs were alive, they thrashed against him, the hooves kicking in his hands, clubbing his ribs. Healey's head and shoulders were now on the wrong side of the wire, his face pressed deep into the sheep's side—a suffocating warmth in there—the barbs cutting into his shirt collar. He was winded, about to let go, but maneuvering himself into a sitting position, his school shoes braced against the fence for support, he gave one final heave. The sheep screamed—a ghostly, quavering soprano—and Healey screamed, too, as they both came flying back through the wire. When they landed, the sheep's belly covered his face. He was breathing in a thick pile rug. Wool was in his mouth, in his nose. Its fibers woven hard into his cheeks. He could feel himself sinking, as if beneath a team's worth of waterlogged sweaters. He freed an arm and, swinging a fist where he thought the animal's head would be, he punched the sheep as hard as he could, crying out as he swung, "On its stupid snout!"

He was sickened, triumphantly repelled. It felt like he was pushing his hand through honeycomb, hearing the dreadful crunch of its sticky, delicate latticework caving in, his knuckles instantly hot and coated. The sheep's bleat was altered, it was lower, a querulous note introduced. Neither of them could quite believe it. Healey had broken the sheep's nose.

It sat on his face awhile longer, stunned, then the sheep bolted, hopping over Healey's prone body with surprising elan, a pert little shake of its dirty, woolen rump, and, baaing peevishly, kicked on up toward the path. Healey watched it slipping, finding traction, falling back, before leaping out of sight.

Then he began hearing the voices of the couples above him on the path, among which he thought he made out Karen's.

"Oh, look," someone was saying "it's been hurt—the poor thing has been hurt."

Healey closed his eyes. In that moment he believed they had found *him*—that he was being attended to, that hands were being laid upon his body.

"All gather round," Karen was saying. "Don't alarm it. We're moving in slowly now. Now we're going to lift our arms quite gently, like that, and now we're closing them, oh, so slowly, around you. There."

Healey opened his eyes. There was no one over him. He crawled up the bank toward the sound of the voices and stopped where he could make out several sets of bare legs, lost among which were those pear-shaped calves. From the dense center of this human circle came the softened cries of animal satisfaction and, Healey believed, even smugness.

While crouching in the bush, waiting for his classmates to finish the business of revival and return to the barbecue, Healey thought about lying faceup on his bed on those weekends when he had decided to sleep through the daylight hours and when he could hear people moving around the house and going about their business as if it were a normal day. In the time he imagined himself falling asleep, the path was again quiet.

Healey and Pickering sat on the veranda, looking out over the harbor toward Wellington. From the extravagant disarray in the kitchen, which Pickering described as "the fallout of my new bachelorhood"—he was, he said, currently in the middle of a bitter divorce—two tall glasses of iced tea had been brought forward, though not on a tray, for which Pickering again apologized, explaining that he was sure his wife had hidden the trays somewhere or cleared out with them. "Don't ever get divorced, Brett," he said. "Don't ever get married, but certainly don't ever go and get yourself divorced. Are you married? Divorced?"

"I'm neither," said Healey.

"Then you're one of the blessed, my boy. But here's a

word for you if you ever, you know, worse comes to the worst, one word in these situations: *inventory*. There, I've said all I'm going to on the subject."

Pickering's "book," which Healey was careful to refer to as a "manuscript" so that his client might begin to have the idea of a process and perhaps a long one, too, was basically the story of his great uncle. "Believe it or not," Pickering had said on the phone, "but I'm part Jewish and my uncle was the first Jewish Lord Mayor of Dublin." At least that was how Pickering had first sold the idea to Healey. With their iced teas in the Eastbourne sunshine, however, Pickering had begun to talk less of his extraordinary relative and the tour of America in the 1950s—the uncle had been interviewed by *Life* magazine and had given speeches at many of the top universities—and more of himself. Or rather, he had begun to so mix details of his life with the life of the uncle, speaking with such a rapid delivery—it appeared that Pickering, too, had done some lecturing in the States, where he had apparently lived for a time, although it was difficult to pin him down to any particular place in any particular year, and where his principal topic had been the uncle ("More modest in scale, Brett, but with full return airfares and, you know, an honorarium, the works")—that Healey grew quickly tired and began to think of the train journey back around the harbor in his almost-private compartment.

"I'm okay with an audience, see," Pickering was saying. "You know, jokes and little anecdotes. But it's the writing gets me. Live, I'm fine—had some pretty big names, you know, tell me I should have been this or should do that with my talent, as they're kind enough to call it. I could have been in entertainment—well, it runs in the blood, of course; my uncle, he was a comedian. I mean, he was Lord Mayor, but at heart, you know, he just loved an audience. But with the book, it's a different kettle of fish, and I can see I need someone such as yourself—"

"Would it be possible to look at the manuscript?" Healey interrupted. "I could take it away with me and then give you a clearer idea of what might be involved."

"Oh, the book's here!" said Pickering.

"Here?"

"All around us. I mean it's in boxes and boxes. I keep everything, Brett. That is, everything my wife doesn't walk off with."

"I see."

"I'll tell you something. If you took away all the stuff that's here, the house would fall down."

"So you haven't actually written anything yet—you've been collating?"

"*Ruminating!*" cried Pickering, tapping his finger against his temple. "I've been sitting here ruminating. For years people, you know, have been telling me I had this book *already written* virtually. After the talks I gave, people always wanted, you know, to read it and were surprised when I said there was no book, that it was all in my head. Well now, my head, you know . . . I'm not getting any younger, Brett." Pickering thoughtfully stroked his remaining hair. "And my wife leaving like that—you become aware of all the other things which are, you know, leaving."

Healey watched Pickering's jaws working on the ice he had picked from the glass with his fingers and plopped into his mouth. His eyes were blinking rapidly as he chewed.

"Mr. Pickering," said Healey.

"Sakes," said Pickering, "call me Fred—I'm nothing on formality, you know."

"Fred, I wonder whether I could see some of the boxes?"

Pickering spat the ice back into his glass and looked at Healey. "They'll have to stay here, Brett," he said sternly. "The boxes stay here with me."

"Of course, but to get some idea I need to look."

"I'll tell you something else, Brett," said Pickering. "There's things in there even my wife hasn't seen. Not in twenty-two years. Maybe that's why my book is being written—wouldn't that be something! The woman takes all my trays and the dinner set, and I write a book for her. She doesn't want me entertaining guests, see, Brett. I love people, see. So she takes all the good stuff. Hitting me where I live. But she doesn't know everything about me, and that's what the book's for, to tell her I live in other places, too."

Pickering paid Healey an hourly rate, though Healey agreed, against his better judgment, to receive the money on a monthly basis, if only to avoid the stories of Pickering's wife's attempts to "bleed him dry" that accompanied all financial transactions. He couldn't bear to listen to this every week. It was agreed that Healey would come to the house in Eastbourne every other afternoon to sit with Pickering on the veranda and sift through the material, and that he would tape record conversations pertinent to the book. After the material had been sorted out and they had an idea of the main elements in the narrative, the most significant taped conversations would be transcribed, becoming another source of reference. Then, before starting on the draft chapters, they would plot out the book. Pickering responded with great excitement to all these ideas, which Healey was adapting freely from his two years of thesis work, and often spoke of Healey as exactly the type of person he had been searching for.

Now as he looked across the harbor at Eastbourne, Healey realized he could remember little of the details of the project itself, which had occupied his afternoons for those months, nor could he account for the diligence with which he had applied himself to a task that he knew from the start to be doomed, since it soon became clear that in hiring him Pickering was simply using up the long summer days, assuring himself of at least one regular houseguest at a time when he felt abandoned, and that for all his talk about "the book," Pickering would have been content to have Healey simply sitting at his elbow, appearing to work, while he talked about himself and occasionally furnished his listener with iced tea.

Finally, after struggling for weeks to find any shape or pattern in the material or in Pickering's talk, and feeling guilty for the hours he had spent being paid for following the wrong scent, Healey decided, while climbing the path to the house one day, that this was a perfectly legitimate occupation—companionship—and he would no longer worry that the book was no closer to realization than when they had started. After all, Pickering's mood—good humor, occasionally interrupted by bursts of maudlin introspection and self-pity—had gone unchanged through these fruitless weeks, and he continued to express satisfaction with Healey's work.

They would sit together and move the boxes around a little while Pickering told Healey stories of the time he had been invited to a small women's college in upstate New York. They had been snowed in and he had been forced to spend the night in the attic room of one of the dormitories. "That's a later chapter, I think, Brett," he would say, nudging Healey, who, as with many of the stories, could see little connection with the Jewish Lord Mayor. Pickering would often exclaim that "Uncle would have seen the irony there!" or "I know who would have enjoyed that!" but these seemed rather half-hearted attempts to tie it all together, and after a time neither the uncle nor Dublin figured much in the conversation.

Nor were the details of how it all finally came to an end any clearer in Healey's mind, except that he recalled not being paid fully for the last month. Pickering had phoned him late one night. He said that he was in a panic and told Healey that he had urgent business overseas and that their contract would have to be put on hold. Pickering was profusely apologetic and began speaking as if it were Healey who had initiated the whole project, even using the phrase "your book." Healey had been surprised, not that Pickering was pulling out, but at himself; he felt a curious sadness at this departure. This had been the last he heard of the Lord Mayor's great-nephew. "My love to Louise," Pickering had said. "Snagged one there, you crafty devil."

The only times he did remember with any clarity were

the ferry rides back to Wellington in the evenings. It was on one of these trips that Healey met Louise and there began that process by which Eastbourne was, in a sense, redeemed for him, causing him for the first time to see himself clearly as a boy in the last weeks of high school, hiding from his classmates in the bush.

At the time, Louise was working not as a journalist but as a picture researcher and librarian at a Wellington newspaper. She was then living in Eastbourne and often commuted by ferry.

At first, Healey had rejected the idea of taking the short-cut by boat, preferring to catch the bus to Lower Hutt and then the train. By this route he saw himself tracing the edges, rather than being tossed into the middle. Later, he would come to see this odd characterization of the daily journey as a variation on his mother's earthquake preparedness; in the middle you would be hit by everything.

Then late one Saturday afternoon Pickering announced that he had some business to conduct and that he would accompany Healey into town. Leaving the house together, Pickering didn't pause at the bus stop but marched on toward the jetty, and Healey, dreading a lengthy discussion about the comparative advantages and disadvantages of each method of transportation, found himself pretending that this was the way he, too, always went. On the small boat—smaller than he had hoped for—Healey leaned back and closed his eyes, as if he were one of the habitual sea commuters and nothing on this trip could possibly surprise him. He also wanted to avoid talking to Pickering, since Healey was now off work and every sentence Pickering addressed to him he regarded as a kind of unpaid overtime.

The journey, however, was smoother than he expected, and soon they were approaching Wellington. Pickering had also found several people onboard whom he could talk to for free, as it were, and it occurred to Healey that his employer might have saved himself some money by forgetting about the uncle entirely and spending his days instead plying these waters, going backward and forward from Eastbourne with a captive audience.

One of the victims was a woman of about Healey's age—he had opened his eyes when he thought it safe—carrying a large art folder, which, he overheard her telling Pickering, contained a photograph she was taking to be framed. Immediately, Pickering had moved closer to her and had begun rehearsing everything he knew or had heard about picture framing, including the many framing disasters that he and his wife had suffered over the years. At certain points in the telling Pickering had put his hand on the woman's knee.

Yet the woman had remained calm throughout and had even laughed at several of the things Pickering said, although not at the so-called jokes but only at times when Pickering himself was not expecting it. Whenever Pickering mentioned his wife, he always made it into a joke. The woman, however, tended to nod seriously at these "wife jokes" and to laugh only when Pickering began to talk seriously of himself dealing with a framer who had split the canvas on one of their paintings. And Pickering, dismal with the failure of the "funny" parts, began to seize on the woman's laughter whenever it erupted. He was joining in now at these apparently random moments, looking a little perplexed as he did so, as if each time he thought this might be the last rise he would get out of her.

While listening to them, it suddenly struck Healey that the woman with the folder was in the business of discovering a pattern in Pickering's speech that might, somehow, turn his often overbearing nature against itself, causing him to speak about his wife and her "abandonment" of him in new ways, and that in the few minutes of this casual encounter, she had accomplished more than Healey had in weeks of paid employment. When Healey had pretended to wake up, stretching his arms above his head as they came into dock, Pickering introduced the woman as Louise, warning Healey that she had "a wicked sense of humor."

"Brett here," Pickering told Louise, "is involved in what I'm afraid is a most dreadfully dull task of editing the reminiscences of a foolish old man—I mean, how would you like to sit all afternoon with such a character while he rattles on about the old days, eh?"

Again, Louise let the comment pass. Yet, as Pickering, slightly put out that no one had rushed to disagree with him, went on, earnestly now, about the highly professional methods with which the project was being carried out, she did suddenly laugh and said it didn't sound like the worst thing in the world.

"It's not," said Healey. "Throw in the iced teas and the harbor views—it beats working any day, right, Fred?"

"Eh?" Pickering hadn't heard him. "What's that? See, even my hearing's going on me."

"He said you're a generous employer," said Louise.

"Do my best," said Pickering. "No one has it easy these days."

"Dead right," said Louise. "I'd say you're lucky to have each other."

"I wouldn't go that far," Healey said quietly.

"What's he whispering for?" said Pickering. "Brett?"

As they were docking, and Louise and Healey were swapping notes on their respective newspapers, Pickering, wedged between them, having spent the last part of the journey sulkily looking back across the water to Eastbourne and muttering loudly to himself about forgetting something, suddenly leaped up and moved to the front of the boat. When the gangplank was in position, Pickering was first off, responding to Louise's calls with a wave over his shoulder and striding along the quay. When they caught up with him, Louise said, "We're all going for a drink, aren't we?"

"A drink?" said Pickering, still moving fast. "Well, I won't. Got some business, you know."

"I guess I will," said Healey. "I don't have any business tonight."

There was a silence while, three abreast, they hurried along the waterfront.

"Well, I suppose I could," said Pickering. "If I'm not, you know, interfering."

"Is he interfering, Brett?"

"Always," said Healey.

"Then we'll get him drunk and leave him somewhere."

"Drunk!" said Pickering, now stopping. "There's not a pub in the city with enough grog to get me going, and that's a fact."

"That's not a fact, Frederick," said Louise, "that's an opinion, which I say needs testing in the old-fashioned way. Wouldn't you agree, Brett?"

"I would," said Healey. "Though I should warn you, Louise, this man's great-uncle was known throughout Dublin for his hollow legs. He has breeding, this man."

"Now there, matey, we don't want to go giving away the book's secrets, do we," said Pickering. "I'll drink with you young people, I will. No Irishman descended from a Jew could sleep at night knowing he'd turned down an invitation to go to the pub with his pals."

In the drinking sessions, which soon became a regular feature of the weekends, Healey's and Louise's courtship, as Pickering once referred to it, investing the word with all the drama of his own losses, began to take on its own odd pattern. The three of them would start off together, making their way from pub to pub, playing pinball or darts, and buying the losing tickets in various charity raffles where the prize was often a big tray of beef leaking its juices onto the bar. But soon they reached the stage when it was preferable to leave Pickering in the bar, once he had assured himself of new partners, for the occasional evening that Healey and Louise now felt they should make more their own.

Yet they found they had imposed certain limits on themselves. They couldn't do just anything. It had to be something

Pickering had ruled himself out of. So they conspired to go dancing, an activity Pickering said he only indulged in when truly inebriated and, since there were no "real" bars in Wellington, he told them they should run along by themselves. Pickering also claimed never to have risen from the table fully sated by a meal from the Orient, as he called it, so they found themselves hiding out in the Chinese restaurants of Courtenay Place. In pursuing only those activities Pickering had singled out as not to his taste, they felt they were avoiding cheating on him.

Yet even when they succeeded in the not too difficult task of losing the third member of their party, they could not fully rid themselves of the peculiar tension that gripped them the moment they left Pickering. When the three of them were together, Healey felt that an energetic, even erotic sparring was taking place in which Pickering was often the unknowing dupe, a kind of backboard for their exchanges. Yet when they were alone, there persisted a feeling of responsibility toward the old man, which caused a certain timidity and cautiousness between the two of them, as if they were junior employees, rivals in the favors of a boss to whom each suspected the other reporting any out-of-hours indiscretions.

Pickering was the source of many of their frustrations and yet, somehow, he had also become the repository for an exciting frankness which, in his absence, tended to dissipate into, if not outright guilt, then a dutiful politeness. With Pickering, Healey felt his affection for Louise becoming almost painfully animated, so that he would be filled with a sudden desire to reach for her across the table in a crowded pub. On those occasions when they were alone, however, and he might well have reached across, as certain as he could be that she would not have resisted, he felt somehow obstructed.

It was not until a number of weeks had passed since the first Saturday afternoon, not until Healey described what he had overheard on the ferry with his eyes closed, asking Louise how it was that she knew immediately the way to deal with Pickering, that a new and independent ease made itself felt. In listening to the story of her time at the girls' boarding school outside Christchurch, it was as if the specter of Pickering finally began to lift.

Louise told him that she hadn't really thought about it but guessed she treated Pickering exactly as she had treated the fathers of her girlfriends at school. Each year, she said, there had been an event called Father's Day, although it didn't correspond with the calendar date, nor was there a Mother's Day. "Of course, the mothers came often," Louise said, "whereas the fathers waited for the annual invitation." Father's Day was a kind of midyear Christmas, she said—"You never knew quite what you were getting."

One winter morning, the fathers' cars would start pulling up the long, sloping driveway. Some came in chauffeur-driven limousines with dark windows, others in old bombs—the fathers of the scholarship girls. Actually, Louise said, the cars were as various and deceptive as the fathers who drove in them. The lost-looking, silver-haired, second and third husbands of the mothers of senior girls; the newish, proud fathers of the infant school; the middle-aged, worried fathers; "alternative" dads; the occasional famous father, for whom the girls would post a watch at the windows of the dorms where they were supposedly readying themselves for morning tea in the Great Hall looked over by the Board of Directors; then the *boyfriends* of the mothers would drive up. It was among this last group, Louise said in reply to Healey's question, that she would have to look for her own father-of-the-day. Her parents had divorced when she was twelve, and since then her real father had lived mostly overseas.

After morning tea—which was always stiff and mildly embarrassing, since the fathers, in the course of a term, had seemed to have forgotten who their daughters were, and, in front of the board and staff, had decided to treat everyone in the room with the same exaggerated sense of decorum, talking to girls of fifteen about the state of the trees and how well the grounds were looking—the fathers were led away on a tour of the buildings by the principal. This took the form of a kind of site inspection, as if the fathers were a team of contractors forced to look at the shoddy work of their predecessors. After being softened by the lavish production of scones and cream, washed down by tea served in the silver teapots which otherwise remained under lock and key in the staff room, the fathers were now stung back into reality by the principal's talk of drain blockages, leaking roofs, and the thought of the chill drafts that the principal vividly described as "whistling" across the beds of the dormitories in which their girls were sleeping. Some of the elderly fathers, Louise said, in the early stages of the rigorous tracking down of cracked masonry and bad floorboards, had been seen to sit down quietly and write out their checks there and then rather than risk pneumonia by continuing on to inspect the "appalling" condition of the downspouts.

Braced and a little haggard, the fathers would then take part in a daughter/teacher conference, where a full assessment of each girl's progress—academic and social—would be undertaken. By this stage, Louise said, the fathers had remembered their daughters, and with thoughts crowding their buffeted heads of the vast expenditure needed to bring this "once great school back up to the mark" (as the windswept principal had repeatedly suggested to them on their little walk), they were in no mood for any girlish "nonsense." If they were paying for it all, they reasoned, no child of theirs was going to ruin things.

The stifling ceremoniousness of morning tea now gave way to frightening acts of collusion between father and teacher in the guise of furnishing an "objective" report on the daughter. "Of course, I never had it so badly," Louise told Healey, "because my mother's boyfriends were really in no position to pull rank. They often didn't know quite how they stood with my mother, and the daughter, I guess, was one more variable. Generally, they'd sit there smiling, or sometimes serious, shooting looks at me to see if this was what was called for at that moment. They were there as a favor. But other girls came out in tears, or vowing never to speak again to their mothers, who'd not only had the stupidity to take up with these men but also the cruelty to inflict them on others."

Lunch, Louise said, was less formal and represented, in the beautifully constructed psychological scheme of the day, a kind of truce, a thawing. Now the fathers were distributed among the long tables of the main dining hall and ate elbow-to-elbow with the girls of their daughter's class. In this way, it was hoped, the fathers might gain an insight into the girls' daily environment. It also allowed each girl, surrounded by other fathers, to believe at least for a short time that these men were in fact different from the figure who in the previous hour had used against them, without pity, the language of economics.

The fathers were by now very hungry after their trekking and the refreshmentless conferences, so hidden, as it were, by the mass of girls, they often grew silent, except for the noises of their voracious eating. Indeed, they might entertain the table by showing what was meant by "a male appetite," competing against neighboring fathers to see how many girl-sized meals they could finish off before the lunch bell sounded and all plates had to be passed to the front.

The afternoon was their own, Louise said, and the fathers, if they did not already have chauffeurs, now became chauffeurs, as the girls, having been forced to look at objective views of themselves all morning, were now rewarded with shopping expeditions into the city, where they hoped to purchase those things which, in the coming term, might give them the edge. In the large department stores, they readily lost the fathers for long enough to collect those special items the fathers might not have understood, concealing them under more "solid" purchases, and then finding the fathers in time for these men to produce the charge cards to pay for, in the words of the mothers, which, under instructions, the fathers quoted at the daughters, "only the things you really need."

The boyfriends, Louise said, were usually generous, top-ping up the sum allowed by her mother, although she guessed her mother found out about this and so began subtracting from her total a corresponding amount. Also, whereas some of the other fathers persisted in following the principal's advice and sought in this afternoon to achieve "quality time" with their daughters, her mother's boyfriends usually backed off when it became clear that Louise would rather find her own way to impart quality to these hours. There were rendezvous with other escapees; long, delicious intervals of sitting in coffee shops; break-ins at the vacant houses of girls' relatives where gin was tasted; prearranged dates with boys from the neigh-boring school.

This once-a-year official afternoon of wickedness was perhaps, Louise said, another tool in the exercise of control, since the school had engineered it so that final responsibility for anything that happened during these hours rested not with the school but with the fathers. "Still," she said, "prisoners don't usually quibble over the terms of their release. We were out there—that was the only thing on our minds."

Even after the delirium of the afternoon, Louise said, the evening of Father's Day often provided the highlight—if it could be called that—climaxing in a strange ritual which had its origins in the years of the Second World War when the supply of fathers had dried up and which still went on despite the present-day participants' vague uneasiness with its form. The father and daughter were to "double-date" with another father and daughter; for the duration of the evening the girls were to swap fathers. On this night, the finest restaurants in

Christchurch were to host squadrons of these peculiar four-somes. And it was at this point, Louise told Healey, that the boyfriends, with their uncertain status, caused the school's forty-year-old good intentions to become somewhat clouded.

Among her girlfriends, she said, there was often a rush to become Louise's double, since the notion of a boyfriend seemed more alluring than that of a plain father, with whom, of course, they all had experience. Even when Louise explained that the man who was currently seeing her mother was, if not Louise's, then certainly someone else's father, they would not listen; they could only truly hear the word *boyfriend*.

At dinner her mother's boyfriends were not exactly hit upon, Louise said, but rather made to feel a certain pressure to be attentive to their dates. This winning of male indulgence was achieved through a variety of tactics, since a girl could easily manufacture an incident calling upon her date, sitting beside her, to enter into a silent pact against the other side of the table where her father sat. She might appear wounded by something the father said under the subtlest provocation, or she might, in a private moment, confide in Louise's mother's boyfriend things that would cause him to see the man across the table in a new light. "It was a game, Brett," Louise said. "And although the men must have known something was up, they'd been worked on so thoroughly throughout the day that at the dinner they were a little punch-drunk and walked into combinations they might normally have ducked."

As for herself, Louise told Healey, she was also involved in some delicate maneuvering, since it happened that the "outcast" father beside her, tired of monitoring his daughter, might sometimes turn to Louise with what she called a "cut my losses" look. She always knew when this time had come: he would lower his voice. Then he would move a little closer to her, and if, in this approach, there was an accident of knees under the table, he would not, as he had at the beginning of the dinner, apologize, but rather excuse himself by looking too long into her eyes. It was in these moments, she said, that she learned—if this was not too dramatic—how to survive, discovering the methods which Healey had witnessed on the Eastbourne ferry and which she said she now, perhaps unconsciously, applied in certain similar situations.

On being stared at, if she looked down, as she had the first few times, the father would get it into his head that she was a shy young thing who needed drawing out, and the eye contact would only become more pronounced. The trick was to stare back for a little while, though emptying the look of anything but a kind of pure objectivity. "Never look into the eyes, though," she said. "Choose a point on the nose, a mark, a dent—that's how I learned. Then I'd quickly turn from him and ask the boyfriend a loud question about my mother. In the end, I guess, the success of the dinner depended on the men being constantly put off guard, and in this our tactics, if not our motives, were no different from those of the school."

Nothing ever really happened on these evenings, Louise said, except, she supposed, a swelling of a few tensions, the entertaining of some mutual fantasies, and yet in the months that followed the big event, the cold, dull months going toward spring, every minute of the date was played over and over again. The smallest movement each person had made gathered a meaning, and missed opportunities were analyzed until next year's plan was finally agreed upon.

When Louise finished telling him the story of Father's Day and the shadow of their friend Pickering had lifted, Healey understood that now was his opportunity. There was not a minute to lose. To waver for even a second, to be caught edging closer or looking into her eyes as if for a signal, would ruin everything. Any hesitation and he felt sure he would appear as impotent and conniving as the fathers of the girls of her school. Nor did he dare to close his eyes when her face was drawing near. He continued to study her skin until it was too close, until he could no longer think of Eastbourne as the source of a schoolboy humiliation, or of the colored water of the bay as belonging to a schoolgirl writer, or the surrounding bush tasting of wet wool—until in his mind he saw a pair of calf muscles shaped like two long glasses of iced tea.

Standing on the newly laid paths, which had finally restored the harborfront to the occupants of the city, Healey watched the inter-island ferry take its sharp turn past the jagged heads and into Cook Strait. The water of the harbor was a browny green and was swollen from the recent rains. Tomorrow, he thought, on his return to Christchurch, he would be looking back at this spot from the same deck, which now caught a fugitive ray of sunshine and from which he imagined someone looking at him and wondering about the paths he had taken that had led him to this viewing position. And somewhere on the ferry—wasn't it just possible?—there would be a girl returning to boarding school from the August holidays, in whose luggage might be secreted those things she hoped would give her the edge over her fellow sufferers.

9

Neptune's
Trident

"WHAT I'M SAYING," THE JOGGER WENT ON, "IS THAT YOUR
so-called all-purpose shoe, in effect, has a set of in-built lim-
itations. It's not a specialist, see. Being good for all some-
times means being good for none—"

Healey was trotting a little behind the veteran jogger, so
that in the tailwind the jogger's words were being blown off
ahead of them toward the child whom Healey had seen fall
and who was still sitting slumped on the wet surface of the
deck as they approached. The boy was six or seven years
old. He was crying, his knees hugged to his chest, and when
they passed him he attempted to hide his face. The other chil-
dren were no longer on deck; their fainting game was over.
Healey then thought that just as the embracing couple had

abandoned him, so the boy had been left behind by his friends. Of course, the couple were not Healey's friends as such, and perhaps the boy had, in fact, chosen to remain outside. The appeal of the weeping boy, whom Healey had instantly seen as an "outcast," as if in this small circle of the poop deck they had come across a desert island and its single forlorn occupant, arose from the wrongheaded impulse to see in the plight of others no more than the reflection of his own condition.

An image now occurred to him of the lightning boy lying in the clouds, black in the white. He remembered that in the darkness of the Kelburn Meteorological Office viewing room, in the silence that was broken only by the elderly guide's sniffing, Healey had dreamed of taking that poor boy's place so that he might become the object of the terror, the awe, and the affection of his classmates—a heroic figure struck down in the noble quest of better seeing the lightning from the lookout of a high branch. He had never thought of the boy as dead but only as lying down and of the *effect* of this lying down. He had imagined himself as that person who might cause the girls in the class to shift in their seats and dab at their eyes with the tissues they have secreted in their sleeves.

But how cold the metal surface of the deck must be. How pathetic the balled-up figure of the boy. He might catch his death out here, Healey suddenly thought. Already he had decided that he would move toward the boy, offering him the remaining napkin. He would let the boy wipe his eyes and blow his nose into the napkin, and then they would go down the stairs together, to be reunited below deck with the other passengers. The complete action now appeared in Healey's mind as a series of images that had about it a certain right-ness and inevitability. This was his path.

Yet again, before Healey could act, the jogger with his perpetual head start had run over to the boy and was now consoling him. When Healey arrived, the jogger reached out and snatched the prized last napkin from his hand. "Here you go, sonny," he told the boy, pushing it into his face.

"Easy," said Healey.

"The kid's lost his parents," said the jogger.

"Have you?" asked Healey.

"Where's Mum and Dad, sonny?" asked the jogger.

The boy appeared to be cringing under the shadow of the jogger, retreating behind his knees, peering up at the men as if, Healey thought with horror, he expected at any moment to be tossed overboard.

"Give him some air won't you?" said Healey.

"What's that?" said the jogger. "Air, you say? No, that's not it. What this kid needs is to be on his feet. It's the worst thing, the very worst thing to sit down in this state. Here, sonny."

"Listen," said Healey, "I've got him. Why don't you, you know—I can handle it from here."

The jogger, however, had taken the boy by the shoulders and was lifting him up. "The feet," he told Healey, "get the feet."

"What are you doing?"

"The kid's not well. Get the feet—he can't stand up, see."

Healey looked at the boy's legs, which hung loosely from

his waist, trailing on the deck and refusing to take the weight of his body as the jogger attempted to "right" him.

"What's wrong with his legs?" said Healey. "He's not moving his legs."

"Sonny, can you move your legs?"

The boy said nothing, but lay limp in the jogger's arms. He was looking straight at Healey, although his gaze seemed directed at some distant, private object that had little to do with his immediate circumstances. Indeed, he seemed scarcely aware of the men wrestling with him, the look of fear now replaced by one of dreamy amusement. This new blandness, however, disturbed Healey more than the fright which had previously been in the boy's eyes. He found himself grabbing the oddly slack ankles and tucking them under his arms, and as he did so one of the boy's sneakers fell off.

"Leave it be, son!" the veteran jogger told Healey.

"It might blow off by the time we come back," said Healey.

"Then it's gone. It's history."

"Wait," said Healey. Carefully, he lowered himself down on his haunches, the boy's legs still gripped under his arms. It was a difficult maneuver, this balancing, the reaching. Why did he have to pick up the sneaker? Was it that the jogger had given the boy the napkin and now Healey had to come up with his own gift? Did he expect gratitude? He finally hooked the sneaker with his fingers, then with some effort rose to his feet again.

The boy lay slung between them, inert and smiling, while Healey backed across the deck, taking small, hurried steps.

"Turn around, why don't you," the jogger told him. "Makes it easier."

"The shoe," said Healey. "I don't want to drop the shoe."

Arriving at the flight of steps to the lower deck, Healey, still in the lead and having managed to turn around, paused for a moment. The giddiness had returned. "How should we play this?" he asked.

"Go on down now, son," the jogger told him.

"Maybe sideways would be better?"

"Christ, just keep moving—the kid's heavier than he looks."

Only by concentrating on putting one foot on the first step, he thought, then following it with the other could he hope to make it down without falling.

"I'll go first then," said Healey.

"Right."

"This is the first step I'm going down now."

"I see you."

"Here we go."

"Just do it! I'm going to drop him soon."

"Shall we rest?"

"No rest. Go!"

Behind him, Healey could hear the jogger's heavy breath.

"What do you think is wrong with his legs?"

"Don't talk—'serve energy."

"Here's the second step—"

"Third."

But now the jogger was coming down too quickly behind him, bending the boy between them and pushing Healey so that he was forced to take the remaining steps two at a time to keep his balance. "Hey!"

"I tell you—the kid's lead. Move it!"

Finally, they crashed through the swinging doors and dropped the boy on a wooden bench. The door had struck something on opening. Turning around, Healey saw that it was the steward, the same one who had handed him the napkins. He was lingering in the doorway, smoking a cigarette, which he immediately tossed outside, saying, while rubbing the shoulder that had taken the impact, "No damage done, sir, and it is a nasty habit, I know." Then he saw the boy. "What's happened here?"

The jogger was tending to the boy and appeared not to hear the steward nor even to have noticed him. And Healey saw, again, how the veteran jogger eliminated from each situation what he considered to be unnecessary. Everything extraneous was removed and this usually included the feelings, even the sense of others. On the poop deck, what had been significant was his running, an activity to which he subordinated every other possible response. Once they had come across the boy, the jogger had placed at his mercy everything but the idea of the boy as someone he was helping. Now, if the steward existed at all he might do so only as part of this focus. Such fierce, blind economy, Healey then understood, was related to the jogger's singleminded pursuit of the best time a man in his position could achieve in competition over a distance of some twenty-six miles. Though he was repelled by the man and continued to have the idea of leaving him as quickly as possible once the boy, whom the jogger had made into "his" boy, was shown to be all right, there was, Healey thought, a certain doggedness in the veteran jogger's purpose—even dedication, a kind of passion—which Healey was powerless against and which he could only, finally and despite himself, marvel at. Meanwhile, the jogger was explaining to Healey why they'd had to hurry. "The kid wasn't helping us, see; he was dead weight. That's when you know there's a problem."

"What problem?" asked the steward.

"Get us a doctor, will you," the jogger said, without looking at the steward. "Possible exposure. We need blankets. Hurry!" He then turned to Healey. "Give me your coat, son. Anything warm."

"Christ, he's shivering, the little bugger," said the steward, peering at the boy. "I told those kids up there, you know, I told them."

"Quickly now!" said the jogger.

Healey handed his coat to the jogger, who tied it around the boy so that the arms of the coat were knotted over the boy's chest.

"Gloves!" cried the jogger.

"I don't have any," said Healey.

"Okay. These wet ones come off." The jogger began pulling at the boy's gloves, and Healey also, not to be outdone, took one, though in placing the exposed hand inside the folds of the coat he suddenly gave a cry and dropped it.

"What is it?" said the jogger.

"They're cold."

"Sure they are."

"Shouldn't we give him something? Some—I don't know—hot tea perhaps?"

"Not yet."

"Why not?"

"You ever poured boiling water into a frosted glass?"

Healey watched the jogger working swiftly on the boy. "How do you know all this stuff?" he said.

"Running," said the jogger. "Marathons. You see every-thing in a marathon. The extremities. Don't you have a hat?"

"No."

"I thought I saw you in a hat."

"I haven't got a hat."

"Okay—what are your socks made of?"

"My socks?"

"What are they—synthetic?"

He felt so stupid; he didn't even know this. "Wool, I guess."

"Good. Let's have them. Mine, see, running socks, no good. Like this nylon windbreaker. Come on, man, come on."

The jogger had removed the boy's remaining wet sneaker and then the socks. Healey, however, couldn't work the laces on one shoe; they were wet and his fingers cold.

"The whole thing, son," the jogger told him, bending to help him, actually taking hold of Healey's shoe. "Just pull the whole thing. There we go."

On the boy's feet, Healey's socks wagged comically. He looked down at his own feet. They were gray. Gray like the feet he had seen years before moving along the corridor in the house of the friend where a code of silence was being enforced. They were tired, sunless feet and the veins showed as raised, blue lines, the toes retreating in that familiar curl Healey shared with his brother and sister, though now it seemed even more pronounced, as if the feet could barely stand to be looked at.

"Put your shoes back on, son," said the jogger. "We don't want you coming down with anything now, do we."

As Healey looked at these familiar yet unfamiliar feet— the pallid flatness of them, which only now appeared to have an interest, as if he were seeing them for the first time—he had an image of himself driving through, or rather hovering above the Canterbury Plains. He had always thought of that drive, hopefully, as a kind of lifting above the surface. Driving in and around Christchurch he had always driven fast, his only thought being the *next stop, the next town.* And just as he had left the Canterbury Plains, so he had left Louise, so he had left the scrapbook—his grandfather's precious scrapbook, which his aunts had entrusted to him in the hope of preserving what was essential—this scrapbook he had left on a table in a bar with a complete stranger!

When looking at the ferry leaving the harbor the day before, he had imagined the figure of a schoolgirl on deck. He had thought she would be of the age Louise had been when she suffered the accident of knees under the tables of the restaurants of Christchurch. Here, today, was a boy of six or seven, and only now did it strike Healey—though he himself had used the phrase "catch his death"—that the boy might easily die.

"Here's what we're going to do," the veteran jogger was

explaining, lifting the boy from the bench. "Up we come—now you take him there like this, son."

The jogger pressed the weight of the boy into Healey's arms.

"Wrap him tight, son. Hold him like you'd hold a girl on a date. Trap that air!"

Then Healey could feel the jogger's arms around him. The boy's face was hard against Healey's chest; the jogger's hands gripped at Healey's shirt around his ribs.

"Now we're going to walk him, understand? We're going to take one step to the right, then we're coming back again. Circulation, circulation."

Where Healey's feet were, there were too many other feet, so that when he tried to move he stumbled and all three of them—Healey, the veteran jogger, and the boy pressed between them—tottered dangerously for a moment before steadying.

How flat the body of the boy had appeared lying on the wooden bench, and yet pressed against him like this the imprint suggested angles, depressions, sharpnesses—the nose in his chest, the hip in his thigh, the knees in his shins—a sandwiching of the tiers, Healey thought.

Only by leaving, Healey had always said to himself—when a certain gecko reaches maturity, his brother had said, only when Handsome says you can—would he come to a decision; only by leaving his precious scrapbook in the hands of a stranger, by rising a certain distance from the surface of the Canterbury Plains, and never paying attention to the city of Christchurch but always thinking about the next stop; only by reaching the sunlit, virgin citadel of the grandfather's knee, would he be able to begin this collecting of himself, he had always said.

"Watch it, son! Follow me, like a dance, I'm leading— first this way, then back."

Only from the height of a sofa—the sofa from which his aunts had played out their parts—he had said to himself, only from the snowy reaches of the pages of books.

The three of them stumbled about as one, the jogger continuing to call out instructions, though now Healey could not hear him. He was imagining again that figure on the poop deck who would raise the alarm—man overboard—a figure he had never thought of as himself while listening to the words of the American. Of course it was absurd that he should have given the American even the slightest impression that he had found his man. Healey had never thought for an instant that he might agree to such a proposition. Entertained it as a possible fiction, perhaps—played a part, and done it seriously, too. Was this what had given the American hope? Healey's wrongheaded attentiveness, the questioning, his earnestness? This posture was what the poor man was clinging to, waiting in the bar with Healey's food. Every minute Healey was up on deck, the man's belief in him, which had been mistakenly instilled and was in truth utterly groundless, continued to firm—wasn't this so?—until shortly he would be convinced that a deal had been struck.

Healey would, he said to himself, stumbling around, waiting for the return of the steward, go down. Staying up here had been a mistake. He would, he had decided, finally enter the below-decks area where the other passengers were, and in the bar, from under the fluorescent lighting, he would retrieve the brittle pages of his grandfather's scrapbook containing the story of his record-breaking triple-jump, which he had left in the hands of a complete stranger. *Sapere aude.* If anything, he felt he owed the man an apology. A mistake had been made—perhaps on both sides, though it was Healey who had not thought to immediately correct it, which he might have done had he not felt the attraction of sitting and listening to the American's story, of observing the man, of weighing his claim, of behaving like an interested party when he should have simply walked away. Of course, when he had walked away, it had been at the wrong time, always at the wrong time.

In the bar, as he imagined it, he would be suddenly calm. He would no longer speak in the voice of the journalist, of the therapist, or in any other "voice." He would look directly into the American's eyes and, seeing there his perfect audience, finally, give himself away. "Now!" he said, stumbling about with the boy wedged hard, painfully, against him and the veteran jogger hanging on desperately around his middle. "One foot then the other," the jogger was saying. "Walk him awake, here we go, one foot then the other."

Toward the end of his time in America, a period of his life still too close for it to appear in his mind in anything more than the most fragmentary images and sentences, Healey had found himself in front of an audience of international students. He had been signed up for a panel discussion before he had the chance to refuse. The director of the International House had asked him to speak about his home country, to provide a geographical, social, and cultural profile of a place that no one else in the international student community had visited or knew much about. "I'll put you down as final speaker, then," the director said, "since you're the farthest away."

In planning his little talk, Healey had struggled to find a central metaphor by which something of the truth might be communicated. Finally, in a large, glossy picture book given to him by one of his Auckland uncles at the airport just as he was about to board the plane—a book he had never bothered to open until this moment, and which he had considered leaving behind in the departure lounge because of its bulk; a gift that had annoyed him; a silly, impractical gift—Healey found a certain sentence. The sentence was unremarkable in every way, yet it caught his attention. It simply stated that whereas for every million Americans there were 94 kilometers of coast, a million New Zealanders could look forward to sharing 3,333 kilometers. He passed over the figures several times in dim comprehension. What exactly did these numbers mean? He stared at the photographs. Land against sea. Green and blue, and white where the surf broke and for the mountains. The book, he now saw, was an aerial circumnavigation of the North and South Islands, and he studied it for several hours. Perhaps finally he was holding in his hands his required theme.

He could talk about edges, uncovering the network of rivers and ridges, peaks and valleys, lakes and beaches that was shown in the book. But he could not stop there, at the picturesque. Wasn't there also an historical angle that might be applied? Abel Tasman, traveling in 1642 from the East Indies, had sailed right past the continent of Australia, the one he was looking for, so making possible the "discovery" of the west coast of New Zealand, the sight of which did not, however, impel the Dutchman to land; he merely traced its edge onto the blank space of his map, not seeing it as an island at all but connecting it to land off the southern tip of the South American continent. The true shape would have to wait more than a century for James Cook to claim it and color it empire pink.

This gap, from 1642 to 1769, from European knowledge to actual settlement, lodged in Healey's mind and tempted him with a range of analogies he thought he might deploy in his talk, even though they remained largely undigested. The momentousness of discovery is tempered with an odd indifference, an absentmindedness almost, a curious forgetting.

Healey applied himself with unusual vigor and dedication. No other time in the two years stood out in his mind as being so productive and intense as the evenings that followed his discovery of the once-despised picture book.

The panel discussion took place on a cold afternoon toward the end of the fall semester in the lounge of International Students' House. The large room was filled with comfortable sofas and armchairs. Oil paintings mounted in gilt frames hung on the walls, mostly portraits of various alumni whose beneficence had made possible the furnishings—men with rosy cheeks, their arms crossed over expansive, suited chests. An impressive marble fireplace provided the focal point. Healey had never seen it lit, although there was always a small stack of logs ready on the hearth and a set of brushes and pans in a tarnished brass holder. On this occasion, a large heater had been moved in front of the fireplace. The students and the house staff sat in the sofas and chairs and on the carpet in front of the heater.

The panel members spoke from behind an oak table, the legs of which, Healey noticed, were elaborately carved with figures from mythology. At the far end was Medusa with her locks, and at his end Neptune riding the waves.

While Healey waited for his turn to speak, he had the impression of a fireside chat, the coziness of the setting only increased by the sight through the windows: American undergraduates hurrying from the dorms to class in their winter coats, turning their collars against the bitter wind, ice hanging in the trees.

Gradually, however, as the members of the panel introduced their respective countries, the atmosphere inside the lounge, at least for Healey, seemed to change, so that when it came to his turn he had already begun to envy the figures on the other side of the icy glass. Clearly he did not belong in the room. He should run outside. After the rather halting, winningly difficult accounts from the other students—the Chinese, the Hungarian, the Sudanese, the Czech, all of whom were speaking English as a second language and whose regular appeals to the audience whenever the right word had momentarily abandoned them made for an exciting communal activity—Healey felt increasingly like an impostor. There would be no warming acts of reciprocity when he spoke.

What a thesis he had concocted! How stiff and lifeless it appeared now against these deeply human stories. A sister in prison. One's first encounter with a microwave. The vagaries of postal systems. One of the panelists had brought along some pottery typical of his area; another distributed small pastries to be eaten while she spoke so that everyone might have a taste for the region she was describing.

Healey had no props. He had not even thought to bring a map. As he was being introduced, he entertained notions of deliberately tripping over his words, of playing to the audience, and yet, looking at their faces, he knew he would never fool them. These people ate language, it was their daily grind. Perhaps, he thought, he should simply rely on his natural terror of public speaking. The tutorial mortification that had held him as an undergraduate might easily be transported across the Pacific to this room. But when he opened his mouth, he found that his English immediately took on an unusual ease and fluidity, its sudden oiliness betraying him at every turn as the true foreigner in the room. The notes to which he believed he would be returning again and again were quite superfluous. The facts, the statistics, all the impressive numbers came to Healey at will.

New Zealanders, he was saying, cannot ever be much farther than one hundred miles from the ocean. We have thirty-five times more coast to play with than Americans. The land is constantly interrupting our designs on it. In a sense, we have no interior. We are all edge.

While he was talking on—now about the frequency of earthquakes, the streets of towns rippling and breaking like waves—he grew impatient with the abstract level at which he had pitched everything, and he began to think that a better subject, a way of "humanizing" his speech might be, say, the story of those evenings when the grandfather would come to their house with his blackboard and make the children recite the only French phrases that Healey could now be sure of pronouncing perfectly. Healey imagined himself speaking these phrases with ringing clarity in the International Students' lounge and the appreciative laughter that would follow such an outburst. He could also talk about the popularity in his home country of gambling on horse racing, and even speak briefly on certain schemes that could be indulged in with regard to the collection of horse manure. That might offer some insight into a certain native tenacity, cunning even. He could mention hiking in the mountains, its perils and rewards. His mind was made up. Soon he would finish with all the tortured stuff about edges and begin with the people who had mattered most to him in his life.

Yet when Healey finally paused and was about to begin again, he heard a sharp clapping of hands from the back of the room. It was the director. Only then did he realize he had gone well over his allotted time. He had seen the director get to her feet several minutes earlier, but had thought she was just stretching her legs. In fact, she had been attempting to catch his attention and bring the event to a close. People had to get to classes. The lounge had been booked for the next hour. Through the glass doors, Healey could now see a crowd waiting.

The director clapped her hands once more and announced

that question time would have to be arranged on an informal basis. She wanted to thank the panelists for their fascinating insights. Each of them, she said, had offered a wide, clear window into what was unique in their cultures. At this point there was a loud and extended round of applause, and the audience started moving off.

Healey felt a momentary sense of panic. An injustice had been done, but by whom he couldn't yet say. Too much had been left unsaid. They had been given the wrong idea. He had not even started to speak. He had been cut off by the director. Well, no, he had used up his time in the wrong way. There had been that rehearsed quality, that awful glibness. Now everyone was leaving.

The panelists were also getting to their feet, smiling at each other in mutual congratulation and relief. Healey's hand was being clasped. Someone had found it fascinating. There was a genuine air of goodwill and it was clearly, though bafflingly, embracing him too. Healey suddenly felt weak against the enthusiastic responses of his fellow speakers. Perhaps his sense of being the outsider had been an overreaction, a simple product of nerves. By dint of their membership on the panel, they had formed a group. The experience had brought them close.

China had kept an immaculate set of notes on each country, which he was now distributing to the respective authorities for checking. Everyone was laughing and thanking one another. Then Healey caught the eye of Czechoslovakia. His had been one of the most impressive contributions. Healey had listened while the Czech student, a political science graduate in his late twenties, delivered a broken and moving plea on behalf of his compatriots, full of convincing detail and dignified restraint. Now the Czech winked at Healey—an unsettling, conspiratorial wink. At first Healey thought it was some fun at China's expense, some relief from the excessive studiousness, from the prospect of correcting the tiny, dense script covering the pages China was pressing excitedly into their hands. Then Czechoslovakia touched Healey on the arm and whispered to him, "Thank God, no one knows the difference, eh. If my father had been here. If my friends!"

"What?" said Healey.

"I feel freedom," said the Czech. "Making speeches—I no longer hear what I am saying. Do you understand?"

"You're not used to it. Well, neither am I—"

"No. Yes, I am not used to it, so perhaps, you know, I make things sound . . . If my friends are here they will correct me."

"They have a different version. A different view."

"Yes, yes! Mine is no good. You are right. Mine is only half, not even half."

"Neither is mine," said Healey.

"Ah, but we shake hands! Half and half!"

In the weeks that followed the panel, Healey had avoided the International House and had even passed up the free Tuesday lunch. The Czech had been right. How false and ludicrous the whole thing had been. What a charade and how the audience had lapped it up. It had been a waste of time, just as the previous three semesters, in which he had pretended to work on a thesis with a writer he had been mistaken about, were a waste of time. He now understood that, once he had met with the writer and realized his error there had been no point in pursuing his studies. Yet he had continued pretending to work on the thesis, just as he had pretended to himself for a moment that he had done a good job on his home country in the International lounge while beneath the thick, ugly, showy table the toe of his shoe traced the oak scrolls of Neptune's trident.

Now, on the ferry, gripping the veteran jogger, attached to the boy who was pressed tightly between them and was surely beginning to move, to struggle, his lips working against Healey's middle, even tickling him—although Healey wanted to hold on for longer—even complaining it seemed, even saying in a weak voice "Hey," the exhaled breath coming up in a small cloud stronger than the word which was its weight and striking Healey on the cheek, Healey thought how he might have once said to himself that he constantly altered the facts to suit his thesis, to suit himself, and that he often appeared to be interested in others but that he was only truly interested in himself. All the time we say it's others—he imagined he might have said to himself—when really we will do anything in our power to make these others fit into our scheme. We let something slip about a person who means something to us, which instantly creates a false impression or rather a not-quite-true image, and still we are impelled to give to this half image, this almost true lie, the semblance of life. Our parents and our relations, the voice went on, our friends, everyone, how often we imagine we have pinned them all mercilessly.

Despite all our efforts, however, despite this unbroken series of misreadings, people, he says to himself, do, of course, escape. The cousin from his hellish vortex, the brother from his beehives, the aunts from their husbands—they get away from whatever we have used against them. Even Daddy, even his grandfather whom he has often during the past three days mistakenly thought of as his subject, with whom he has often paired himself—even that character escapes, is, on his aunt's evidence, lightening, rising hopefully against that thin ceiling of earth, which is the grassy floor played upon without a care by his great-grandchildren.

The phone call from his mother three days before, a call which finally lifted him from his desk, has now made him think of what he told himself in the weeks following the panel discussion: I will remember with the utmost accuracy—that is, simply, in a voice of feeling that restores to them their fullest context—all those details and moments that make up the story I regretted not having told in the room of the rosy-cheeked alumni who looked down from the walls as I stood in front of those fellow internationals sitting in the sofas and long, plush armchairs and on the carpet by the unlit fireplace, and in whose faces I saw reflected, as I again see reflected, to be true to the moment, though I could scarcely recognize it then and am only able to do so now, what I must faithfully record here as tenderness.